365 AMAZING DAYS ★ IN SPORTS

A DAY·BY·DAY LOOK at SPORTS HISTORY

ERIC SHERMAN

D1506266

A *Sports Illustrated For Kids* Book

First Edition

Library of Congress Cataloging-in-Publication Data

Sherman, Eric, 1962–
    365 amazing days in sports : a day-to-day look at sports history / by Eric Sherman. — 1st ed.
        p.   cm.
    A Sports Illustrated for kids book.
    Summary: Presents five amazing sports happenings for every day of the year.
    ISBN 0-316-78537-7
    1. Sports—History—Juvenile literature. [1. Sports—Miscellanea.] I. Title. II. Title: Three hundred sixty-five amazing days in sports.
GV576.S53   1990
796—dc   20 89-48216
                                                                                CIP
                                                                                  AC

SPORTS ILLUSTRATED FOR KIDS is a trademark of THE TIME INC. MAGAZINE COMPANY.

Sports Illustrated For Kids Books is a joint imprint of Little, Brown and Company and Warner Juvenile Books. This title is published in arrangement with Cloverdale Press Inc.

10   9   8   7   6   5   4   3   2

C-W

For further information regarding this title, write to Little, Brown and Company, 34 Beacon Street, Boston, MA 02108

Published simultaneously in Canada by Little, Brown & Company (Canada) Limited

Printed in the United States of America

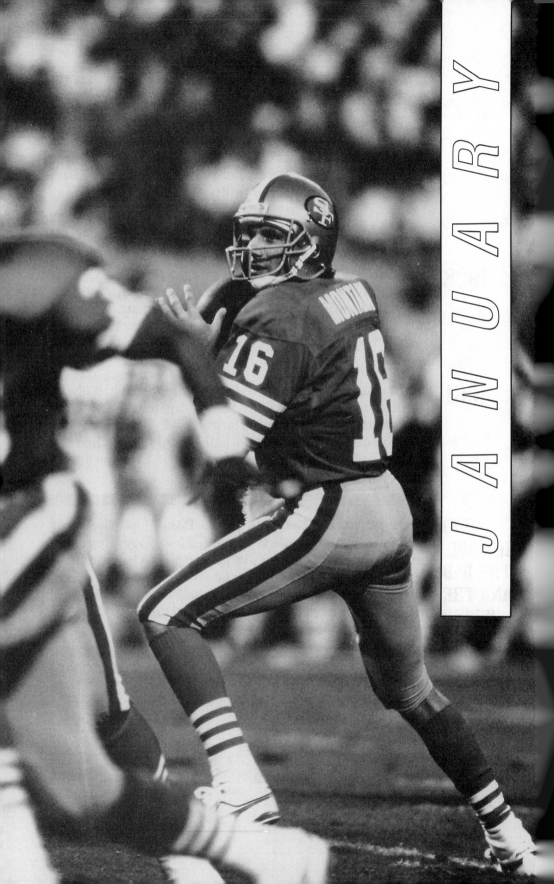

JANUARY

1902 At the first college football bowl game ever, the University of Michigan stomped Stanford 49–0 to win the Tournament of Roses association game in Pasadena, California. That was the first Rose Bowl. Unfortunately, the game was such a flop that it was not played again until 1916. Instead, Tournament of Roses officials held such events as a chariot race and a race between a camel and an elephant, as well as the famous parade that still takes place on New Year's Day.

1938 In a basketball game against Duquesne University, Hank Luisetti of Stanford University became the first college player to score 50 points in one game. Two years earlier, he had made history by sinking basketball's first one-handed shot. Before that, players always used both hands to shoot the ball.

1961 The Houston Oilers won the first championship of the brand new American Football League (AFL). They defeated the Los Angeles Chargers, 24–16. The AFL is now part of the National Football League (it's called the American Football *Conference*), and the Chargers have moved down the freeway to San Diego.

1929
THE GOOD,
THE BAD
AND THE
WEIRD
You could have called this year's Rose Bowl the Woes Bowl for all the trouble it caused. First, Roy Riegels of the University of California picked up a Georgia Tech fumble and ran 60 yards ... *the wrong way*. Then, California kicked off, and while the ball was in midair, all the air went out of it! The ball fell to the ground as flat as a pancake. Breakfast, anyone?

Joe Montana, the quarterback who has passed for more yards in a Super Bowl than any other. (See January 22, 1989)

1961 Grandmaster chess player Bobby Fischer, age 17, won his fourth U.S. chess championship in a row in New York. He kept his title because he played to a draw against Pal Benko, a Hungarian grandmaster. Fischer had defended his title in New York exactly one year earlier.

1965 Joe Namath, the colorful University of Alabama star, became the richest rookie in football—or any other sport—by signing a $400,000 contract with the New York Jets. The flashy quarterback known as "Broadway Joe" turned the Jets from an average team into Super Bowl champions in just four years.

1982 This AFC playoff game has been called "The Game That Would Not End." That's the way it looked to the San Diego Chargers, who jumped out to a 24–0 lead, but watched that lead get smaller and smaller as the game wore on. The Chargers finally squeaked by the Miami Dolphins, 41–38. The winning play was a field goal by Rolf Benirschke with just over a minute remaining in sudden death overtime.

1985 It took three overtime periods, but the Running Rebels of the University of Nevada-Las Vegas (UNLV) finally out-ran, outsmarted and outlasted Utah, 142–140. At the time, it was the highest scoring game in National Collegiate Athletic Association (NCAA) basketball history. What game holds the record today?

1920 The Boston Red Sox, World Series Champions two years earlier, traded a pitcher named Babe Ruth to the New York Yankees. As a great hitter, Ruth would lead the Yanks to seven pennants. The Red Sox would not win a pennant for 26 years. They still have not won another World Series. And you thought being a Red Sox fan was fun!

1925 Have you ever seen greyhounds race? No, not the buses, the dogs! They chase fake rabbits on special racetracks. On this day, the Saint Petersburg Kennel Club in Saint Petersburg, Florida, opened for greyhound racing. It's the oldest greyhound track in the world still open on its original site.

1931 Nels Stewart of the Montreal Maroons set a National Hockey League (NHL) record today by scoring two goals in just four seconds in a game against the Boston Bruins. If he had played the whole game at that rate, Stewart would have scored 900 goals by the time the game was over.

1983 The Dallas Cowboys were in a hole. They had the ball on their own one-yard line in a game against the Minnesota Vikings. Running back Tony Dorsett got the ball, hoping to squirm for just a little breathing room. He did more than that. Dorsett ran for 99 yards and a touchdown. That's a National Football League record for longest touchdown run. Nice squirm, Tony.

1981 The Dallas Cowboys made one of football's most amazing comebacks. With only one quarter to go in a playoff game against the Atlanta Falcons, the Cowboys trailed, 24–10. But then they began to lasso touchdowns like real-life cowboys roping cattle. They scored three TDs in the final minutes and ended up winning the game, 30–27. The winning touchdown came with 52 seconds left when quarterback Danny White zipped a pass between two Atlanta defenders to receiver Drew Pearson.

1984 Adrian Dantley of the Utah Jazz tied an NBA record no one thought could ever be matched. Dantley hit 28 of 29 free throws in his team's 116–111 victory over Houston, tying Wilt Chamberlain's mark for free throws made in a single game, which was set on March 2, 1962. Chamberlain had scored an incredible 100 points in all on his record-setting night. (See March 2, 1962.)

1984 The Edmonton Oilers gushed past the Minnesota North Stars 12–8 in the highest scoring game in modern NHL history. (The modern era is said to begin in 1924, when American teams first joined the NHL.) Oilers Center Wayne Gretzky scored four goals and four assists, but he didn't come close to the record for most points in a game by one player. That mark was set by Toronto's Darryl Sittler in 1976 with 10 points.

1986 Navy basketball star David Robinson, now a member of the San Antonio Spurs, set an NCAA record by blocking 14 shots in a game against North Carolina-Wilmington. By the end of the season, Robinson had set another mark with 207 rejections—an average of 5.9 per game.

1964 The San Diego Chargers lived up to their nickname in the American Football League championship game as they charged up and down the field against the Boston Patriots. The Chargers gained an incredible 601 yards total offense and walloped the Pats, 51–10.

1971 The Harlem Globetrotters are known for their silly antics on the court—and for always winning. Not today. The all-black basketball squad lost a game to the New Jersey Reds, 100–99. It was the Globetrotters first loss in 2,496 contests. Let's see the Los Angeles Lakers top that!

1976 Kevin Doherty of Davidson College set an NCAA record when he fouled out of a basketball game just five minutes and six seconds after he entered it, midway through the second quarter. No other player has picked up five fouls so quickly. Doherty's very first infraction—a charging penalty—came only two seconds after he touched the ball. He picked up the next three in 36 seconds.

1986 The Chicago Bears shut out the Los Angeles Rams 24–0 in an NFL playoff game. They had already blanked the New York Giants 21–0 in the opening game of the playoffs. The victory over the Rams made the Bears the first team in NFL history to go through the playoffs without giving up a single point. They would go on to win the Super Bowl two weeks later by squashing the New England Patriots, 46–10.

1896 The first bicycle marathon for women began today in New York's Madison Square Garden. When the six-day race ended on January 11, a woman named Frankie Nelson had won by pedaling further than anyone else—418 miles.

1951 The Indianapolis Olympians nipped the Rochester (New York) Royals 75–73. Does the score seem low? Consider this: It was the final after six overtimes! That was the longest game in National Basketball Association history. The reason the score was so low is that the NBA had not yet introduced the 24-second clock so teams could stall as long as they wanted—and score very few points.

1957 Talk about family feuds. Two cousins from the Asian nation of Pakistan battled each other on Long Island in New York for the U.S. Open Squash Championships. Hashim Khan—one of the greatest players in the history of the game—defeated his cousin Roshan Khan 12–15, 15–5, 15–3, 15–9. Squash is similar to racquetball. It is played in a small room with the ball bouncing off all four walls.

1986 Boing! Boing! Boing! Six students at Cleveland State University in Ohio set out to bounce their way into the *Guinness Book of World Records*. Taking turns, they began jumping up and down on a trampoline in the college gym. Fifty-three exhausting days later, the six dizzy students stopped jumping. They had set the record.

1988 English lesson: Alex English of the Denver Nuggets became only the 14th player in the history of the NBA to score 20,000 points in his career. He scored 35 points to lead his team to a 98–93 victory over the New Jersey Nets.

1785 Jean Pierre Blanchard of France and J. Jeffries of the United States became the first men to travel between France and England in a hot-air balloon. The balloon just barely made it. The men were forced to throw everything out of the basket—including their clothing—to stay up in the air.

1972 The Los Angeles Lakers beat the Atlanta Hawks, 134–90. It was the Lakers 33rd win in a row—an NBA record. In fact, the Lakers hadn't lost since October 31, 1971. Two days later, though, the streak would come to an end. The Lakers lost to the Bucks, 120–104, before a sellout crowd in Milwaukee, Wisconsin.

1980 In NHL action, the Philadelphia Flyers record-setting streak of 35 games without a loss came to an end when they were tripped up by the Minnesota North Stars, 7–1.

1936
THE GOOD,
THE BAD
AND THE
WEIRD
Bounce-thwat. Bounce-thwat. Bounce-thwat.... well, you get the idea. Tennis champions Helen Wills Moody and Howard Kinsey made that sound a lot when they volleyed a tennis ball back and forth 2,001 times in a row without stopping or missing. Finally, after 1 hour and 18 minutes, Kinsey had to stop to teach a tennis lesson. Thank goodness. Otherwise, they might still be hitting that ball today.

1940 Boxer Al Hostak agreed to do a radio interview before his middleweight fight with Tony Zale. But then, as thousands of people listened in, he refused to speak. Hostak thought it was bad luck to talk before a fight, so his brother spoke for him. Al stood by his side and nodded— but nobody could see him, since it was on radio.

1945 Arkansas State University tied an NCAA record for the fewest points scored in a Division I basketball game when they lost to the University of Kentucky, 75–6. There's a saying that "it isn't over till the fat lady sings." Well, today the fat lady must have started singing *very* early.

1955 Perhaps you have heard of the home court advantage—the benefit a team gets by playing in front of its own fans. The Kentucky Wildcats certainly had. They won 129 games in a row at home before losing today to Georgia Tech, 59–58. The winning streak dated back an incredible 12 years—to January 14, 1943.

Bill Shoemaker, the winningest jockey in horseracing history. (See January 24, 1964)

1793 Hot-air balloonist Jean Pierre Blanchard made the first balloon flight in the United States. Blanchard took off from a prison yard in Philadelphia and spent 46 minutes in the air with his dog. President George Washington, Thomas Jefferson, James Madison and James Monroe watched from the ground.

1942 It didn't take heavyweight boxing champion Joe Louis very long to finish off opponent Buddy Baer and keep his title. Louis knocked out Baer in the very first round. It was the 20th time he had successfully defended his title. Not too surprisingly, many consider Louis the greatest fighter of all time.

1977 The NFL's Minnesota Vikings were a talented team in the 1970s. They had a tough defense called the Purple People Eaters, and a superb quarterback named Fran Tarkenton. So why did they keep losing Super Bowls? In bowing to the Oakland Raiders 32–14 in the 11th championship game, the Vikings lost their fourth Super Bowl. Only the Denver Broncos, who lost their fourth Super Bowl in 1990, have matched that number.

1979 High school basketball player Daryl Moreau of New Orleans went down in the record books when he hit his 126th free throw without a miss. In fact, it had been a year since the teenager had missed a shot from the foul line.

1988 Minnesota Vikings wide receiver Anthony Carter was considered too small for football, weighing only 166 pounds. But that didn't stop him from setting a playoff record. He caught 10 passes for an incredible 227 yards in a playoff game against the San Francisco 49ers.

1920   The Montreal Canadiens and Toronto St. Patricks set an NHL record for most points in a game (21) in Montreal's 14–7 victory. Only three months later, the Canadiens would set an NHL mark for most points by one team when they beat the Quebec Bulldogs, 16–3.

1931   What was the worst team in the history of the NHL? For a long time it might have been the Philadelphia Quakers. On this day, they finally snapped the longest losing streak in the league's history. They somehow beat the Montreal Maroons, 4–3. It was their first win after 15 straight defeats. In 1975, the Washington Capitals broke that embarrassing record with a total of 17 losses.

1980   Boston Bruin rookie Jim Stewart played his first NHL game as goalie—and his last. Stewart gave up three goals in the first four minutes, and five in the first period. He was benched very quickly, and would never play in the NHL again. If you were a coach, would *you* play him?

1982   Have you ever tried to catch a football when the weather is freezing? How about when it's 59 degrees below zero? That's what it was in Cincinnati for the AFC championship game—the coldest playoff game on record. The temperature was minus 9 degrees, but the wind chill factor was 59 below. It's no wonder the Bengals bombed the San Diego Chargers, 27–7. It never gets that cold in San Diego, California.

1970 The Kansas City Chiefs beat the Minnesota Vikings 23–7 in Super Bowl IV in New Orleans. Kansas City quarterback Len Dawson threw for 122 yards and a touchdown, and kicker Jan Stenerud set a record for the longest field goal in a Super Bowl—48 yards.

1973 The American League voted to use designated hitters on a trial basis. Under the experiment, another hitter would bat for the pitcher, but would not take the field. Three years later, the American League decided to keep the designated hitter on a permanent basis. The National League has never used the DH.

1976 The NHL was seeing red. The league had invited a hockey squad from the Soviet Union to play exhibition games against seven teams in the United States and one Canadian team. Everyone expected the Americans to win the series easily, but the Soviets were 5–2 going into the last game. In the finale tonight, the Philadelphia Flyers helped the league—and all of North America—regain some pride. They outskated the Soviets, 4–1.

1931
SAD SACKS
OF SPORTS
Well, at least they weren't shut out. The girls' basketball team from the Jonesboro Baptist School in Monticello, Arkansas, made one foul shot in its basketball game against Magnolia A & M. And for 40 minutes, that was it. Magnolia held on to win this nail-biter, 143–1. The top scorer, Louise Hicks, scored 69 points—68 more than the entire Jonesboro squad.

1958 Adolph "Dolph" Schayes set an NBA scoring record today. In helping the Syracuse Nationals beat the Detroit Pistons, Schayes scored his 11,770th point. By the time he retired, he had raised that total to an impressive 19,249 points. Now Schayes's son Danny plays for the Denver Nuggets, and the scoring record is held by Kareem Abdul-Jabbar with 38,387 points.

1969 Quarterbacks often predict that their team will win the Super Bowl. But they don't usually *guarantee* it. That's what New York Jets QB Joe Namath did before the third Super Bowl. Everyone thought he was crazy. The Jets were an AFL team, and no AFL team had ever won the game. Besides, their opponent—the Baltimore Colts—was clearly a better team. But when the talking stopped and Namath started quarterbacking, he proved he was right. He led the Jets to a 16–7 upset.

1975 The Pittsburgh Steelers defeated the Minnesota Vikings, 16–6, to win Super Bowl IX in New Orleans. It was the Steelers' first championship since entering the league in 1933. Running back Franco Harris was the star of the game, rushing for 158 yards—a Super Bowl record. The record is now held by Tim Smith of the Redskins, who ran for 204 yards in Super Bowl XXII.

1961 Basketball great Wilt Chamberlain set an NBA record by scoring 78 points in a game. Chamberlain's record didn't last long, however. Two months later, a player scored 100 points in a game for the first—and only—time in history. That player: Wilt Chamberlain. (See March 2, 1962.)

1974 The Miami Dolphins easily defeated the Minnesota Vikings, 24–7, in Super Bowl VIII. It was the Dolphins' second Super Bowl win in a row. Miami's Larry Csonka (pronounced *Zonka*) was so successful, running for 145 yards, that quarterback Bob Griese only had to throw seven passes the entire game.

1985 It's pretty amazing that Otto Bucher of Switzerland was still playing golf when he was 99 years old. But it's even more amazing that he was able to get a hole-in-one. Otto aced the 12th hole of a golf course in Spain to become the oldest person ever to get a hole-in-one.

1969
THE GOOD,
THE BAD
AND THE
WEIRD
A day after their shocking Super Bowl upset over the Baltimore Colts, the New York Jets got on a plane in Miami to fly home. At the airport in New York, thousands of fans waited to meet them and see the Super Bowl trophy. There was only one problem. The Jets had left the trophy in a hotel room. Ooops.

1940 Do you think the idea of free agents in baseball is new? Think again. On this day, baseball commissioner Kenesaw Mountain Landis made four players for the Detroit Tiger club—plus 87 members of its 15 farm teams—free agents. Landis released the 91 players after he ruled the Tigers had unfairly handled players.

1951 The first NFL Pro Bowl game was held at the Los Angeles Memorial Coliseum. Actually, a Pro Bowl of sorts was held in 1939 (see January 15), but that contest pitted the NFL champion New York Giants against an all-star squad. This time, both squads were made up of the league's best players from different teams. The American Conference defeated its National foes in a squeaker, 28–27.

1968 Legendary Green Bay coach Vince Lombardi coached his final game with the Packers. But what a way to go. A year after winning Super Bowl I, the Packers defeated the Oakland Raiders, 33–14, in the second Super Bowl contest.

1973 The Miami Dolphins zapped the Washington Redskins, 14–7 to win Super Bowl VII, and become the first—and only—team to go through the regular season and the playoffs without a single loss. Still, the Dolphins proved no team is perfect. After missing a late field goal attempt, Miami kicker Garo Yepremian picked up the ball and then fumbled it. The ball was then recovered by Washington's Mike Bass, who ran it back for the Redskins' only touchdown.

1892 Rules for a new sport were made public. The newfangled game was called basketball. It had been invented a month earlier by Dr. James Naismith in Springfield, Massachusetts. An official ball for the game would not be invented for years. In the meantime, the sport was played with a soccer ball, and a peach basket at each end of the court.

1939 The first Pro Bowl was held in Los Angeles—sort of. (See January 14.) The NFL champion New York Giants beat a squad of all-stars, 13–10. It is now held every year in Honolulu, Hawaii.

1967 The first Super Bowl was held in Los Angeles Memorial Coliseum. Green Bay Packers quarterback Bart Starr was just that—the star of the game. He passed for 250 yards and two touchdowns as the Packers beat the Kansas City Chiefs, 35–10. For his efforts, Starr was named the first Super Bowl Most Valuable Player.

1978 The Dallas Cowboy defense was nicknamed the "Doomsday Defense" because they were the toughest in the NFL. In Super Bowl XII, they proved it. They caused seven turnovers and the Cowboys beat the Denver Broncos, 27–10.

1984 In a battle of Czechoslovakian tennis stars, Hana Mandlikova beat Martina Navratilova to bring Martina's 54-match winning streak to an end. Hana won the match 7–6, 3–6, 7–4.

1896 The first basketball game with five players on a side was held. Before this, nine men (or women) from each team were on the court at one time. In this "new" game the University of Chicago beat an Iowa YMCA team, 15–12.

1952 What would football be like if there were no "points after touchdowns"? We almost found out. On this date, the NFL Rules Committee discussed getting rid of the "PAT" and making each touchdown automatically worth seven points. The vote was 7–5 in favor of this proposition, but a 10–2 vote was required for passage.

1962 In one of the highest scoring NBA All-Star Games, the West beat the East, 150–130. Bob Pettit of the St. Louis Hawks set a record for the most rebounds in an All-Star Game with 27. Not to be outdone, Wilt Chamberlain of the Philadelphia Warriors set his own record for the most points (42). Who got the MVP award? Pettit.

1970 In a college basketball game at Pacific Lutheran University, Steve Myers made a shot while standing out of bounds... at the *other* end of the court. Myers' shot was later measured at 92 feet, $3\frac{1}{2}$ inches. Since he was standing out of bounds, the basket was declared illegal. But the officials changed their minds after the crowd booed. It's still the longest shot in basketball history.

1972 This was not a super Super Bowl for the Miami Dolphins. In losing Super Bowl VI to the Dallas Cowboys, they became the first team *not* to score a touchdown in the annual football showdown. The Cowboys won, 24–3.

1916 The first organizational meeting of the Professional Golfers' Association (PGA) was held today in New York City. The first PGA Championship was held Sept. 9–14 at the Siwanoy Country Club in Bronxville, New York. James Barnes of Great Britain won. In fact, an American didn't win the contest until Walter Hagen defeated Barnes in 1921. Hagen would make the United States proud, however. He won every PGA Championship between 1924 and 1927.

1971 You can say one thing about Super Bowl V: It wasn't boring. Between them, the Baltimore Colts and Dallas Cowboys had 11 turnovers. The game was so sloppy, many people called it "The Blooper Bowl," yet the game is still one of the most exciting of all the Super Bowls. The Colts won on a late field goal, 16–13.

1942
SPORTS
PROFILE

Cassius Marcellus Clay, Jr., was born in Louisville, Kentucky. Cassius who? In later life, he changed his name to Muhammad Ali, after becoming a devoted follower of the Islamic faith. But no matter how he was known, he will always be regarded as one of the greatest—and most colorful—boxers ever.

By the time he retired in 1980, Ali had a record of 56–4. He had been heavyweight champion three times. His most famous opponent wasn't another fighter, but the U.S. government. Ali refused to be drafted into the army during the Vietnam War because of his religious beliefs, and the Supreme Court agreed. Nonetheless, he had to give up his title. In 1974 he regained it by knocking out George Foreman.

Ali was as good at bragging as he was at fighting. Some of his most famous lines are: "I'm the greatest," "Ain't I beautiful?" and "Float like a butterfly, sting like a bee."

1941 Epinard was once considered one of the greatest race-horses of the early 1900s. Today, he was found by the Paris police being used to make deliveries. The poor horse had been stolen by the Nazis when the Germans occupied France during World War II, and for years no one knew who he was.

1958 Willie O'Ree became the first black player in the NHL when he was called up from the Boston Bruins' Canadian farm team and played in a game against the Montreal Canadiens. The Bruins beat the Canadiens, 3–0.

1959 Marion Ladewig of Grand Rapids, Michigan, won the American Bowling Congress' (ABC) annual all-star women's bowling championship for a record seventh time. Considering that the event had only been around for 18 years, you might say she was on a roll.

1976 The Pittsburgh Steelers won Super Bowl X by defeating the Dallas Cowboys, 21–17. Pittsburgh receiver Lynn Swann made four spectacular catches for 161 yards. His accomplishment was even more incredible considering he had just gotten out of the hospital after suffering a concussion in the AFC championship game against the Oakland Raiders.

1982 The first jets to fly around the world nonstop landed in Riverside, California, today. The three B-52 Air Force Stratofortress bombers had flown 24,325 miles in just over 45 hours. That's an average speed of 525 miles per hour. The planes were refueled in flight by aerial tankers.

1880 William Muldoon defeated Thiebaud Bauer to win the Greco-Roman wrestling championship of America. Greco-Roman is a type of amateur wrestling in which the use of the legs is not allowed. Muldoon went on to become the most famous wrestler of the 19th century.

1898 In the first college ice hockey game ever played, Brown blanked Harvard, 6–0. By the 1940s, the college version of hockey would become as popular as the professional game. The first NCAA hockey championship was held on March 20, 1948, with Michigan defeating Dartmouth.

1931 For the first time ever, a basketball game was held at a major sports arena rather than a small gym. More than 15,000 fans attended a charity tripleheader held at New York's Madison Square Garden. Columbia University beat Fordham, 26–18, Manhattan College edged New York University, 16–14, and St. John's crushed City College, 17–8. Add up all their scores, and you still wouldn't have one average basketball game today.

1974 Time was running out in a college basketball thriller between Notre Dame and the University of California at Los Angeles (UCLA). With 29 seconds left, Dwight Clay of Notre Dame took a shot. Everyone held their breath. Swish! It was good! The final buzzer sounded and fans in South Bend, Indiana, Notre Dame's hometown, went crazy. Notre Dame had beaten UCLA 71–70 to snap the Bruins' record 88-game winning streak. Ironically, Notre Dame had been the last team to beat UCLA back in 1970.

1977 Norm Van Lier of the Chicago Bulls scored only two points in an NBA game against the San Antonio Spurs. But it was the longest shot in NBA history—84 feet. Standing under the Spurs' basket, Van Lier heaved a shot the length of the entire court toward his own basket. A ball thrown from that far couldn't possibly go in . . . or could it? It could.

1952 Patricia McCormick of Big Spring, Texas, became the first woman bullfighter in North America. She killed two of three bulls she faced in a ring in Juarez, Mexico. McCormick dedicated the second bull to her mother, who might have preferred flowers and a nice card. Patricia's bullfighting success so pleased the crowd, she decided to make bullfighting a long, exciting career.

1968 An NCAA record crowd of 52,693 fans in the Houston Astrodome watched the University of Houston beat UCLA, 71–69. The loss ended the Bruins' winning streak at 47 games.

1974 In the worst rout in college basketball history, Essex Community College defeated Englewood Cliffs College 210–67 in a game between two small New Jersey schools. Essex hit 97 of 129 shots from the floor and had an incredible 89 rebounds.

1980 The United States announced it would not participate in the 1980 Summer Olympics in Moscow. President Jimmy Carter said he was protesting the Soviet invasion of Afghanistan. After the Americans backed out, some 50 other Western nations also boycotted the Games.

1985 Super Bowl XIX was *supposed* to be the best yet. But the battle of the two best quarterbacks in the league — Joe Montana of the San Francisco 49ers and Dan Marino of the Miami Dolphins — turned out to be a laugher. San Francisco easily ran away with a 38–16 victory.

1954 In one of the most exciting NBA all-star games in history, the East squad squeaked by the West 98–93 in overtime. Bob Cousy of the Boston Celtics scored 10 of the East's 14 overtime points and won the MVP award.

1975 Tonight's NHL All-Star contest made history... but not because of anything that happened on the ice. For the first time in professional sports, female reporters were allowed to enter the players' locker rooms. The coaches of both teams allowed a woman to interview the players as they got ready to take their showers.

1979 Thirteen (or XIII as it is written in Roman numerals) is a lucky number for the Pittsburgh Steelers. They defeated the Dallas Cowboys in Super Bowl XIII to become the first team in football history to win three Super Bowls. The Steelers won the exciting seesaw battle, 35–31.

1986 New York Islander Denis Potvin tied an NHL record for defensemen by scoring the 270th goal of his career. The previous mark had been set by Bobby Orr back in 1977, when Orr was playing with the Chicago Blackhawks.

1986 More than 100 naked Purdue University students participated in the school's Nude Olympics. The runners dashed through the streets of West Lafayette, Indiana, even though the temperature was only a few degrees above freezing.

1857 The newly formed National Association of Baseball Players met in New York. The group agreed on several important new rules, including limiting games to nine innings. Until then, baseball contests went on until one team scored 21 runs. There were a lot of *very* long games.

1951 A young Cuban pitcher with his heart set on a career in baseball was thrown out of a winter league for hitting a batter with a pitch. The pitcher—Fidel Castro—decided to give up sports and look for another career. Today, he is the dictator of Cuba.

1983 Maybe the Houston Rockets ran out of gas. They were on the short end in the most lopsided overtime period in NBA history. At the end of regulation time, the Rockets and Portland Trail Blazers were tied at 96. When the final buzzer went off five minutes later, Portland had 113 points, and Houston still had just 96. Overtime scoring: Blazers 17, Rockets 0.

1984 Except for one play, Super Bowl XVIII was pretty boring. But that was some play. The Los Angeles Raiders were leading the Washington Redskins 28–9 at the end of the third quarter, and about the only excitement left was trying to guess the final score. Then Raider running back Marcus Allen sent everyone to their feet with an electrifying 74-yard touchdown run that set a new Super Bowl record for the longest run from scrimmage. The Raiders went on to triumph, 38–9.

1989 By the time Super Bowl XXIII was over, one thing was clear: No one is better than San Francisco quarterback Joe Montana. He set a Super Bowl record by passing for 357 yards as the 49ers dumped the Cincinnati Bengals, 20–16. San Francisco's John Taylor set another Super Bowl mark for the longest punt return—45 yards.

1893 Some people can barely stand up in a pair of ice skates for a minute. Joe Donoghue *raced* in skates for 7 hours, 11 minutes and 38.2 seconds. That was the winning time in a 100-mile skating race that was held in Stamford, Connecticut.

1933 How times have changed! On this day, baseball's Pacific Coast League announced a mimimum price of 25 cents for bleacher seats and 40 cents for the grandstand. You can't buy a bag of peanuts at those prices anymore.

1944 There are some days it's just better to stay in bed. The New York Rangers lost to the Detroit Red Wings today, 15–0, which was the worst loss in NHL history. Things only got worse—the Rangers record would be 0-21-4 over the next 25 games. The Rangers had been a first-place team two years earlier, but their best players had been drafted into the armed service because of World War II.

1988 For the first time ever, a perfect game was bowled on TV in a title match. Bob Benoit bowled a 300 to take the Quaker State Open in Grand Prarie Texas. His perfect game earned him a $100,000 bonus.

Bart Starr, the first Super Bowl's Most Valuable Player. (See January 15, 1967)

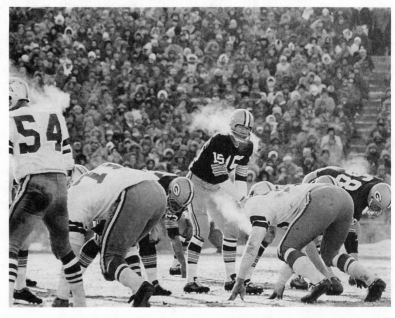

1955 Major league baseball gave new meaning to the word "fastball." It announced a new rule that required pitchers to deliver the ball within 20 seconds after taking the pitching position. Before that, pitchers could take as long as they wanted. Fans were complaining the game was becoming slower than a snail with arthritis.

1959 Walter Stolle of Czechoslovakia set out on what would be the longest bicycle tour in history. Over the course of 17 years (yes, *years*) he visited 159 countries. Along the way, he had more than 1,000 flat tires.

1964 Jockey Bill Shoemaker today set a new earnings mark for horseracing. The famous jockey rode four winners at Santa Anita race track in Arcadia, California to become the first man to earn $30,043,792 in a lifetime.

1976 The George Foreman-Ron Lyle heavyweight boxing match may have gone only 5 rounds, but it had more knockdowns than most 15-rounders. In the fourth round, Lyle kissed the canvas once and Foreman went down twice. The last time, Foreman got up just in time to beat the count. Then he knocked down Lyle for the second—and final—time in the next round.

1982 Finally, a Super Bowl that really *was* super. Cincinnati Bengals tight end Dan Ross caught 11 passes from quarterback Ken Anderson, who passed for a record 300 yards. That still wasn't enough. The San Francisco 49ers held on to win Super Bowl XVI, 26–21, thanks to Ray Wersching's record-tying four field goals. Whew!

1924 The first Winter Olympics officially opened in Chamonix, France. Some 281 men and 13 women representing 18 countries participated in 14 events, including figure skating, speed skating, hockey and skiing. Before this, the few winter Olympic sports were actually played during what are now called the *Summer* Games. By the way, the United States came in fourth in this Winter Olympics, winning one gold, two silver and a bronze medal.

1968 Pole vaulter Bob Seagren set a world record at the Millrose Games in Madison Square Garden. Seagren became the first man to clear 17 feet, $4^{1}/_{4}$ inches. On July 2, 1972, he broke his own record by vaulting 18 feet, $5^{3}/_{4}$ inches. That's higher than a two-story building.

1987 Phil Who? Like Rodney Dangerfield, New York Giants quarterback Phil Simms got no respect. Few considered him an excellent passer. But in Super Bowl XXI, Simms made a lot of believers by leading the Giants to a 39–20 victory over the Denver Broncos. Simms set records for percentage of passes completed (22 of 25 for 88%) and for the most passes completed in a row (10).

1988 Quick—how many zeroes are there in five million? Utah Jazz guard Rickey Green scored the NBA's 5,000,000th point in a game against the Cleveland Cavaliers. The record shot was a three-point goal at the buzzer to end the third quarter of the Jazz's 119–96 win over the Cavs.

1989 Michael Jordan of the Chicago Bulls scored the 10,000th point of his career in a 120–108 loss to the Philadelphia 76ers. Jordan isn't the first basketball player to reach the 10,000-point level, but only Wilt Chamberlain did it in fewer games. Chamberlain hit number 10,000 after 236 games; Michael Jordan needed 303.

1960 Danny Heater couldn't have been hotter. In one basketball game, the high school student from Burnsville, West Virginia, scored 135 points—more than any other schoolboy in history. He went on to earn a basketball scholarship to the University of Richmond in Virginia.

1986 The Chicago Bears bombed the New England Patriots 46–10 in Super Bowl XX in New Orleans. Along the way, the Bears set 11 Super Bowl records and tied 15 others. They held New England to only seven yards rushing.

1961

SPORTS PROFILE

Wayne Gretzky was born in Brantford, Ontario, Canada. "The Great Gretzky" is a long way from retiring, but he's already established himself as perhaps the greatest hockey player ever. He has set records for most points in a season (215), most goals in a season (92), most goals in a period (4), most hat tricks in a season (10), most hat tricks in a career (45), most assists in a season (163) and most assists in a career (1,200). Whew! In 1988, Gretzky broke the hearts of his fellow Canadians when he agreed to be traded to the Los Angeles Kings.

27

1927 The Harlem Globetrotters were born today in (where else?) Harlem, New York. The team was originally known as the New York Rens. They were the first all-black professional basketball team. They later changed their name to the Globetrotters and opened their first world tour in Hinckley, Illinois. Over the years, the Globetrotters have appeared all over the world, entertaining millions with their zany antics.

1973 The UCLA basketball team set a record for the longest winning streak in college history. The Bruins beat Notre Dame's Fighting Irish in South Bend, Indiana, 82–63. It was their 61st win in a row, breaking a record set by the University of San Francisco in 1956. Notre Dame would end the streak the next year. (See January 19, 1974.)

1984 For the first time in 51 games, Edmonton Oiler center Wayne Gretzky didn't score a goal or an assist. His scoring streak set an NHL record. The team that stopped him was none other than the Los Angeles Kings—the team he plays for today.

1989 Kenny Anderson, a high school student at Archbishop Molloy High School in New York City, set a New York state basketball scoring record. Going into the game against Holy Cross High School, Anderson needed 15 points to break the record of 2,391 points. He did it on a free throw late in the second quarter. The game was stopped to give him a standing ovation. Anderson, who dedicated the record to his mother, now attends Georgia Tech.

1933 Tennis star Helen Wills Moody scored a big win for women. Moody, who won tennis's most important tournament (Wimbledon) seven times, defeated Phil Neer in a tennis match before 3,000 fans in San Francisco. It was the first time a woman beat a man in a professional tennis match.

1943 Believe it or not, sometimes brothers do get along. And it's a good thing for the Chicago Blackhawks. Forward Max Bentley scored four goals on assists from his brother Doug, and added an assist to set an NHL record for most points in a single period.

1961 An indoor basketball game... rained out? It happened at a contest between two Pennsylvania high schools—West Hazleton and McAdoo. The heated gym had become too hot, so someone opened a window to let cold air in. Unfortunately, when very cold air enters a very hot room, you get rain. The game was called with West Hazleton winning, 31–29.

1989 Steffi Graf defeated Helena Sukova 6–4, 6–4 to win the Australian Open tennis championship and become only the fourth woman to win five Grand Slam events in a row. In addition to the Australian Open, the Grand Slam events are: the French Open, the U.S. Open and Wimbledon in England. A player is said to win the Grand Slam when he or she captures these four tennis tournaments in the *same season*.

1921 Great actors often get to take an extra bow at the end of a show. Horses usually don't. But today, Man o' War, perhaps the greatest racehorse of all time, got to after he made his final appearance. He went up and down the homestretch twice, as the fans at the Kentucky Jockey Club in Lexington cheered wildly. Man o' War was a Triple Crown winner. That means he won the Kentucky Derby, Preakness Stakes and Belmont Stakes all in one year.

1936 The first inductees into the Baseball Hall of Fame were announced. The Baseball Writers Association of America chose 5 men out of a field of 33. Ty Cobb captured the most votes—222 of 226. The other inductees were: Babe Ruth, Honus Wagner, Christy Mathewson and Walter Johnson. The Hall of Fame Museum would not open until June 12, 1939.

1961 This is a day for the track-and-field record books. American high jumper John Thomas set a world record by clearing 7′ 3″ at the Athletic Association Games in Boston, Massachusetts. Unfortunately, Valeri Brumel of the Soviet Union picked the same day to jump 7′ 4½″ in Leningrad, U.S.S.R. The two men met head-to-head for an exciting showdown at a packed Madison Square Garden in New York City a month later (February 16, 1961). Once again, Brumel came out on top.

1988 The Detroit Pistons delighted a hometown crowd of 61,983 by defeating the Boston Celtics, 125–108. The crowd at the Pontiac Silverdome was the largest in the history of the NBA, breaking the record of 52,745 set on February 14, 1987 in the same building.

1971 Russell Thompson of Birmingham Southern State College led all scorers in his basketball team's 55–46 victory over Florence (Alabama) State University. But he didn't sink a single field goal. How did he do it? All 25 of Thompson's points came from the free throw line.

1983 The Washington Redskins defeated the Miami Dolphins 27–17 in Super Bowl XVII at the Rose Bowl in Pasadena, California. Redskins running back John Riggins rushed for 166 yards, including a 43-yard touchdown.

1936

THE GOOD, THE BAD AND THE WEIRD

What's in a name? When you're talking baseball, a nickname can be important. On this day, the owners of the old Boston Braves asked their fans to suggest a new name for the team. The winning choice: The Boston Bees. But it was changed back to the Braves five seasons later.

A similar thing happened to the New York Mets 25 years later, also in the month of January. The Mets weren't the Mets yet—just a new team without a name that was scheduled to play their first season in New York in 1962. The owner of the unnamed New York club decided to let the fans make some suggestions. Here's what some of those clever (and rather strange) New Yorkers came up with:

The New York Muggers
The New York Slumlords
The New York Mothers-in-law
The New York Farmers (In New York City?)

1920 The Quebec Bulldogs of the National Hockey League are long since gone, and few people remember their star linesman, Joe Malone. But Malone set a record for goals in a game that still stands. In a game against the Toronto St. Pats, he scored seven goals, as his team beat the Pats, 10–6.

1934 These days, it's not that unusual to see 20,000 people pack an auditorium to watch a professional wrestling match. But back in 1934, the 20,000 Chicago fans who watched Jim Londos defend his title against Joe Savoldi set an attendance record for wrestling. Savoldi was a former Notre Dame fullback.

1988 They might as well have stopped Super Bowl XXII at half-time. The Washington Redskins scored five touchdowns in the second quarter to put away the Denver Broncos early. Washington quarterback Doug Williams passed for a record 340 yards. Tim Smith and Ali Haji-Sheikh smashed some records of their own. Smith rushed for 204 yards and Haji-Sheikh kicked six extra points—both totals were the most in any Super Bowl.

1989 In a college basketball game in Los Angeles, Loyola Marymount University beat U.S. International University, 181–150, and set two records. Loyola's 181 points were the most ever scored by a college team, and the teams' combined score of 331 points was also the highest ever.

1919
SPORTS
PROFILE
Jack Roosevelt Robinson—known to the world as Jackie Robinson—was born in Cairo, Georgia. Despite a wonderfully successful baseball career, he will always be best remembered for one thing. In 1947, Robinson became the first black man to play major league baseball. In 10 years with the Brooklyn Dodgers, he batted .311, with 1,518 hits, 137 home runs and 197 stolen bases. He was named Rookie of the Year in 1947, MVP in 1949 and appeared in six World Series. In 1962, he became the first black player elected to the Hall of Fame.

FEBRUARY

1914 For the first time, a baseball game was played in the Egyptian desert. The Chicago White Sox and New York Giants played an exhibition game in front of the Great Pyramids. The exhibition was part of a 56-game world tour to promote baseball. The final score: 3–3. A tie in baseball? Maybe the players were thirsty.

1950 Green Bay Packers coach Curly Lambeau resigned after 31 years of running football's most successful team. His career with the Packers included six titles and seven divisional championships.

1956 It sounds like a fancy New York law firm: Jenkins, Robertson & Jenkins. Not quite. That was the order of finish in the men's figure skating competition at the Winter Olympics as Americans swept the event. Two brothers—Hayes and David Jenkins—won the gold and bronze, and Ronnie Robertson won the silver.

1968 February 1 is not a good day for Green Bay coaches. On this day, the Packers great coach, Vince Lombardi, announced he, too, was stepping down. In nine seasons, he had a record of 89-29-4. He led his team to five NFL titles, six conference titles and victories in the first two Super Bowls.

1970 How many shots could a Sawchuk stop if a Sawchuk could stop shots? If he's New York Rangers goalie Terry Sawchuk, the answer is "a lot." The 40-year-old veteran recorded the 103rd shutout of his 21-year career by blanking the Pittsburgh Penguins, 6–0. Sawchuk was the first man in NHL history to shut out 100 teams.

Eric Heiden, the first athlete to win five individual medals in one Olympics. (See February 23, 1980)

←

1954 A record for most points by a college basketball player was set by Clarence (Bevo) Francis of Rio Grande College in Rio Grande, Ohio. He scored an unbelievable 113 points in his team's 134–91 thrashing of Michigan's Hillsdale College.

1962 With fans like these, who needs enemies? John Uelses became the first man to pole vault over 16 feet which he did at a track-and-field meet in New York City's Madison Square Garden. Unfortunately, a throng of fans ran over to congratulate him, and accidently knocked the bar off. That meant the jump no longer counted. The very next day, however, at a meet in Boston, Massachusetts, Uelses cleared 16′ 3/4″ for the record. This time, everyone stayed in their seats.

1964 Soviet speed skater Lidia Skoblikova took the gold medal in the 3,000-meter competition at the Winter Olympics in Innsbruck, Austria. For Lydia, it meant a sweep of all the women's speedskating events. She became the first athlete to win four gold medals in the Winter Games, and the first to win six in two Olympic Games (she had won twice in 1960).

1970 "Pistol" Pete Maravich became the first college basketball player in history to score more than 3,000 points. The Louisiana State University star pumped in 49 points in a game against Mississippi State University.

1977 Toronto Maple Leaf defenseman Ian Turnbull hadn't scored a goal in 30 games. So who would have guessed he'd suddenly set an NHL record for defensemen by scoring five goals in one game? That's what he did against the Detroit Red Wings. The previous record of four goals had been set 47 years earlier.

1956 The pairs figure skating competition at the Winter Olympics in Cortina D'Ampezzo, Italy was interrupted when angry fans began to throw oranges at the referee and judges. The audience disagreed with a low score a German pair received and began to hit the judges with a year's supply of vitamin C—unpeeled. Orange you glad you're not a figure skating judge?

1964 Two days after winning the gold and silver medals in the slalom competition at the Winter Olympics in Innsbruck, Austria, French sisters Marielle and Christine Goitschel struck again. The skiing sisters won the two top spots in the giant slalom. (The slalom is a downhill race with skiers zig-zagging between flags.) Then the sisters played a little joke. Marielle announced she was going to marry fellow French skier Jean-Claude Killy, who had fininshed fifth in the men's giant slalom. The press ran off to find Killy, who quickly put an end to the rumor. Girls!

**1940
SPORTS
PROFILE** Francis Asbury Tarkenton is born in Richmond, Virginia. With a name like that, it's no wonder he became known simply as Fran Tarkenton—one of the greatest quarterbacks of the modern football era. In 18 years with the Minnesota Vikings and New York Giants, he completed 3,686 passes. That's more than any other player to this day. In fact, he holds more career passing records than any other quarterback. Tarkenton also led Minnesota to three Super Bowls, although he never won the big game.

1932 For the first time, the Winter Olympics were held in the United States. New York Governor Franklin D. Roosevelt (who would later become president) welcomed 306 athletes to Lake Placid, New York, the site of the games. His wife, Eleanor, took a ride down the bobsled course. Lake Placid hosted the Olympics again in 1980.

1964 Terry McDermott, a 23-year-old barber from Essexville, Michigan, had a close shave at the Winter Olympics in Innsbruck, Austria. He almost didn't participate in the 500-meter speed skating competition because he didn't have skates. At the last minute, he borrowed a pair from the U.S. coach and pulled one of the biggest upsets in Olympic history—he won the gold medal.

1987 The cup came home—sort of. Four years earlier, the United States lost the America's Cup trophy for yachting (boating) to Australia for the first time in 132 years. Today, the man who lost in 1983—captain Dennis Conner—won it back in four straight races against the Australians. Unfortunately, his ship—the Stars & Stripes—was later disqualified by an American court. They ruled the boat breached the spirit of America's Cup charter of 1887. An appeal has been launched. The next America's Cup will be held in 1992.

1974 In a regional boys' basketball tournament in Stockholm, Sweden, 13-year-old Mats Wermelin scored an unbelievable 272 points. He was the only player in the game to score a single point, as his team won 272–0. Once before, in 1963, an American high school student scored all his team's points—although it wasn't quite 272. Walter Garrett of Birmingham West End High School in Birmingham, Alabama scored 97 points in the school's 97–54 romp over Birmingham Glenn Vocational. It was Walter's final game, so his teammates passed up all shots so he could take them.

1976 Bill Koch of Guilford, Vermont, became the only American ever to win an Olympic medal in a cross-country skiing event. Koch took the silver in the 30-kilometer race in Innsbruck, Austria. In fact, before Koch's medal, no American had even finished in the top eight in this event.

1978 Ever hear some kid brag: "I can shoot more free throws blindfolded than you can with both eyes." Well, Fred L. Newman wasn't just bragging when he said it. He made 88 free throws in a row while blindfolded, at a YMCA in San Jose, California. Six years earlier, on May 18, 1972, John T. Sebastian had hit 63 consecutive free throws while blindfolded.

1984 Professional bowler Mark Baker gave the crowd quite a scare at the Miami, Florida, Miller Lite tournament. Only he didn't do it on purpose. Baker's pants suddenly ripped open while he was bowling—and he wasn't wearing any underwear. The crowd didn't notice!

1925 In a New Jersey high school basketball match, Hackensack High dunked Passaic, 39–35. So what? Well, the loss brought to an end the longest winning streak in basketball history—159 consecutive victories. In more than five years without a loss, Passaic had outscored its opponents, 9,435 to 3,236.

1932 The Olympics went to the dogs this year. For the first time, a dogsled race was included as an Olympic demonstration sport at the Games in Lake Placid, New York. The two-day, 25-mile race was won by Canadian Emile St. Goddard.

1937 The United States was hungrier than the Hungarians in the men's world table tennis championships in Austria. The Americans captured the team title by defeating Hungary five and a half matches to three and a half. One match was declared a draw because it had not been decided after more than an hour of play.

1988 Michael Jordan of the Chicago Bulls today scored a perfect 50 on his final flying dunk to win the NBA's Slam-Dunk Championship before 18,403 fans at Chicago Stadium.

1895
SPORTS
PROFILE
Babe Ruth, probably the greatest baseball player of all time, was born in Baltimore, Maryland. He was named George Herman Ruth. He began his career as a pitcher for the Boston Red Sox. Although he was excellent on the mound (he had a lifetime winning percentage of .617), his true talent was hitting. When the Sox traded Ruth to the New York Yankees in 1920, he was quickly moved to the outfield, because he could hit more often if he played in every game. And hit he did. Known as the "Sultan of Swat," Ruth hit 714 homers in his career, a record that would not be broken until 1974. In 1936, he was inducted into the Hall of Fame. Only Ty Cobb got more votes for the honor than Ruth did.

1949 It seems like today's highest-paid baseball players make $100,000 practically every time they hit a home run. But it wasn't all that long ago that outfielder Joe DiMaggio became the first man in baseball to earn $100,000 in one **year**. He signed his historic contract with the New York Yankees today.

1969 The good news is that Diana Crump made history. At Hialeah Race Track in Florida, she became the first woman jockey to compete in an American thoroughbred horse race. The bad news is Crump's horse came in 10th out of 12 horses.

1970 In the history of NCAA college basketball, no one had ever scored like Pete Maravich of Louisiana State University. In a game against Alabama, "Pistol Pete" set a record that has never been matched. He scored 69 points, the most ever in a game against a Division I opponent. Four other players have outscored Maravich, but they were playing opponents from smaller schools. In fact, Maravich had three of the highest-scoring Division I games in NCAA history—pumping in 69, 66 and 64 points.

1976 Center Darryl Sittler set an NHL record for most points in a game as the Toronto Maple Leafs beat the Boston Bruins, 11–4. Sittler had a hand in all but one of his team's 11 goals, with 6 goals and 4 assists.

1985 Marshall University's Bruce Morris was standing about as far back as you can go when he sank an unbelievable basket in a college basketball game. At 89 feet, 10 inches from his basket, Bruce was only a few inches from being out of bounds at the wrong end as time was running out. The shot went up, up, up... and in! It was the longest measured basket in a college game. (On January 16, 1970, Steve Myers of Pacific University sunk a 92-foot shot while standing *out of bounds*. Although his shot was technically illegal, the officials decided to count it.)

1887 The first ski jump competition in the United States was held in Red Wing, Minnesota. Mikkel Hemmestveidt soared to victory with a jump of 37 feet. That was impressive at the time, but the current world record is more than 636 feet.

1936 University of Chicago halfback Jay Berwanger was chosen by the Philadelphia Eagles to become the first player selected in the first NFL draft. Back in 1935, he had been the first player to receive the Heisman Trophy, given to the nation's top college football player.

1986 Let's face it: Atlanta's Spud Webb does not look like he should be playing basketball. At 5' 7", he's at least six inches shorter than most players. But Webb proved today that when it comes to talent, he's one of the tallest guys around. He won the NBA's Slam-Dunk Championship by defeating the 1985 champ (and his teammate) Dominique Wilkins. The next time someone tells you you're too short to play basketball, just say two words: Spud Webb.

SPORTS QUIZ If Spud Webb is 5' 7", how much shorter is he than the height of the basket?

Answer: 4' 5". The basket is 10 feet above the floor.

1895 The final score was 9–3, but not a single field goal was kicked. How can that be? Easy—this was a *basketball* game, not a football game. In fact it was the first basketball game ever between two colleges. Tiny Hamline College of St. Paul, Minnesota, defeated the Minnesota State School of Agriculture, 9–3. Instead of each team having five players on the court at a time, each side had nine. It made for a very crowded (and low-scoring) game. About a year later, the rules were changed to allow only five players on a side.

1971 Baseball legend Leroy "Satchel" Paige became the first player from the Negro Leagues to be elected to the Baseball Hall of Fame. He was elected in a separate category for Negro League players who did not qualify under the regular rule of a minimum of 10 years of service in the majors. Before Jackie Robinson broke baseball's color barrier in 1947, blacks were only allowed to play in their own leagues.

1987 What a nice guy. Tony Fairly of Baptist College was the most generous guy on the court in a game against Armstrong State College. Rather than keep all the good shots for himself, he dished off 22 assists to set an NCAA record. His mark was later tied by another considerate fellow, Avery Johnson of Southern University, on January 25, 1988.

1989 Sometimes records last for decades before they are broken. Sometimes they don't. When the Sacramento Kings beat the Golden State Warriors 142–117 they hit 16 three-point field goals—the most ever in an NBA game. The Kings broke the record of 11 three-pointers set by the New York Knicks. The Knicks' record lasted exactly two months and one day.

1920 The Joint Rules Committee of the National and American Leagues outlawed the spitball, shineball, emeryball and all other pitches using substances to wet or mark the ball. Until then, pitchers could rub sandpaper or emery paper against the ball to suddenly make it drop or take a wild turn at the last minute.

1932 The first major international ski meet in the United States began at the Winter Olympics in Lake Placid, New York. In the first event—the 18-kilometer cross country—skiers from the Scandinavian nations of Sweden, Finland and Norway took the top 11 places.

1962 American Jim Beatty became the first man to run a mile in less than four minutes *indoors*. He did it in 3 minutes, 58.9 seconds in a track meet in Los Angeles, California. Less than five years earlier, Don Bowden had become the first American to run a mile in under four minutes outdoors.

1971 Bill White today became the first black announcer in the history of major league baseball. The New York Yankees announced the former star first baseman would begin calling games for their team on New York's WPIX-TV. In 1989, White was named president of the National League, making him the first black to head a major sports league.

1972 At the Winter Olympics in Sapporo, Japan, American speed skater Anne Henning won a gold medal twice in the same event. How is that possible? In the 500-meter competition, Henning's opponent failed to switch lanes as required and almost knocked Henning down. Yet, Henning's time of 43.31 was still good enough to win the gold medal. The judges decided to let Anne run the race a second time to try to set an Olympic record. And she did, with a 43.33 performance. Which means she won the event twice. She only got one gold medal, however.

1905 This is one for the folks at *Ripley's Believe It or Not*. James Blackstone, a bowler from Seattle, Washington, was robbed of a perfect game when a pin cracked in half after his ball hit it in the last frame. The bottom of the pin remained standing while all the others fell. Officials decided to give him a score of 299½.

1956 It was a basketball free-throw bonanza. The University of Cincinnati and Morehead State attempted a total of 111 free throws and made 88 to set an NCAA record for free throws made. Morehead State also set an individual mark for most free throws in a game, hitting 53 of 65.

1968 America's sweetheart, figure skater Peggy Fleming, won the only U.S. gold medal in the 1968 Winter Olympics in Grenoble, France. She earned every first place vote from the judges, beating the silver medal winner by 88.2 points. Fleming went on to become a professional skater with the Ice Capades, and now does television commentary at skating events.

1989 No one expected New York's Kenny Walker to win the NBA's Slam-Dunk Championship. He was only a last-minute replacement for another player who had to drop out. And even then, it was doubtful whether he'd participate, since his father had died earlier in the week. But a great athlete can overcome personal tragedy, and that's what Walker did. He put on a slamming, jamming, dunking exhibition to take the crown.

1908 The first around-the-world auto race began in New York City. Cars from the United States, Germany, Italy and France entered the race, which ended in Paris, France. The route was across the United States to Seattle, by boat to Siberia in Russia, then through Europe to France. The American team of four drivers arrived first, completing the 13,341-mile race in less than six months. Their car broke down a number of times along the way, but that was nothing compared to what happened to the Italians. They were given a ticket by the New York State police when their noisy car scared a horse. It didn't make much difference, though. They arrived in Paris third—almost a month and a half after the Americans.

1949 Paul Arizin of Villanova University set an NCAA basketball record by scoring 85 points in a game against the Philadelphia Naval Air Command. Five years and one day later, Frank Selvy of Furman University easily outdid that. He became the first college player to score 100 points in a game.

1934
SPORTS
PROFILE
Basketball great William Fenton (Bill) Russell was born in Monroe, Louisiana. He captained the University of San Francisco basketball team to a record winning streak of 60 games, before leading the 1956 U.S. Olympic team to gold. Drafted by the Boston Celtics, Russell helped them win 11 championships in 13 years. He was known for his superb shot-blocking and was named the NBA's most valuable player five times. Russell later went on to coach his old team, becoming the first black coach in the history of the NBA.

1930 At the Meadowbrook Games in Philadelphia, Pennsylvania, a 17-year-old runner named Stella Walsh made news by setting her second world record in a week. She won the 220-yard girls' sprint in a time of 26.8 seconds.

1954 Only a year after scoring 63 points in a game against Mercer College, Frank Selvy of Furman University became the first college player to hit the century mark. The 6-foot, 3-inch senior scored an even 100 points in his team's 149–95 victory over Newberry College. No other player has even come close to breaking his record.

1971

SAD SACKS OF SPORTS

Duck! The Vice President is teeing off. On his very first shot in a golf match in Palm Springs, California, Vice President Spiro Agnew took a swing at the ball and ... OUCH! The ball smacked a 66-year-old spectator in the arm. If that wasn't bad enough, the ball then bounced off the man and hit his wife. Agnew's next shot smashed into the left ankle of a woman who had to be rushed to the hospital. She was released an hour later. As a result, Agnew skipped the first hole and started on the second.

1934 Thirteen years before the first official NHL All-Star Game, an all-star game of sorts was held in Toronto, Canada. Called the Ace Bailey Benefit Game, it featured the entire Toronto Maple Leaf squad against the best players from the NHL's seven other teams. The Leafs won, 7–3. The game was played to raise money for Toronto's Ace Bailey, who had suffered a fractured skull on December 2, 1933.

1953 Bill Chambers of William & Mary College set an NCAA basketball record today by pulling down 51 rebounds in a game against Virginia. Another player would set an NCAA record for most rebounds in a *season* that very same year. Walt Dukes of Seton Hall University grabbed 734 rebounds in 33 games, for an average of 22.2 rebounds a game.

1966 Rick Dean of Syracuse University became the first college basketball player to hit all of his shots (minimum of 13) as he went 13 for 13 in a game against arch-rival Colgate. As of the 1989 season, only five other players had gone 13 for 13, most recently Brad Daugherty of North Carolina on November 24, 1985.

1975 The San Diego Conquistadors and the New York Nets (who later became part of the NBA and moved to New Jersey) played the highest scoring game in the American Basketball Association. After four overtimes, San Diego finally beat the Nets, 176–166. The game took more than three hours to complete. The Nets Julius Erving scored a career-high 63 points in the losing effort.

1932 The four-man bobsled team from the United States won the gold medal in the Olympics at Lake Placid, New York. On board was Edward F. Eagan, who also won a gold medal in boxing in the 1920 *Summer* Olympics. Eagan is the only man to win a gold medal in both the Winter and Summer Olympics.

1953 Figure skater Tenley Albright made history by becoming the first American woman to win the world title in skating. She also won the North American and U.S. championships that year, and medals in the 1952 and '56 Olympics.

1978 In one of the most remarkable boxing upsets in history, heavyweight Leon Spinks won a 15-round split decision over the great champion Muhammad Ali. Spinks had been such an underdog, few gambling houses had been willing to take bets on the fight.

1980 Edmonton center Wayne Gretzky tied an NHL record with seven assists in the Oilers' 8–2 victory over the Washington Capitals. The Great Gretzky tied a record set by Detroit's Billy Taylor in 1947. (See March 16, 1947.) Since then, Gretzky has had seven assists in two more games.

1953 Gordie Howe of the Detroit Red Wings became the first player in the NHL to score 40 goals in each of three seasons. He slapped in numbers 200 and 201 during a 4–1 win over the Chicago Blackhawks. With those goals, Howe also became the 25th hockey player in history to score 200 goals in his career. Howe went on to score 801 goals in his 24-year NHL career.

1984 On this day, Bill Johnson became the first American skier to win the Olympic downhill event.

1987 Cindy Brown of Long Beach State University set an NCAA women's basketball record by scoring 60 points against San Jose State University. In the game, Brown had perfect 20/20 vision—she scored 20 field goals and 20 free throws. That season, she also set an NCAA mark for most points— 974.

1988 King Kong isn't the only one who made a name for himself by climbing up the Empire State Building. Every year, runners compete to see who can dash up the 86 flights of steps in New York's famous skyscraper the fastest. This year's winner was an Australian named Craig Logan. It took him only 11 minutes and 29 seconds to run up to the top.

1899 The first two-man, six-day bicycle race came to a close in New York's Madison Square Garden. Each team of riders took turns going round and round the sports arena for six days. Then their distances were combined. The winners were Charles Miller and Frank Waller, who rode a combined total of 2,733 miles.

1951 Jay Handlan sure loved to shoot the basketball. Handlan, of the University of Washington and Lee, set an NCAA record for shots when he attempted 71 field goals in a game against Furman University. Handlan made 30 of those shots, for a .422 shooting percentage.

1975 Victor Niederhoffer defeated Peter Briggs in three straight sets to win his fifth U.S. squash singles championship. Squash is a fast-paced racquet game played in a small room with the ball bouncing off the floor and all the walls.

1985 Johnny Walker's name should have been Johnny Runner. In a track-and-field competition, the New Zealander ran a mile in under four minutes for the 100th time in his career.

1951 For weeks, a scandal had been brewing around college basketball. Today, it broke wide open. Three players from national champion City College of New York were arrested for accepting bribes from professional gamblers. The gamblers were also charged. What followed was one of the biggest scandals in the history of college sports, which eventually included schools around the country.

1967 Any baseball fan who thinks that softball is a baby's game should take a look at the results of a special exhibition game held today. Softball pitcher Eddie Feigner struck out six of baseball's greatest hitters in a row: Willie Mays, Willie McCovey, Brooks Robinson, Roberto Clemente, Maury Wills and Harmon Killebrew.

1967 Pole vaulter Bob Seagren set a world indoor record of 17 feet, 3 inches at the Knights of Columbus meet in Cleveland, Ohio today. Seagren would go on to smash his own record on July 2, 1972, when he jumped 18 feet, 5³/₄ inches.

1979 Richard Petty drove his Oldsmobile at an average speed of just under 144 mph to win the Daytona 500 in Daytona Beach, Florida. This made him the first race car driver to win the event six times.

1928 As soon as the Canadian ice hockey team arrived in St. Moritz, Switzerland, for the Winter Games, Olympic officials knew they had problems. It was obvious that the Canadians were far better than any other squad. To avoid embarrassing the other teams, the officials quickly changed the rules so that Canada would only have to play in the final round, and all 10 other teams would have to compete in the earlier rounds. As expected, team Canada dominated and won the gold medal. And they did it without giving up a single goal. The final score of their three games: 11–0, 14–0, 13–0.

1984 How many Mahres [pronounced Mares] does it take to dominate an Olympic event? When you're talking about twin brothers Phil and Steve Mahre, the answer is two. The look-alike Americans finished first and second in the slalom skiing competition at the Winter Olympics in Sarajevo, Yugoslavia. Phil took the gold and Steve won the silver.

1952

THE GOOD, THE BAD AND THE WEIRD

If at first you don't succeed, fall, fall again. Greek skier Antoin Miliordos found a unique way to ski the slalom. After falling down 18 times in the Olympics in Oslo, Norway, he became so disgusted, he sat down and slid backwards past the finish line. His final time for the one run was slower than the winner's combined time for *two* runs. Don't worry Antoin, we've all had days like that.

1952 Five years after Jackie Robinson became the first black baseball player in the major leagues (see April 15, 1947), Emmett Ashford continued to chip away at the color barrier. He became the first black umpire in organized baseball. He was a substitute umpire in minor league baseball.

1982 In NHL action, the New York Islanders outskated the Colorado Rockies 3–2 for their 15th regular-season win in a row—an NHL record.

1988 It was "The Battle of the Brians," one of the most closely watched events of the 1988 Winter Olympics. The competition for the gold medal in men's figure skating was considered a toss-up between American Brian Boitano and Canadian Brian Orser. The battle was as close as people had expected, and tonight Boitano finally eked out the victory with his brilliant "free skate." The scene of Boitano standing at the medal ceremony with tears in his eyes as *The Star Spangled Banner* was played is still a highlight of the Games.

Muhammad Ali, the heavyweight boxer who defeated Sonny Liston to win the first of his three world championships. (See February 25, 1964)

1952 Figure skater Dick Button of the United States introduced a daring new move at the Olympics in Oslo, Norway. He became the first man to do a triple loop jump—three complete turns in the air followed by a smooth landing. Button admitted he was terrified as he prepared to do the difficult move. But he did it perfectly. It was the second straight Olympics in which he had won the gold medal after introducing a new figure skating move. In 1948, he introduced the double Axel, another difficult jump.

1980 It was a great day for Liechtenstein, a tiny country of only 25,000 people which is usually overshadowed by neighboring Germany. If you took everyone who lived in Liechtenstein and put them in the Rose Bowl, you'd still have room for three more Liechtensteins. But at the Winter Olympics in Lake Placid, New York, one of those 25,000 people—a woman named Hanni Wenzel—made history. She became the first person from Liechtenstein to win an Olympic gold medal when she came in first in the giant slalom. Two days later Wenzel took the gold in the slalom.

1979

THE GOOD, THE BAD AND THE WEIRD

What if you held a basketball game and no one scored? That's what happened at a girls' high school basketball contest between two schools from Sheldon, Iowa. The score at the end of four quarters: Melvin 0, Sibley 0. In fact, it took four *overtimes* before these two teams suddenly came alive (sort of). Melvin finally won it, 4–2.

1906 Using a stroke called the "modified Australian crawl," Charles M. Daniels became the first American to swim 100 yards in less than a minute. His time of 57.6 seconds, at the New York Athletic Club, tied the world record. On March 23, 1906, Daniels shattered the world mark, swimming 100 yards in 56 seconds flat.

1936 Norwegian figure skater Sonja Henie (pronounced SEWN-ya HEN-nee) completed her brilliant career by winning her 10th world championship in a row. A week earlier she had won her third straight gold medal in the 1936 Olympics in Garmisch-Partenkirchen, Germany. During her career Sonja collected 1,473 cups, medals and trophies. She changed the sport of figure skating by introducing many of the graceful spins and jumps that are now common. After retiring from skating, Sonja became a successful Hollywood actress.

1937 Robert Grant III defeated Ted Edwards in straight sets to take the 46th U.S. Racquets Championships in New York City. Grant soon established himself as one of the greatest racquet tennis players ever by winning another nine titles through 1953.

1980 It's called the "Miracle on Ice" and shall always be remembered as one of the greatest moments in the history of American sports. The United States ice hockey team was a heavy underdog when it faced the superior Soviet squad at the Winter Olympics in Lake Placid, New York. Trailing 3–2, the Americans rallied to score two quick goals for an awesome 4–3 upset. Goalie Jim Craig held off one Soviet shot after another, and the largely American crowd went wild as the final seconds ticked off. Hundreds of American flags waved throughout the arena, and millions of fans cheered around the country. The U.S. went on to win the gold medal.

1960 This is one of those stories that make you feel all warm inside. Four years after her mother died from cancer, American figure skater Carol Heiss vowed to win a gold medal at the Winter Olympics in her honor. And that's exactly what she did. If that wasn't a happy enough ending, Heiss ended up marrying the 1956 gold medal winner in the men's figure skating event—Hayes Jenkins.

1967 In a track meet in Lawrence, Kansas, runner Jim Ryun set an indoor half-mile record of 1 minute, 48.3 seconds. It was only one of seven world marks he would set, despite the fact he suffered from severe nearsightedness, hearing impairment and allergies. He set the record for the two-mile and the 1500-meters, and five records for the mile. (He kept breaking his own record.) Ryun went on to win the silver medal in the 1500-meter run at the 1968 Olympics.

1968 In a game against the Detroit Pistons, Wilt Chamberlain of the Philadelphia 76ers became the first man to score more than 25,000 points in his career. By the time he retired in 1973 after 14 years in the NBA, Chamberlain had scored 31,419—a mark that has been surpassed only by Kareem Abdul-Jabbar.

1980 In the Olympics at Lake Placid, New York, American speed skater Eric Heiden won the gold medal in the 10,000-meter event. It was his fifth gold medal in five events—a sweep of the men's competition. Heiden was the first athlete to earn five individual medals at one Olympics.

1987 Seattle's Nate McMillan proved he was one super Super-Sonic when he handed out 25 assists in a game against the Los Angeles Clippers. His performance tied an NBA record for most assists by a rookie. The mark was first set by Ernie DiGregorio of the Buffalo Braves in 1974. By the way, the Sonics clipped the Clippers, 124–112.

1942 Most dog owners are happy if Fido brings their slippers and and waits until it's time to be walked. But Everett Heseman expected a free ride from his four-legged friends. And he got it. Heseman became the first man to win the American Dog Derby three times. Contestants sat in a sled and were pulled by a team of dogs around a two-mile track. What a life.

1978 Kevin Porter of the New Jersey Nets went down in the record books tonight, even though he only scored 14 points. His 29 assists set an NBA mark for the most in one game. New Jersey topped the Houston Rockets, 126–112. Porter's record has yet to be broken.

1980 The United States ice hockey squad beat the Finnish team 4–2 to win the gold medal in the 1980 Olympics. The victory came two days after the Americans had shocked the powerful Soviets (see February 22, 1980) and performed their Miracle on Ice. It was the Americans' first gold medal in the sport since 1960.

1985 The United States Football League (USFL) may no longer be around, but here's a record to remember. Houston Gamblers quarterback Jim Kelly (now with the Buffalo Bills in the NFL) passed for 574 yards in a 34–33 victory over the Los Angeles Express. That's more yards than any quarterback in the NFL or any pro football league has ever thrown. Kelly broke the record of 554 yards set by Norm Van Brocklin of the Los Angeles Rams in 1951. (See September 28, 1951.) Kelly also threw for five touchdowns in that game.

1929 Marie Boyd of Lonaconing Central High School in Maryland set a record for the most points scored in a high school basketball game. Boyd poured in 156 points in her team's 163–3 thrashing of Ursuline Academy.

1940 For the first time in history, a hockey game was televised. The New York Rangers took on the Montreal Canadiens at New York's Madison Square Garden, and television station W2XBS was there to call the action.

1962 Mike O'Hara competed in his 97th marathon—New York's Cherry Tree Marathon. No man—or woman for that matter—had ever run that many long-distance races. Since marathons are 26 miles, 385 yards long, O'Hara ran more than *2,500* miles in competition.

1964 Cassius Clay (who later changed his name to Muhammad Ali) was given little chance of beating Sonny Liston in the world heavyweight boxing title match. But Clay fought a calm and calculated fight for five rounds, then he got tough in the sixth. Liston quit before the seventh round. It was Clay's first heavyweight championship, but not his last. He won a total of three. Whatever name he fought under, Clay was one of the greatest boxers of all time.

1977 Pete Maravich of the New Orleans Jazz (now the Utah Jazz) set an NBA record by scoring the most points ever by a guard. Maravich, who also set many records scoring in college, hit 26 of 43 shots from the field and 16 of 19 from the free throw line for a total of 68 points.

1988 You're pulling my Oleg. Seventy-four-year-old fashion designer Oleg Cassini is probably the last man you'd expect to see driving a horse to victory at harness race. But only a day after his first race, Cassini drove a 10–1 shot to victory at New Jersey's Freehold Raceway. For his win, the Italian millionaire earned $67.50.

1960 In the final round of the men's figure skating competition, American David Jenkins staged a dramatic comeback today to win the gold medal in the Winter Olympics at Squaw Valley, California. Four years earlier, his brother, Hayes, had won the gold medal in the same event. And three days earlier, David's soon-to-be sister-in-law, Carol Heiss, won the gold in the women's competition. Call it a family affair.

1962 It may not have been a brilliant career, but at least it was short: Junior middleweight boxer Joseph "Ace" Falu was knocked out after only 14 seconds of the first round of his very first professional fight in New York City. Falu wisely decided never to fight again.

1887
SPORTS
PROFILE Baseball great Grover Cleveland Alexander (no relation to U.S. President Grover Cleveland) was born in tiny Elba, Nebraska. One of the greatest right-handed pitchers in the history of the game, Alexander won more games (373) than any other player except the great Cy Young. In 20 years with the Philadelphia Phillies, Chicago Cubs and St. Louis Cardinals, he had a career earned run average of 2.56 and pitched 90 shutouts (once again good enough for second on the all-time list). He also had a total of 2,199 career strikeouts. Alexander, who retired in 1930, was elected to the Baseball Hall of Fame in 1938. In 1952, an actor named Ronald Reagan portrayed the pitcher in the film *The Winning Team*. Whatever happened to that Reagan guy anyway?

1874 England's first baseball game was played today. Teams were made up of English soccer and cricket players, plus a handful of American baseball players. Cricket is a British game that is somewhat similar to baseball, only it is played with flat bats and with very different rules. Despite today's attempt, American baseball never caught on in England.

1980 The Major Indoor Soccer League (MISL) held its first All-Star Game before 16,892 fans in the Checkerdome in St. Louis, Missouri. The Central Division defeated the Atlantic Division, 9–4.

1982 Earl Anthony became the first bowler to win $1 million in his career. The Hall of Famer from Dublin, California, has won more than 40 Professional Bowlers Association titles in his career, which dates back to 1970.

1988 Katarina Witt of East Germany thrilled the figure skating world when she became only the second woman ever to win back-to-back gold medals at the Olympics. Four years earlier, in Sarajevo, Yugoslavia, Witt narrowly defeated American Rosalyn Sumners to win her first medal. In 1988 she again triumphed at the games in Calgary, Canada. The only other woman to win back-to-back gold medals in figure skating was Sonja Henie, who did it in 1928 and 1932—and in 1936!

1940 For the first time a basketball game was broadcast live on television. The University of Pittsburgh Panthers whipped the Fordham University Rams 50–37 in New York's Madison Square Garden.

1960 After two periods in the hockey game for the gold medal at the Winter Olympics, the United States was trailing Czechoslovakia 4–3, and the players looked exhausted. During the break between periods, the captain of the Soviet squad (which had lost to the Americans the day before) came into the U.S. locker room. He offered one piece of advice: Get some oxygen—fast. The Americans took his advice, hunted down an oxygen tank, and went back on the ice to score six unanswered goals. They won 9–4.

1967 Wilt Chamberlain missed a shot tonight from the field for the first time in 36 attempts. He didn't miss a single shot in an astounding 11 days. His 35 field goals in a row set a NBA record.

1960
SAD SACKS
OF SPORTS
While the United States hockey team was taking the gold medal in the Olympics, the unfortunate Australians were struggling to a last-place finish. One of their many defeats was at the hands of Finland, who beat them 14–1. After Australia scored its only goal, center Ivor Vesley was so excited, he forgot to stop himself from going straight into the net. He smashed his head on the iron crossbar and had to be rushed to the hospital.

1964 For the first five overtime periods, it was exciting. During the next few periods, it began to get boring. And by the 13th overtime period, the players from Boone Trail and Angier High Schools in Mamers, North Carolina, must have needed oxygen tents! Finally, Boone came out on top, 56-54. That was after 13 overtime periods.

1964 Badminton is a game that is similiar to tennis, except the racquet has a longer handle and instead of hitting a ball you hit a lightweight object with a feathered top called a shuttlecock. Today, Frank Rugani set a record when he hit a shuttlecock 79 feet, 8½ inches in San Jose, California. The feathers on his shuttlecock must have had wings.

1980 Howe right you are! In the final season of his incredible 28-year career, Gordie Howe became the first player in the history of the NHL to score 800 goals. Before he retired a few months later, he had added an 801st goal.

Phil and Steve Mahre, the twin skiiers who won the gold and silver medals in the 1984 Olympic slalom. (See February 19, 1984)

MARCH

1973 Jockey Robyn Smith became the first woman to win a stakes horse race. She rode North Sea to victory in the $27,450 Paumanauk Handicap at New York's Aqueduct Raceway.

1988 Hockey great Wayne Gretzky set an NHL record by scoring the 1,050th assist of his career. The Edmonton Oilers center broke Gordie Howe's record while leading the Oilers over the Los Angeles Kings. It took Howe 26 seasons to set the record. Gretzky needed less than 9 seasons to break it.

1989 This New York Knicks team wasn't afraid to shoot from downtown. Tonight, they broke the NBA record for most three-pointers in a season by scoring their 272nd in a game against the Milwaukee Bucks. Even with all the three-pointers, though, the Knicks lost to the Bucks, 121–111.

1989 In an effort to cut down on steroid use among athletes, the United States and the Soviet Union announced an unusual agreement today. In all events leading up to the 1992 Olympics, American officials would test Soviet athletes in the Soviet Union and the Soviets would test U.S. athletes in the States. Steroids are illegal, dangerous drugs used by some athletes to build muscles.

Caption:
Figure skater
Katarina Witt, winner
of four world championships and two
Olympic gold medals.
(See March 26,
1988)

←

1940 The 19th annual Intercollegiate AAAA track-and-field competition became the first track meet ever shown on television. New York station W2XBS showed the important college meet live from Madison Square Garden. Some 23 colleges participated.

1951 The first NBA All-Star Game was played. More than 10,000 fans at the Boston Garden watched the East beat the West, 111–94. "Easy" Ed Macauley led all scorers with 20 points. How did he do it? It was easy.

1962 Some basketball *teams* are lucky to score 100 points a game. But Wilt Chamberlain did that all by himself. Playing for the Philadelphia Warriors, he hit 36 field goals and 28 free throws for an even 100 points. No professional has ever come close to beating that record. With Wilt's help, Philadelphia beat the Knicks, 169–147.

1970 Jacksonville University in Florida became the first college basketball team in the nation to average more than 100 points per game for an entire season. Today they defeated Miami University, 108–97, to close their regular season on a winning note.

1982 Game forfeited on account of . . . meat loaf? The Pembroke State University baseball team walked off the field with the score tied at eight in the ninth inning of a game. The players forfeited because the cafeteria was closing in five minutes. Maybe they preferred french fries to pop flies.

1938 A record 24,765 people showed up for the the American Bowling Congress tournament at Chicago's Coliseum. No, not spectators, 24,765 *competitors*. It was the largest field ever for a bowling competition.

1985 Bill Shoemaker became the first jockey to win $100,000,000 (yes, $100 million) in purses. Shoemaker was atop Lord at War when it won the Santa Anita Handicap at Arcadia, California. Bill wasn't done yet, though. When Bill retired in 1990 at the age of 58, his total number of winners was 8,833.

1920
SAD SACKS
OF SPORTS
Their name was the **Quebec Bulldogs**, but tonight they played more like chihuahuas. This NHL team (which no longer exists) gave up 16 goals, the most in NHL history, in a 16–3 loss to the Montreal Canadiens. But that was nothing compared to what the New Zealand national hockey team did on March 15, 1987. They lost a world championship match to Australia by the score of 58–0.

Jean-Claude Killy, winner of the World Cup in skiing and three Olympic gold medals. (See March 11, 1967)

1861 Edward Payson Weston travelled to Washington, D.C. to see the inauguration of President Abraham Lincoln. Unfortunately, Weston arrived late, and missed the ceremony. You can't really blame him. After all, he walked all the way from Boston, Massachusetts—that's a stroll of 478 miles! Weston had made the walk, which took 10 days, on a bet—for a bag of peanuts. He got mentioned in a lot of newspapers, and decided to become a professional walker. In 1867, he made $10,000 for walking from Portland, Maine, to Chicago, Illinois. And that's not peanuts.

1930 Bowler Emma Fahning of the Germain Cleaning Team really helped her squad clean up. During a match in Buffalo, New York, Fahning became the first woman to bowl a perfect 300. And while we're on the subject, the record for the most perfect games by a woman is held by Jeanne Maiden of Solon, Ohio. She rolled 17 in her career. The oldest woman to bowl a perfect game was 65-year-old Helen Duval.

1941 The least the Chicago Blackhawks could have done was win the game! But even though goaltender Sam LoPresti set an NHL record for stopping 80 shots in a game against the Boston Bruins, his team still lost, 3–2. LoPresti averaged a save every 45 seconds.

1924 Frank Carauna of Buffalo, New York, did what most bowlers dream of—he rolled a perfect 300 game. Then he did what few people would even *think* to dream of—he turned around and rolled a second perfect game. In his third game, Carauna rolled five more strikes in a row before finally missing a pin. In all, he had a record 29 strikes in a row.

1953 Gordie Howe of the Detroit Red Wings scored two goals and had three assists in a 7–1 NHL victory over the New York Rangers. Howe's five points for the game brought his season total to 90—breaking the old record of 86. Who held the old record? Gordie Howe.

1983 Cris Collinsworth, a wide receiver with the Cincinnati Bengals, wasn't just horsing around when he challenged the thoroughbred Mr. Hurry to a man-against-horse race at the Latonia Racetrack in Florence, Kentucky. Unfortunately for Collinsworth, Mr. Hurry did indeed hurry, and easily won the 40-yard race.

1923 Swimmer Johnny Weissmuller must have set a record for breaking records. He set his 47th world mark at a meet in New Haven, Connecticut. Weissmuller, who later played Tarzan in the movies, today became the first person to swim the 440-meter freestyle in less than five minutes.

1930 Georgetown High School in Illinois beat neighboring Homer High, 1–0, in basketball. That's right—1–0. After scoring a free throw, the Georgetown players froze the ball. The Homer boys got angry, then bored, then they just sat down and gave up. The referees, meanwhile, read the newspaper. Not one of the most exciting games in basketball history.

1981 Kris Anderson took off from Lakeland, Minnesota, this morning in a hot air balloon called *Knight Hawk*. Some 600 miles later, he landed in West Virginia, setting a record for the greatest distance traveled in a hot air balloon.

1984 Dale Hawerchuk of the Winnipeg Jets set up five goals in the second period to lead the Jets to a 7–3 win. That set an NHL record for the most assists in a period. Hawerchuk needed only two more assists in either period to tie the NHL record for the most in a game, but he didn't get them.

1954 For the first time ever, the Soviet Union was allowed to play in an international hockey match. And, boy, did they play! The Soviets defeated the Canadians in Stockholm, Sweden, to take the world ice hockey championship. The final score: 7–2. The Soviet Union has dominated international hockey ever since.

1959 Oklahoma State's Arlen Clark set an NCAA record when he hit all 24 of his free throws in a basketball game against the University of Colorado. Twenty-two years later, Western Illinois's Joe Dykstra set another free-throw mark, hitting every shot from the penalty line for eight games in a row. Dykstra hit all 64 of his free throws between December 1, 1981, and January 4, 1982.

1970 SPORTS QUIZ Austin Carr of Notre Dame University was in the driver's seat today. He set a record for most points in an NCAA Tournament game by scoring 61 points in a first-round game against Ohio University. The Fighting Irish won easily, 112–82. Carr's 61 points beat the record of 58 points held by Bill Bradley of Princeton University. Do you know what Bradley does for a living now?
A: He is a United States Senator from New Jersey.

1958   Talk about come-from-behind victories. In the running of the horse race at the Santa Anita Derby in California, a horse named Silky Sullivan was in last place. He trailed the leader by an overwhelming 40 lengths. But just when Silky's bettors thought they couldn't look any more, the horse actually rallied and managed to win the race.

1971   It was called "The Fight of the Century," and it lived up to its billing. In a match held at New York City's Madison Square Garden, Joe Frazier sent champion Muhammad Ali crashing to the canvas with a left hook in the 15th round. Clay staggered to his feet, but Frazier was given the victory and declared heavyweight champ of the world. The fighters were paid more than $2.5 million, making it the richest sports event ever at the time.

1986   Tennis sensation Martina Navratilova today became the first player to earn more than $10 million in tournament play. Since then, she has won over $5 million more. Martina also holds the record for a single year—she took home a whopping $2,173,556 in 1984, including a $1 million bonus for winning the Grand Slam of tennis (Wimbledon, the U.S., Australian and French open championships).

1989   Try saying this three times fast: Swiss miss goes shush down Shiga slalom. What does it mean? Well, Vreni Schneider, a skier from Switzerland, went shushing down the women's giant slalom in Shiga Kogen, Japan today. She won the race—her 13th skiing victory of the season— to tie a record set by Ingemar Stenmark of Sweden in 1979.

1931 George Godfrey, a former heavyweight boxer, threw his opponent, John Grandovitch of Yugoslavia, to win a wrestling match in Newark, New Jersey. Godfrey became the first black man ever to wrestle against a white opponent. In those days, segregation was common in sports and in American life in general. Blacks and whites were not allowed to wrestle together.

1948 Everyone knows about the trouble Cincinnati Reds manager Pete Rose got into for gambling. But Pete wasn't the first sports star to find himself in hot water. On this day, the NHL banned New York Ranger Billy Taylor for life because he bet on a hockey game.

1981 The Buffalo Sabres set an NHL record for goals in one period by scoring nine goals in the second period of a 14–4 win over the Toronto Maple Leafs. Toronto had set a similar scoring record itself 43 years earlier. They scored eight goals in less than five minutes in a game against the New York Americans.

1989 The Eastern Collegiate Athletic North Atlantic Conference held the opening round of its championship basketball tournament today at the Hartford Civic Center. But they wouldn't let any fans in. A measles epidemic was spreading through the two colleges playing—Siena College and Colgate University (both in New York state)—and officials decided the disease would spread like crazy if thousands of students sat close together in the stands. So Siena beat Colgate, 61–51, in front of just a handful of school officials and journalists.

1896 The first marathon of the modern age was held in Athens, Greece. The race was really a trial run for the marathon to be held at the first modern Olympic games in Athens a month later. A Greek runner named Charilaos Vasilakos won the 26 mile, 385 yard race with a time of 3 hours, 18 minutes. According to ancient history, the first marathon was in 490 B.C. when a messenger ran the 26 miles back to Athens to say the Greeks had won the Battle of Marathon. As soon as he gave the good news, the messenger dropped dead from exhaustion.

1913 William Knox struck gold at the 13th International American Bowling Congress Tournament in Toledo, Ohio. He became the first man ever to bowl a perfect 300 game in a tournament.

1963 It was only a spring training game, but it was quite a nice debut. A young player named Pete Rose had two hits in two at-bats in his first big league game for the Reds—an exhibition game against the Chicago White Sox. A great start to a great career for the man who became known as "Charlie Hustle."

1987 Kareem Abdul-Jabbar may hold a hoop-ful of NBA records, but this is one he's probably not so proud of. The Los Angeles Laker center was whistled for the 4,194th personal foul of his career. That set an NBA record, but you can bet there was no ceremony at halftime.

1892 The first public basketball game was played between students and teachers at the YMCA training school in Springfield, Massachusetts. The students beat their teachers five field goals to one. A gym teacher at the school had invented the game only a few months earlier. (See January 15, 1892.)

1967 Jean-Claude Killy, considered the greatest skier of his time, won the World Cup of skiing by winning the North American alpine giant slalom in Franconia, New Hampshire. Killy went on to win three gold medals in the 1968 Olympics.

1971 One assist, two goals, two records. Not a bad night for Boston's Phil Esposito. In one game, the Bruin center set records for most goals in a season (60) and most points in a season (128). Even more important for his teammates, the Bruins crushed the Los Angeles Kings, 7–2.

1979 Was this a hockey game, or a boxing match? In a fight-filled contest that went down in the record books, the Philadelphia Flyers beat the Los Angeles Kings, 6–3. Thanks to a gigantic, bench-clearing brawl in the first period, the Flyers set a mark for most penalty minutes in a period by one team (188). The Kings were a close second with 184 minutes. And Los Angeles defenseman Randy Holt set another record by tallying 67 penalty minutes all by himself. (Not bad, considering there are only 60 minutes in a game.) How did Randy do it? With three major penalties, one minor, and five misconducts. In the words of Lou Costello, Randy was a baaaaaad boy.

1956 There is no shame in fouling out of a basketball game in its closing minutes. The most aggressive players in the NBA do it from time to time. But what about fouling out in just five minutes? That's what Dick Farley of the Syracuse Nationals did in a game against the St. Louis Hawks. In doing so, he set an NBA record no player has ever matched—and no player wants to.

1956 Two teenagers stood out at a swimming meet in Chicago for a couple of reasons. First, Joan Page and Jane Peterson both broke their own personal best records in the 100-yard butterfly. But the really odd part was that both were under post-hypnotic influence at the time. In other words, both girls had been hypnotized before the meet and told they would swim better than they ever could.

1966 He was known as the Golden Jet—and he was fast. Bobby Hull of the Chicago Blackhawks was considered the best left wing in the history of hockey. One of his shots was timed at 118.3 mph! Today, he set an NHL record for the most goals in a season by scoring his 51st against the New York Rangers. By the end of the year, he would have 54.

1915 SPLAT! As a stunt, Brooklyn Dodgers manager Wilbert Robinson tried to catch a baseball dropped from an airplane during spring training in Florida. The pilot, though, played a joke on Robinson, and threw out a grapefruit instead. When Robinson tried to catch it, the grapefruit splattered all over the place. Maybe that's why they call spring training in Florida the Grapefruit League.

1948 Dr. Reginald Weir won his first-round match at the U.S. Indoor Lawn Tennis Association Championship in New York City to become the first black player ever to play in the championship. He was eliminated from the competition two days later. Two years later, Althea Gibson became the first black person to play in the more important U.S. Open Championship.

1981 Kevin Slaten of the St. Louis Steamers got thrown out of a Major Indoor Soccer League playoff game for trying to punch a player from the other team. Happens all the time, you say? Not exactly, Slaten was the *announcer* for the Steamers, not a player.

1983 Neither colds nor injuries nor.... In fact, nothing could keep guard Randy Smith out of a basketball game. For 11 years with the Buffalo Braves, the San Diego Clippers, Cleveland Cavaliers and New York Knicks, Smith didn't miss a single game. His 906-game playing streak set an NBA record. Only Ron Boone of the Utah Jazz played more professional basketball games in a row—1,041—but most of those were played for teams in the American Basketball Association which no longer exists.

1929 The puck stops here. Montreal Canadiens goalie George Hainsworth recorded his 22nd shutout of the season to set an NHL record. He did it in the Canadiens 1–0 victory over the Montreal Maroons. Hainsworth posted shutouts in exactly half of the 44 games in which he played that season.

1936 Tennis players Alex Ehrlich of Poland and Farcas Paneth of Romania held the longest rally in the history of the sport. At the start of a match in Prague, Czechoslovakia, it took them two hours and five minutes to score the very first point.

1953 Put up your Dukes: Seton Hall University's Walter Dukes pumped in 21 points and pulled down 20 rebounds to lead the Seton Hall University Pirates to the National Invitational Tournament Championship over St. John's University, 58–46. Dukes was named Most Valuable Player of the tournament and he set a college mark for most rebounds in a season (734), which still stands.

1962 A year after becoming the first player in the NBA to score 3,000 points in a season, Wilt Chamberlain became the first man to score more than 4,000 points in a season! He scored 34 points to lead the Philadelphia Warriors over the Chicago Packers, and led his season total to 4,029 points. To this day, no one has come close to matching Wilt's mark.

1963 San Francisco Warriors guard Guy Rodgers tied an NBA record by handing out 28 assists in his team's victory over the St. Louis Hawks. The Warriors have since moved across San Francisco Bay to Oakland, where they are known as the Golden State Warriors. The record for assists has since been broken by New Jersey's Kevin Porter, who dished out 29 in a 1978 game against the Houston Rockets.

1869 Baseball's first entirely professional team, the Cincinnati Red Stockings, played their first game, and it was a blowout. They defeated Antioch, 41–7. The Red Stockings were the first team in which all the players were paid. The players' average yearly salary was $950.

1909 This senior citizen wasn't retiring! Edward P. Weston, 70, began a walk from New York to San Francisco today. It took Weston 104 days to walk the 3,800-mile route. Then, just for fun, he walked back the next year. Show-off.

1970 Bobby Orr of the Boston Bruins scored two goals and two assists in a game against the Detroit Red Wings to bring his season total to 101 points. This made Orr the first defenseman in the NHL to score 100 points in a season. By the time the season ended, he had scored 120 points on 33 goals and 87 assists.

1938 College basketball held its first national championships in New York. Surprise! It wasn't the NCAA Tournament but the National Invitation Tournament (NIT). Temple University beat Colorado 60–36 to win the title. The NIT is still held in New York City's Madison Square Garden, but it's the NCAA Tournament that crowns the national champs.

1947 Detroit's Billy Taylor set an NHL record by collecting seven assists in the Red Wings' victory over Chicago. His record would stand for almost 33 years, before being tied by Wayne Gretzky in 1980. The record has since been tied two other times—both by Gretzky.

1937
THE GOOD,
THE BAD
AND THE
WEIRD

Many athletes love to claim they won a game single-handedly. Here's one young basketball player who wasn't exaggerating. Today in Fairmont, West Virginia, during a scrimmage between students at St. Peter's High School, every one of Pat McGee's teammates fouled out. Unfortunately, there were four minutes left to play in the game and the score was tied 32–32. Even without teammates to help him, Pat was able to keep the other team scoreless, plus score a basket and a free throw. His team won, 35–32.

1876 Marshall Jones Brooks became the first man to jump over six feet—just barely—in the high jump. Brooks's jump of 6 feet, $\frac{1}{8}$ inch at a meet in England set a world record.

1955 NHL president Clarence Campbell (for whom the Campbell division is named) suspended the Montreal Canadiens' star player, Maurice "Rocket" Richard (pronounced ree-SHARD), for fighting in a game against the Boston Bruins. Richard was such a hero in Montreal that the fans there started a riot throughout the city. Despite his fans' loyalty, Richard wasn't allowed to play until the next season.

1984 Tracy Caulkins, a University of Florida student, set four meet records and helped Florida win two record-setting relay races at the NCAA women's swimming and diving Championship. It wasn't enough. Despite Caulkins' efforts, the University of Texas won the competition.

1945   Montreal's Maurice "Rocket" Richard soared into the NHL record books when he became the first player to score 50 goals in one season. Goal number 50 came with just over two minutes left to play in a game against the Boston Bruins. Richard retired in 1960 with a total of 544 goals in 18 seasons.

1972   The Cornell University hockey team was shut out for the first time in 225 games. Cornell picked a bad time to go dry. The 4–0 loss to Boston University (BU) cost it the NCAA hockey title. It was BU's second championship in as many years.

1982   Everybody into the pool! The first NCAA women's swimming and diving championship was held at the University of Florida. The Florida squad made the best of the home field (or is it home pool?) advantage by winning the team championship.

1988   Drag racer Eddie Hill set a National Hot Rod Association (NHRA) record for speed. At a race in Gainesville, Florida, Hill pushed his dragster to 288.73 mph by the end of the 440-yard run. And it only took about five seconds! Later that year, Hill would set another mark for running the fastest drag race ever. He completed a race in Baytown, Texas, in 4.936 seconds. (See October 9, 1988.)

1970 Despite playing with an ankle injury, "Pistol" Pete Maravich scored 20 points against Marquette University in his final college game for Louisiana State University. Maravich set a number of scoring marks that still stand, including most points in a season (1,381), most points in a career (3,667), and highest average per game in a season (44.5) and a career (44.2).

1972 March 19 is a big day for basketball blowouts. On this day, the Los Angeles Lakers walloped the Golden State Warriors, 162–99, in the most lopsided defeat in NBA history. Exactly 16 years later—on March 19, 1988—the University of North Carolina crushed Loyola of California, 123–97. UNC set records for most points scored in a regulation NCAA Tournament game, and the highest field goal percentage (79 percent).

1972 Before the NCAA held a women's basketball championship, there was the Association for Intercollegiate Athletics for Women (AIAW) tournament. In the first championship, held today, Immaculata College defeated West Chester State University, 52–48.

1953
SAD SACKS OF SPORTS Bob Lochmueller of the Syracuse Nationals set an embarrassing record that can only be described as foul. He fouled out of a playoff game against the Boston Celtics after only seven minutes. That is the quickest anyone has ever fouled out of an NBA game. The man who holds second place is Al Bianchi, who also played for the Nationals. He, also, fouled out of a playoff contest against the Celtics—but he lasted a full eight minutes.

1897 The first official men's college basketball game with five men on a team was held in New Haven, Connecticut. Yale University defeated the University of Pennsylvania, 32–10. Some basketball historians point to a January 16, 1896 college contest between the University of Chicago and Iowa as the first game under modern rules (five men on a team). But the Iowa squad was really from a local YMCA.

1914 The first international figure skating championship tournament was held in New Haven, Connecticut. In addition to men's and women's singles competitions, other events included pair skating and waltzing. Nowadays, waltzing is known as "dance."

1948 The first college ice hockey playoffs were held in Colorado Springs, Colorado. The University of Michigan defeated Dartmouth College 8–4 to take the championship.

1966 Every basketball coach will tell you how important it is to sink your free throws. So every basketball coach would love Los Angeles Laker star Jerry West. West hit 11 of 12 shots from the line in a game against the San Francisco (now Golden State) Warriors. That set a record for the most free throws in a season—840.

1934 She was one of the greatest all-around women athletes of all time—great in basketball, track, golf, and just about everything else she tried. Today, Babe Didriksen became the first woman to pitch in a major league baseball game. Didriksen pitched an inning for the Philadelphia Athletics in an exhibition game against the Brooklyn Dodgers. The inning almost turned into a disaster when she hit one batter and walked the next. Luckily, the next batter was kind enough to hit into a triple play, and Babe escaped the inning without giving up a hit.

1946 A year before Jackie Robinson broke the color barrier in Major League baseball, tailback Kenny Washington became the first black athlete ever to play with an NFL team. He signed a contract with the Los Angeles Rams.

1953 It took four overtimes, but the Boston Celtics finally defeated the Syracuse Nationals, 111–105. Bob Cousy of the Celtics certainly did his part, scoring a playoff record 50 points in the game. Cousy went on to be named an all-star 10 years in a row. In addition to Cousy's scoring, the game was also noteworthy for the record number of personal fouls called—107. Twelve players fouled out.

1893 Smith College became the first women's school to play basketball. Since there were no other colleges to compete against, the Smith students played against each other. As part of their uniforms, the girls wore bloomers (loose fitting pants) which were considered so shocking that men weren't allowed to watch the game. This *was* 1893, after all.

1894 Hockey's first Stanley Cup game was played, with Montreal beating Ottawa, 3–1. At the time, the Cup was given to the best amateur Canadian hockey team. There would be no professional clubs—or any United States clubs—until the NHL was formed more than 20 years later.

1969 Hey, Kareem, give someone else a chance! UCLA's Lew Alcindor (who later changed his name to Kareem Abdul-Jabbar) was named the MVP of the NCAA basketball championship for the third year in a row. Since college freshmen were not allowed to play at the time, that means he won the award every year he played.

1984 Here's a very good reason not to get to a hockey game late. Bryan Trottier of the New York Islanders tied an NHL record when he scored a goal against the Boston Bruins only five seconds into the game. Three years earlier, on December 20, 1981, Doug Smail of the Winnipeg Jets did the same thing against the St. Louis Blues.

1986 American Debi Thomas became the first black athlete to win a woman's world figure skating championship. The Californian beat two-time winner Katarina Witt of East Germany. Katarina got her revenge by winning the gold medal at the 1988 Winter Olympics.

1935 Oklahoma State University won the NCAA team wrestling crown for the seventh time in the eight-year history of the tournament. Three Oklahoma State wrestlers won their individual weight divisions. Only one school from the Eastern part of the United States—Pennsylvania State University—won any events at all. Oklahoma State has won 29 team titles and 109 individual titles.

1944 The Rocket soars again. Maurice "Rocket" Richard, the Montreal Canadiens right wing, scored all five of Montreal's goals in a game against the Toronto Maple Leafs to set an NHL record for goals in a playoff game. Montreal won the game, 5–1. Richard set two other records—most goals in a career (544) and most goals in a season (50)—which were later broken. But his five-goal game still stands.

1952 If you blinked you missed it. In the final game of the season, Bill Mosienko of the Chicago Blackhawks scored three goals in 21 seconds against the New York Rangers. It is the fastest hat trick in hockey history, shattering the old mark by 43 seconds. The Hawks won the game, 7–6.

1957 In the longest NCAA championship basketball game in history, the University of North Carolina beat the University of Kansas, 54–53, after playing three overtime periods. It was the second time in two nights that the Tar Heels had won a three-overtime thriller. Talk about tired.

1936 The longest hockey game in history went on for six overtime periods. It wasn't over until almost 2:30 in the morning—six hours after it began. That's when the Detroit Red Wings finally beat the Montreal Maroons, 1–0. The game totaled 2 hours, 56 minutes in actual playing time—nearly three times more than the standard 60 minutes.

1973 The International Track Association held its first professional meet in Los Angeles, complete with controversy. In the important showdown between Kip Keino (pronounced KAY-no) and Jim Ryun in the mile run, an official accidentally fired his gun to announce the final lap. But there were still *two* laps to go. Despite being confused at first, Keino held on to win by 10 yards.

1980 The University of Louisville Cardinals shocked the UCLA Bruins, 59–54, to ruin the Bruins' hopes for an 11th national college basketball title. For the Cardinals, it was their first NCAA basketball championship.

1924 The Montreal Canadiens won their first Stanley Cup. They defeated the Calgary Tigers, 3–0, to sweep the two-game series. It would not be the last time Montreal would raise the Cup in triumph. The Canadiens have won 22 total championships—nearly a third of all the Stanley Cup titles.

1944 St. John's University made college basketball history by winning their second NIT title in a row. The Redmen defeated DePaul, 47–39, at New York's Madison Square Garden. St. John's has won five NITs since—more than any other college.

1961 Despite an injury to its top fencer, New York University (NYU) won team titles in two events at the Intercollegiate Fencing Association (IFA) Championship in Princeton, N.J. It was NYU's first triumph since 1952. Gil Eisner, the national college fencing champion, was injured and had to be carried to the sidelines, but that didn't stop NYU.

1967 Kareem Abdul-Jabbar, then known as Lew Alcindor, led the University of California at Los Angeles to its third NCAA basketball championship in four years. The Bruins defeated Dayton, 79–64. They ended the season without a loss, and Alcindor ended the season with a record. He had a field-goal percentage of .667 for the season.

Bobby Orr, the first defenseman in the NHL to score 100 points in a season. (See March 15, 1970)

1966 Perhaps you have seen sumo wrestling on television. Two absolutely gigantic Japanese men try to push each other off a mat. On this day in Tokyo, Japan, a sumo wrestler named Taiho won a record 19th professional championship. Taiho was practically tiny by sumo standards. At 6′ 1″, he weighed only 310 pounds.

1973 The UCLA Bruins were unstoppable. Today they defeated Memphis State, 87–66, to win their record seventh straight NCAA basketball championship. The hero of the game was center Bill Walton, who hit all but one of the 22 field goals he attempted. It was UCLA's 75th win in a row.

1974 Milwaukee Bucks great Oscar Robertson only scored 14 points in the final basketball game of his career, but he still set two records. Robertson made nine assists, for a career record of 9,887, and he hit all six free throws to establish another mark for the most free throws (7,694) in a career.

1979 It was college basketball's dream game finally come true. Earvin "Magic" Johnson of Michigan State University and Larry Bird of Indiana State University went head-to-head tonight in the title game of the NCAA championship. When it was over, Michigan State came out on top, 75–64. These days, Johnson performs his magic for the Los Angeles Lakers and Bird flies high for the Boston Celtics.

1988 East German figure skater Katarina Witt won her fourth world championship in her final amateur competition. In addition to the world titles, Witt established herself as one of the sport's greatest talents by winning the gold medal in the 1984 and 1988 Olympics.

1939 The first NCAA basketball championship was held at Northwestern University outside Chicago. In the finals, a small crowd of only 5,000 fans watched the University of Oregon Tall Firs beat the Ohio State Buckeyes, 46–33.

1949 The University of Kentucky Wildcats became the second team in NCAA basketball history to repeat as tournament champions. They beat the only other team to win twice, the Oklahoma State University Aggies, 46–36. Six-foot-seven Wildcat Alex Groza scored 25 points and was named Most Valuable Player.

SPORTS QUIZ You've just read the names of two college teams. Can you match up the following colleges with their teams' names?

1. Notre Dame   a. Hoosiers
2. Syracuse   b. Seminoles
3. Iowa   c. Razorbacks
4. Georgetown   d. Redmen
5. Arkansas   e. Orangemen
6. Harvard   f. Fighting Irish
7. Indiana   g. Tar Heels
8. North Carolina   h. Hoyas
9. Florida State   i. Crimson
10. St. John's   j. Hawkeyes

ANSWERS:
1.f   2.e   3.j   4.h   5.c   6.i   7.a   8.g   9.b   10.d

1906 It was a busy night for heavyweight boxing champion Tommy Burns. First, he knocked out challenger Jim O'Brien in the first round. Then, later that evening, he did the same thing to boxer Jim Walker. Burns, by the way, was the shortest heavyweight champion in history, at 5′7″.

1944 Utah University shocked the college basketball world by winning the NCAA basketball championship in New York City's Madison Square Garden. Utah was a last-minute, surprise entry into the tournament. It replaced Arkansas University which had to drop out when two key players were hurt in an automobile accident. The Utes defeated Dartmouth College, 42–40, behind Arnold Ferrin's 22 points.

1950 City College of New York, a tiny school, became the only team in history to win both college basketball post-season tournaments. It beat Bradley University in the finals of both the National Invitation Tournament and NCAA championship. After City's double victory, the rules were quickly changed. A team can no longer play in both tournaments.

1982 The final game of the first NCAA women's basketball tournament was held today. Louisiana Technical University beat Cheyney State University of Pennsylvania, 76–62. Before this, the Association for Intercollegiate Athletics for Women held the only national championship for women.

1976 Indiana University beat the University of Michigan, 86–68, to take the NCAA basketball title and complete a perfect season. The Hoosiers became only the seventh team in history to take the championship without losing a game. They ended the season with 32 victories and no losses.

1981 Calvin Murphy of the Houston Rockets hit only four free throws tonight. No big deal. Or is it? Since he only had four chances, Murphy did the best he could. It was good enough for him to set a record for the highest free-throw average ever in one season—.958. By the way, the highest career percentage is held by Rick Barry, who retired from Houston a year earlier. He hit .900 from the foul line over a 14-year career.

1987 A record for indoor attendance at a sporting event was set by the professional wrestling competition, Wrestlemania III, at the Silverdome in Pontiac, Michigan. More than 93,000 fans watched Hulk Hogan become the first wrestler to defeat Andre the Giant and retain his World Wrestling Federation belt.

1867
SPORTS
PROFILE
He was born Denton True Young in Gilmore, Ohio. But he is remembered as Cy Young, the greatest pitcher who ever lived. He was certainly the busiest. By the time he retired in 1911, at age 44, Young had set records for the most games won in a career (511) and the most losses (315). He also started more games (815) and completed more games (750) than any other man during a career that stretched over 22 years and four different teams. Young was best known for a fastball so vicious it was called the "cyclone pitch." That's how he got his nickname. Young was elected to the Baseball Hall of Fame in 1937. The Cy Young Award, given every year to the best pitcher in each league, is named after him.

1946 The underdog East squad won college basketball's first All-Star Game. They beat the West in a thriller, 60–59, at New York City's Madison Square Garden. The hero of the game was a 17-year-old freshman from Colgate University named Ernie Vandeweghe. Ernie, the youngest man on the court, scored 16 points, played excellent defense and was named MVP. His son, Kiki, now plays in the NBA.

1957 The first men's national curling championship ended on this day in Chicago, Illinois. A curling club from Hibbing, Minnesota, defeated another from Minot, North Dakota. Curling is sort of like shuffleboard on ice. One player of a team rolls a specially made smooth "stone" down a lane of ice toward a bullseye. His teammates smooth out the ice in front of it with a broom. The object is to get the stone as close as possible to the bull's-eye.

1985 If there were a record for a championship setting the most records, this would be the event that set it. The NCAA men's national swimming championships saw an incredible 10 marks shattered in 10 different events. Matt Biondi of the University of California set records in the 100- and 200-meter freestyle. Biondi went on to become one of the heroes of the 1988 Olympics in Seoul, South Korea.

1987 The NCAA basketball finals at the Superdome in New Orleans, Louisiana, set a record for attendance at a college game. 64,959 fans watched Indiana University's Keith Smart hit a jumper with five seconds left to edge Syracuse University in a 74–73 thriller.

1923 The first dance marathon began at the Audubon Ballroom in New York City. When it was over, 27 hours later, Alma Cummings ended more than a day of non-stop dancing. Later, dance marathons changed a bit and became a real fad. Dozens of couples would dance until they literally fell down and had to be dragged off the floor. The last couple standing won. (See July 1, 1928.)

1985 The first Wrestlemania was held before 23,000 screaming fans at New York City's Madison Square Garden. In a tag-team match, Hulk Hogan and Mr. T defeated "Rowdy" Roddy Piper and Paul Orndoff. Bob Orton, the corner man for Piper and Orndoff, accidently hit Orndoff with his cast and knocked him out cold for the count. Muhammad Ali was the referee.

1928
SPORTS
PROFILE
Gordon "Gordie" Howe was born in Saskatchewan, Canada. One of the greatest players in the history of hockey, he also played the sport longer than any other man. Howe skated with the Detroit Red Wings for 26 seasons through 1971. Two years later, he came out of retirement to play with his two sons for the Houston Aeros in the World Hockey Association. Then he returned to the NHL for a final season with the Hartford Whalers. By the time he retired in 1980, Howe was 52. But he was still one of the best. He held NHL records for playing in more hockey games than any other man (1,767), for most points in a lifetime (1,850) and for most All-Star Game appearances (21).

1972 As millions of fans were preparing for the start of the baseball season, America got some shocking news. The first players' strike in the sport's history began. The walk-out lasted until April 13, and the season began two days later. Games that were canceled were not replayed.

1985 In one of the biggest college basketball upsets in recent years, Villanova University defeated heavily-favored Georgetown University, 66–64, to take the NCAA championship. Georgetown had won the title the year before and had been rated Number 1 much of the season. But no one counted on Villanova hitting an impressive 79% of its shots.

1989 Thousands of fans cheered swimmer David Wharton to victory in the national collegiate men's swimming championships in Indianapolis, Indiana. Unfortunately, Wharton couldn't hear them. He suffers from severe hearing loss, and wears a hearing aid outside the pool. In the pool, he won the 200- and 400-yard individual medley titles.

1990 President George Bush announced a new sports trivia competition for 8 to 13 year olds throughout the United States. Anyone can enter at any time. The winner will receive a year off from school and a special dinner at the White House. April Fool!

Hank Aaron, the batter who broke Babe Ruth's record for most home runs in a career. (See April 8, 1974)

←

1931 Jackie Mitchell, 17, became the first female pitcher on a men's baseball team when she was signed by the Chattanooga (Tennessee) Baseball Club of the Southern Association, a minor league. In her first start today, Mitchell consecutively fanned two of the greatest hitters of all time—Babe Ruth and Lou Gehrig—in a special exhibition.

1956 For the first time ever, the United States and the People's Republic of China met in an athletic competition. The two nations took part in a table tennis tournament held in Japan. The Chinese defeated the Americans, five matches to four.

1974 It was Jerry West's last game, but he made it memorable. His team, the Los Angeles Lakers, was in trouble. The Lakers trailed the Milwaukee Bucks in the NBA playoffs two games to none, and they were behind in this one. West, their star player, was on the sideline with an injury. Then, in the second quarter, the coach decided to put him in the game. The home crowd at the Forum leapt to its feet. Although he scored only two points in the game, West gave his teammates the spark they needed. Los Angeles rallied to win the game, 98–96. The Bucks, though, would still take the series.

1983 Luther Bradley set a professional football record on this day that may never be beaten. He intercepted an amazing six passes in one game! Bradley was playing for the Chicago Blitz of the United States Football League in a game against the Tampa Bay Bandits. He ran back one of the interceptions for a 93-yard touchdown. Sixteen NFL players have had four interceptions in one game, but no one has ever matched Bradley's record.

1989 Hulk Hogan regained his World Wrestling Federation title by defeating champion Randy Savage in the main event of Wrestlemania V.

1936 The shortest professional boxing match on record took place in New Haven, Connecticut. Heavyweight Al Carr knocked out Lew Massey only seven seconds after the fight began. Fifty years later, Mike Tyson knocked out Marvis Frazier in just 30 seconds for the shortest fight ever seen on TV. The shortest amateur fight took place on November 4, 1974. It lasted four seconds—about one-fifth as long as it took you to read this entry.

1981 Participating in a track-and-field competition in Rome, Italy, Arnie Boldt of Canada cleared 6 feet, 8¼ inches in the high jumping event. Boldt's accomplishment is especially impressive since he has only one leg.

1989 There was enough drama in this year's NCAA basketball championship that you could have turned it into a Broadway play. First there were the University of Michigan Wolverines, whose head coach had been fired just before the start of the tournament. Then there was the Cinderella team, the Seton Hall University Pirates. No one dreamed they would make it to the finals. The two teams played the first title game to go into overtime in 26 years. Michigan won, 80–79, when Rumeal Robinson sank two foul shots with only three seconds left in the overtime.

Kareem Abdul-Jabbar, the highest scorer in the history of the NBA. (See April 5, 1984)

1974 It's a tie. Some 52,000 baseball fans packed Cincinnati's Riverfront Stadium to watch the Reds take on the Atlanta Braves. They were there not only to see the game, but to watch Atlanta's Hank Aaron try to tie Babe Ruth's record of 714 career home runs. Aaron didn't disappoint the fans. In his very first at bat, he smacked a three-run homer. Four days later, in Atlanta, Aaron broke the Babe's record. (See April 8, 1974.)

1986 Wayne Gretzky has set so many hockey records in his career that it's no surprise that he broke two in one night. He recorded three assists, including his 163rd of the year, in the Oilers' 9–3 loss to Calgary. This broke the season record for most assists, and also for the most points (215). In both cases, the record Gretzky broke had been set earlier by—you guessed it—Wayne Gretzky.

1988 George Bell of the Toronto Blue Jays was not a happy man. During spring training, he had been made the designated hitter, which meant he could no longer play in the field. But his unhappiness didn't stop him from setting a major-league record. He went out and belted three home runs in the team's very first game of the season, against the Kansas City Royals. Bell became the first player ever to hit three homers on opening day. All his shots were hit off pitcher Bret Saberhagen. The Blue Jays won, 5–3.

1952 Henry Wittenberg won the Amateur Athletic Union's national wrestling championship in the 191-pound division for a record eighth time. This time, he defeated Enzo Marinelli of Syracuse University. Four years earlier, Wittenberg had won a gold medal in wrestling at the Olympics. In fact, he won more than 350 bouts in his 13-year amateur career.

1984 Los Angeles Laker great Kareem Abdul-Jabbar became the highest scorer in the history of the NBA by breaking Wilt Chamberlain's record of 31,419 career points. But Kareem wasn't done yet. By the time he retired in 1989, he had 38,387 points.

1987 Doug Jarvis of the Hartford Whalers set a whale of a record. He played in his 962nd game in a row to set an NHL mark. Jarvis' streak began an incredible 12 years earlier, on October 8, 1975, when he was playing for the Montreal Canadiens.

1893 Boxers Andy Bowen and Jack Burke participated in the longest fight in history. The two men from New Orleans, Louisiana, slugged it out for 110 rounds! The contest was finally declared a draw because both men were too tired to go on. The fight started at 9:15 p.m. and didn't end until 4:34 in the morning for a total of 7 hours and 19 minutes.

1926 The Montreal Maroons defeated the Victoria Cougars, 2–0, in the fourth game of the Stanley Cup championship to win the title.

1973 New York's Ron Blomberg became major league baseball's first designated hitter. Under the DH rule, a player hits for the pitcher, but does not take the field. The rule was first adopted by the American League on a three-year trial basis, and later became permanent. The National League has never used the DH.

1980 Gordie Howe, 52, played the final regular season game of his brilliant 32-year career. Howe played more seasons in the NHL (26) than any other man. He also played six years in the World Hockey Association. In his last game, Howe helped the Hartford Whalers beat the Detroit Red Wings, 5–3. Gordie still holds four major scoring records. (See November 10, 1963.)

1975 SPORTS QUIZ Dave Schultz of the Philadelphia Flyers spent seven minutes in the penalty box as the Flyers beat the Atlanta Flames, 6–2. That gave Schultz the NHL record for the most minutes penalized in one season— 472. How many hours did he spend in the penalty box?

A: 7 hours, 52 minutes (or: 7.866 hours).

1943 The NFL decided to require that all players wear helmets. Before, many players wore nothing on their head and some got badly injured. The first helmets were nothing like today's, though. They were thin, made of leather and had no face mask. But they were better than nothing.

1969 President Richard Nixon was disappointed. An avid Washington Senators baseball fan, he and 45,000 others were in the stands at Robert F. Kennedy Stadium in Washington, D.C. to see the debut of the Senators' new manager, Ted Williams. Williams may have been one of the greatest players ever, but he couldn't work miracles as a coach. Washington lost to the New York Yankees, 8–4.

1979 Pitcher Ken Forsch of the Houston Astros hurled a no-hitter to beat the Atlanta Braves, 6–0. The previous season, Forsch's brother Bob had thrown a no-hitter for the St. Louis Cardinals. The Forsches are the first brothers ever to do that.

1986 Well, there he goes again. President Ronald Reagan, who announced baseball games over the radio as a young man, tossed out the first pitch at Memorial Stadium in Baltimore, Maryland. Unfortunately, he threw it 10 feet over Oriole catcher Rick Dempsey's head. Better stick to the radio, Ronnie.

1989 John Stockton of the Utah Jazz made his 1,000th assist of the season and led the Jazz to a 99–97 win over the Los Angeles Lakers. It was the second season in a row that Stockton had more than 1,000 assists. He was the first player in the NBA to do so.

1928 More than 16,000 fans gathered at New York's Polo Grounds to watch the American Soccer League championship, called the Challenge Cup. The New York Nationals and the Chicago Bricklayers played to a 1–1 tie. Because the score was still knotted after two overtime periods, the teams later met again for a rematch in Chicago. The Nationals won, 3–0. But the 16,000 who had gathered in the Polo Grounds set an American record for soccer. Some believed the sport would soon overtake football in popularity.

1974 Going, going, gone...again. In the fourth game of the season, Hank Aaron did what everyone had said was impossible. He broke Babe Ruth's record for most home runs in a career with his 715th homer. By the time Hank retired in 1976, the Atlanta and Milwaukee slugger had hammered an amazing 755 homers and driven in 2297 runs. No one has bettered either of these marks yet.

1982 Steve Bentley of Sacramento, California, earned a place in the *Guinness Book of World Records* today. He tossed a Frisbee® farther than any person had before—272$\frac{1}{2}$ feet.

1989 Talk about putting some English on the ball! Alex English of the Denver Nuggets became the first player in the history of the NBA to score 2,000 or more points in each of eight seasons in a row. He scored number 2,000 in the Nuggets' 110–106 victory over the Utah Jazz.

1923 A five-man bowling team from Milwaukee, Wisconsin, won the American Bowling Congress team championship, and set a world record in the process. The men became only the second squad in bowling history to score more than 3,100 points in competition. Their 3,139 points beat the previous mark of 3,115—set just five minutes earlier in the same tournament.

1959 The Boston Celtics defeated the Minneapolis Lakers in four games to win the NBA championship. It was the first sweep ever in title play. It was also the Celtics' first in a record string of eight straight championships. In that stretch, Boston would beat the Lakers four more times. They did it again in 1968 and 1969 but, by then, the Lakers had moved to Los Angeles, California.

1965 The Astrodome—the world's first domed stadium— officially opened in Houston. More than 47,000 fans were on hand, including President and Mrs. Lyndon Johnson, as the Astros played the New York Yankees in an exhibition game. Now, there are domed stadiums in major cities throughout the United States and Canada. There's even one on a college campus—the Carrier Dome at Syracuse University.

1974 The "San Diego Chicken" waddled into Jack Murphy Stadium in San Diego, California, for the first time. A San Diego resident named Ted Giannoulas dressed up as a giant chicken and ran around the stands, the field and the top of the dugout entertaining the fans. As it turned out, it was the Padres who were chicken. They lost to the Houston Astros, 9–5.

1896 With only a few miles to go in the first modern Olympic marathon, an Australian named Edwin Flack was in the lead. But he began to weave back and forth from absolute exhaustion. A kind Greek man came over to help Flack, but the runner, by now totally dazed and confused, thought he was being attacked. So he punched the man to the ground. Flack never finished the race, but he might have won a medal in boxing if he had entered that event.

1934 In one of the great upsets in Stanley Cup history, the Chicago Blackhawks shocked the Detroit Red Wings, 1–0, to win the Cup, three games to one. The Hawks were never given much of a shot to make the finals, much less win. Their regular season record was so bad that they barely even qualified for the playoffs.

1948 It wasn't a very good night for Chuck Reiser of the Baltimore Bullets of the NBA. In a game against the Philadelphia Warriors, he threw up 14 field goal attempts...and missed all 14. That set an NBA record for misses that was unmatched for 30 years. On June 7, 1978, Dennis Johnson of the Seattle SuperSonics missed all 14 of his shots in a game against the Bullets, who had moved to Washington, D.C.

1956 The Montreal Canadiens beat the Detroit Red Wings to capture the NHL Stanley Cup, four games to one. It was the third time in a row the Canadiens had met their American rivals for the Cup. In each of the two previous years, Detroit had won in an exhausting seven-game series.

1962 A new club called the Houston Colt .45s played the first baseball game ever held in Texas. They defeated the Chicago Cubs, 11–2. Three years later, the Colt .45s moved into the world's first domed stadium, the Astrodome, and became known as the Houston Astros.

1912 The New York Giants walloped the Brooklyn Dodgers, 18–3, behind the pitching of Rube Marquard. For Marquard, it was the start of an incredible 19-game winning streak. Most pitchers would be happy to win 19 games in a season, much less in a row!

1962 The New York Metropolitans (more commonly known as the Mets) had high hopes when they took the field for their very first National League game. Unfortunately, the Mets were grounded by the St. Louis Cardinals, 11–4. And that was just the beginning. The Mets would lose 120 games by the end of the season—more than any other team in the history of baseball.

1971 It was one small step for table tennis, one giant leap for world friendship. Fifteen members of the U.S. table-tennis team arrived in Beijing for a match against the Chinese. They became the first American sports team to appear in that Communist nation since 1949.

1896
THE GOOD,
THE BAD
AND THE
WEIRD
The award for the most bizarre event ever held in the Olympics goes to the 100-meter freestyle for sailors. Held at the first modern games in Athens, Greece, the swimming competition was open only to sailors. It was the only time the event was ever held. What a surprise.

1858 The first American billiards championship was held in Detroit, Michigan. And boy, was it a long match. Michael J. Phelan defeated John Seereiter in a game that lasted $9\frac{1}{2}$ hours. Phelan won $15,000, which was a tremendous amount of money in 1858. Come to think of it, it's not too bad now, either.

1953 Ben Hogan won his second Masters golf tournament. He beat Porky Oliver by five strokes. Later that year, Hogan also won the U.S. Open and the British Open. He became the first man to win the three major tournaments in one year.

1957 Jim Spalding of Louisville, Kentucky, set a bowling record by knocking down 2,088 pins in nine games. That's an average of 232 per game. The previous nine-game record was 2,070, set in 1937.

1958 Kiel Auditorium, in St. Louis, Missouri, erupted with joy at the final buzzer. The St. Louis Hawks had just defeated the mighty Boston Celtics to take the NBA Championship, four games to two. Bob Pettit's brilliant 50-point performance led the Hawks to a 110–109 victory. For St. Louis, it was sweet revenge. They lost to the Celtics in the finals the previous year.

1980 Trouble was brewing for the Boston Red Sox. In the second inning of a game against the Milwaukee Brewers, the Sox gave up not one, but two grand slam home runs. Cecil Cooper hit one and Don Money struck gold with another. Milwaukee went on to win, 18–1.

1944 The Montreal Canadiens swept the Chicago Blackhawks in four games to win the Stanley Cup and become the only team to complete an entire season undefeated at home. For a while, it didn't look like there would be a sweep, however. The Canadiens trailed the Hawks 4–1 with only 10 minutes to go in the second period of Game 4. But Montreal rallied to score four unanswered goals and win in overtime.

1957 It was a thrilling double overtime game that ended a thrilling NBA championship series. The Boston Celtics took Game Seven—and the title—by defeating the St. Louis Hawks, 125–123. Forward Tommy Heinsohn scored 37 points for the Celts in the final game. The Hawks and Celtics would clash for the championship three more times over the next four years.

1984 Pete Rose of the Cincinnati Reds doubled off Philadelphia Phillies pitcher Jerry Koosman to become the first National League player to get 4,000 hits. Rose's 4,000th came exactly 21 years to the day after his very first hit.

1986 Forty-six-year-old Jack Nicklaus became the oldest golfer to win the Masters tournament. His dramatic come-from-behind victory set another record: It was his sixth Masters win. Six years earlier to the day, Severiano Ballesteros of Spain became the *youngest* player to win the Masters. He was 23—exactly half Nicklaus' age in 1986.

1987 What a way to start a season. In their first home game of the year, the San Diego Padres set a National League record when their first three batters hit homers. Marvell Wynne, Tony Gwynn and John Kruk all roughed up San Francisco Giants pitcher Roger Mason.

1900 The first 50-mile automobile road race was held on Long Island, New York. Andrew Riker, the only participant who drove an electric-powered car, beat out eight autos using gasoline. His time was 2 hours, 3 minutes and 30 seconds. Today, the same trip would take less than half that amount in the family Chevy.

1910 What a great day for pitchers. Two one-hitters were hurled as the Washington Senators' Walter Johnson gave up only one hit to the Philadelphia Athletics, and Frank Smith of the ChicagoWhite Sox did the same against the St. Louis Browns. This same day in 1915, Philadelphia's Herb Pennock lost a no-hitter when he gave up a hit with two out in the ninth inning. Two years later, on April 14, 1917, White Sox pitcher Ed Cicotte did them all one better. He allowed no hits to the St. Louis Browns in an 11–0 victory.

1957 Her nickname was "ping," which, along with "pong," isn't a bad name for a table tennis player. On this day, Leah "Ping" Neuberger won her eighth women's national singles table-tennis championship in nine years. She won her ninth the next year.

1960 The Montreal Canadiens beat the Toronto Maple Leafs, 4–0, to sweep the NHL championship in four games. It was the Canadiens' fifth Stanley Cup win in a row—an NHL record that has never been matched. In all, Montreal has won the Cup more than any other team—an amazing 22 times in the last 65 years!

1985 Steve Garvey, the first baseman for the San Diego Padres, played in his 193rd National League game today without committing an error. Garvey hadn't flubbed a play in almost two years, since June 26, 1983. That's a major league record for first basemen!

1895 Josephine Blatt set a women's weightlifting record when she lifted an amazing 3,564 pounds. Her accomplishment came while using a hip and harness lift at the Bijou Theatre in Hoboken, New Jersey. No woman has ever lifted that much again.

1947 An historic day for baseball. Jack Roosevelt Robinson became the first black player in the modern major leagues. He took first base for the Brooklyn Dodgers at their home stadium, Ebbets Field. Previously, blacks were allowed to play only in their own leagues. Although he faced a lot of prejudice, Robinson won the Rookie of the Year Award that season and the Most Valuable Player Award in 1949. More importantly, he paved the way for other blacks to enter the majors. In case you were wondering, Robinson's first day wasn't quite so memorable: He had no hits in three at-bats against the Boston Braves.

1952 There's an octopus on the ice. Jerry Cusimano of the Detroit Red Wings decided to play a joke before the start of his team's Stanley Cup game against the Montreal Canadiens. He threw an octopus onto the ice. The slimy creature was removed and the game began. It's a pity. With eight tentacles, the octopus would have made one heck of a goalie. The Red Wings won without his help.

1968 After 24 innings, a run was finally scored in a baseball game between the New York Mets and the Houston Astros at the Houston Astrodome. The Astros won, 1–0, after six hours and six minutes. Les Rohr, the Mets eighth pitcher, took the loss. At the time, it was the longest night game and the longest scoreless game in major league history.

1912 A 28-year-old American named Harriet Quimby became the first woman to fly an airplane across the English channel. The English channel is the famous 21-mile stretch of water between England and France. A journalist, Quimby was the first American woman to get her pilot's license.

1967 A new league is born. The 10-team National Professional Soccer League opened with a match between the Los Angeles Toros and the New York Generals. Some 9,048 fans attended the match in Los Angeles' Memorial Coliseum, which can hold 93,000. The Toros won, 3–2. A year later the league merged with the United Soccer Association to form the North American Soccer League.

1988 Record times for men and women were set in the downhill ski competition at Les Arcs, France. Michael Pruffer of France was clocked at 139 mph and Tara Mulari of Finland went 133 mph. That's speeding!

1947 SPORTS PROFILE Kareem Abdul-Jabbar, one of the greatest players in the history of basketball, was born Ferdinand Lewis ("Lew") Alcindor, Jr. today in New York City. He later took his Muslim name—meaning "generous, powerful servant to Allah (God)"—when he converted to the Islamic religion. In college, he led the University of California at Los Angeles to three national championships. Before retiring from the NBA in 1989 after 20 seasons, Kareem led the Milwaukee Bucks to one NBA championship and the Los Angeles Lakers to a total of five. Along the way, he scored 38,387 points—more than any other player. Jabbar, who had once wanted to become an architect, invented the famous skyhook—a one-handed shot in which the ball arches like a rainbow.

1953 Get out your binoculars. New York Yankees star Mickey Mantle just hit the longest home run in a regular season game. Mantle slammed a 565-footer in a game against the Washington Senators at Griffith Stadium in Washington, D.C. Seven years later, he would shatter his own record with a towering 643-foot shot. (See September 10, 1960.)

1972 For the first time in its 76-year history, the Boston Marathon held a women's competition. Women continued to race beside the men, but their ranks and times were kept separate. The first winner in the women's division was Nina Kuscsik of Huntington, New York, with a time of 3 hours, 8 minutes, 58 seconds.

1976 Let's face it folks, this game was BORING. The Philadelphia Phillies trailed the Chicago Cubs, 13–2. Then, Mike Schmidt of the Phillies hit four home runs in a row including the game-winner in the 10th inning. That was a National League record. The Phillies couldn't help but rally for an 18–16 comeback win.

1977 On the subject of comebacks: The Philadelphia Flyers were trailing the Toronto Maple Leafs, 5–3, with only two minutes left in a Stanley Cup Playoff. If the Leafs won they would be ahead three games to one in the semifinal series. Then, the impossible happened. The Flyers scored two goals in only 16 seconds. Then, they slapped through a third with 50 seconds left in the overtime period to win the game. The Flyers went on to win the series, too.

1987 Dr. J made one big house call. In one of the last games of his career, Julius Erving of the Philadelphia Flyers became the third basketball player in history to score 30,000 points. Only Wilt Chamberlain and Kareem Abdul-Jabbar have scored more. In tonight's game, Erving contributed 38 points in a losing effort against the Indiana Pacers.

1898 In his first game as a major league pitcher, Jim Hughes of the Baltimore Orioles threw a two-hit shutout. Four days later, in his second start, Hughes outdid himself. He didn't give up a single hit against the Boston Beaneaters. The Boston who?

1923 The New York Yankees played their first game in the new Yankee Stadium. For the opener, 74,000 fans saw Babe Ruth hit a three-run homer as the Yanks beat the Boston Red Sox, 4–1. Because of Ruth's popularity, and his ability to bring fans into the ballpark, Yankee Stadium was nick-named "The House that Ruth Built."

1962 Boston Celtic great Bill Russell tied an NBA playoff record by pulling down 40 rebounds in an overtime game against the Los Angeles Lakers. Russell tied the mark he had set in 1960.

1987 There's something fishy about a man whose last name is Land setting records on the water. But Robert Land of New Brunswick, Canada, won the Kenduskeag Stream Canoe Race for the sixth straight year. It took him more than two hours to get through the cold, rocky waters around Bangor, Maine.

1909
THE GOOD,
THE BAD
AND THE
WEIRD

It may not have been the greatest game in baseball history, but it was the quietest. When the New York Highlanders (now the Yankees) played an exhibition game against Jersey City on this Sunday afternoon, the team asked the fans not to cheer. At this time, it was illegal to play baseball on Sunday for religious reasons. The Highlanders didn't want to attract the police to the game with a lot of noise. They won the game 6–3, and the fans were indeed quiet.

1897 The first Boston Marathon was held today. A New Yorker named John J. McDermott won with a time of 2 hours, 55 minutes, 10 seconds. The Boston Marathon, the nation's first, was the only annual major event of its kind in the U.S. until New York City held its first marathon in 1970.

1969 For the first time ever, a horse race is run with only female jockeys. Penny Ann Early beat out six other women in the Lady Godiva $10,000 handicap at Suffolk Downs, near Boston, Massachusetts, atop a horse named Royal Fillet.

1981 The longest game in the history of baseball was so long it took two months to complete. A minor league game between Pawtucket, Rhode Island and Rochester, New York, was suspended at 4:07 a.m. after 32 innings. Pawtucket won the game 3–2 in the 33rd inning when it resumed two months later. By the way, a couple of major league stars, Wade Boggs and Bob Ojeda, were then members of the Pawtucket squad.

1912 Boston's Fenway Park is one of the most famous ballparks in America—the small, old-fashioned, charming home of the Red Sox. Today, 27,000 fans packed Fenway for its grand opening. The Sox defeated the New York Highlanders, later renamed the Yankees, 7–6, in 11 innings.

1982 The Atlanta Braves set a major league record when they won 12 games in a row at the start of the season. The Braves beat the Reds, 4–2, today at Atlanta's Fulton County Stadium for the record-breaking win. The previous record for most wins in a row at the start of the season had been set by the Oakland A's only a year earlier. The Braves would extend their streak to 13 games the next day.

1985 Karyn Tarter Marshall lifted 303 pounds in a weightlifting move called a clean and jerk. It was the greatest overhead lift ever by a woman. Marshall has won U.S. national championships five times in three separate weight classes. There are reports that a German woman named Katie Sandwina once cleaned and jerked $312^{1/2}$ pounds, but that has never offically been confirmed. She is also supposed to have once lifted a 1,200-pound cannon!

1986 Look, up in the sky! It's a bird! It's a plane! It's ... Michael Jordan! The Chicago Bulls star spent most of his time soaring toward the basket today as he set an NBA record for most points in a playoff game. In the Bulls' double overtime loss to the Boston Celtics, Jordan had 63 points to break Elgin Baylor's mark of 61 points.

1951 It was the fifth game of the Stanley Cup finals. The Toronto Maple Leafs and the Montreal Canadiens were tied at two goals each. With time running out, Toronto defenseman Bill Barilko suddenly found the puck in front of him. He took a desperate slap shot from behind the blue line. It's good! Barilko became a hero throughout Toronto. Unfortunately, he would not enjoy it for long. Four months later, he was killed in a plane accident.

1951 In the final game of the NBA Championship, the New York Knicks came back after trailing by 14 points to tie the Rochester Royals at 75 points apiece. With 40 seconds left, Bob Davies of the Royals went to the free throw line for two crucial free throws. The crowd was silent. Up went the ball . . . and in! Davies made both shots and Rochester went on to win, 79–75.

1959 Did you hear about the one that *didn't* get away? Alf Dean of Australia reeled in a 2,664-pound, 17-foot-long great white shark. It's the biggest fish on record ever caught with a regular fishing rod.

1977 NBA star Moses Malone is one of the greatest offensive rebounders in the history of basketball. Today, playing for the Houston Rockets, he set the record for most offensive rebounds in a playoff game (15) in an overtime win over the Washington Bullets.

1980 No one had ever heard of Rosie Ruiz. So when the New Yorker was the first woman to cross the finish line at the 84th Boston Marathon, people were surprised. Then they were suspicious. When the officials investigated, they found she had cheated. Ruiz was disqualified for not having run the entire race.

1876 The first official National League baseball game was played. Boston nipped Philadelphia, 6–5, in a contest at Philadelphia. Jim O'Rourke got the first hit in NL history, and Joe Bordon became the first winning pitcher. Bordon's luck would soon run out and he would be demoted to groundskeeper.

1884 Thomas Stevens set off today from San Francisco, California on an around-the-world bicycle trip. It took $2\frac{1}{2}$ years before the Californian arrived back in San Francisco on January 4, 1887. He became the first man to ever pedal around the globe.

1947 The Philadelphia Warriors defeated the Chicago Stags, 83–80, to win professional basketball's first championship series, four games to one. The series marked the end of the first season of the Basketball Association of America (BAA). The BAA became the NBA two years later.

1970 Tom Seaver of the New York Mets threw 19 strikeouts in one game to tie a major league record for "Ks." His most special K of the day came when he threw his 10th in a row, setting another record. Seaver gave up only two hits as the Mets beat the San Diego Padres, 2–1.

1959
THE GOOD,
THE BAD
AND THE
WEIRD
In what must be the strangest inning in baseball history, the Chicago White Sox scored 11 runs against the Kansas City Athletics ... even though they only had one hit. Three A's pitchers gave up 10 walks, hit 1 batter, and committed 3 errors in a row. It's no wonder Chicago, which had been losing 6–1, came back to win 20–6.

1939 In one of his very first games, rookie Ted Williams of the Boston Red Sox got four hits, including his first homer, in five at-bats. The Sox lost to the Philadelphia Athletics, 12–8, but for Williams it was the start of a brilliant career. Williams would hit 520 more homers, good enough to put him in 10th place on the all-time home run list.

1950 The Minneapolis Lakers won the first NBA championship over the Syracuse Nationals, four games to two, by winning the final game, 110–95. The Lakers would lose the championship the next year to Rochester, and then win the next three in a row.

1950 The Detroit Red Wings and the New York Rangers battled through two overtime periods in the seventh and final game to decide the winner of this year's Stanley Cup. And what a thrilling game it was! In the second overtime, Detroit's George Gee won a face-off in front of the Rangers' net and passed the puck to Pete Babando. Babando shot the puck past Ranger goalie Chuck Rayner to win the game, 4–3. By the way, the Rangers played their two "home" games in Toronto, since the circus was appearing at Madison Square Garden.

1989 In 20 years in the NBA, Kareem Abdul-Jabbar played in more games and scored more points than any man in the history of the NBA. This was the final regular-season game of his brilliant career, and the Los Angeles Lakers center was given a thank-you he would never forget. In a ceremony before the game, Kareem was presented with a special plaque and an emotional standing ovation from the crowd in the packed Los Angeles Forum. Kareem then went out and scored 10 points in his team's 121–117 victory over the Seattle SuperSonics.

1901 The Chicago White Stockings defeated the Cleveland Broncos, 8–2, in the first American League baseball game ever played. The game was as short as it was unexciting. It lasted only 1 hour and 20 minutes. The three other American League games scheduled for the day were rained out.

1909 Would you believe they once kept records for the three-legged race? Well, they did. Today in Brooklyn, New York, Olympic medalists Harry L. Hillman and Lawson Robertson set a world record by "running" 100 yards in 11 seconds with one of each man's legs tied together. Can you run 100 yards that quickly? Most kids can't.

1967 The Philadelphia 76ers took the NBA championship by edging the San Francisco Warriors, 125–122. In the exciting sixth and final game, Wilt Chamberlain blocked 6 shots and grabbed 23 rebounds for Philadelphia, while Rick Barry scored 44 for the Warriors in a losing effort. It was the first time in nine years that the Boston Celtics had not won the title.

1969 What a nail-biter. The Boston Bruins and the Montreal Canadiens were tied 1–1 in the final game of the NHL playoff semifinals at seven minutes into the second overtime period. The Canadiens Claude Provost intercepted a Bruin pass and passed it to Jean Beliveau. Beliveau took a 20-foot wrist shot and prayed. His prayers were answered: The shot was good.

1977 Chess master Vlastimil Hort of Czechoslovakia earned a spot in the *Guinness Book of Sports Records* by playing 550 opponents over two days. At one point, Hort was playing 201 games of chess at one time! Of the 550 games, he lost only 10. For the 540 losers, that really had to Hort.

1950 The Boston Celtics drafted Duquesne University star Chuck Cooper, making him the first black basketball player in the NBA. Within weeks, the Washington Capitols would sign one player by the name of Earl Lloyd and the New York Knicks would acquire Nat "Sweetwater" Clifton from the Harlem Globetrotters. (The Globetrotters are not in the NBA.)

1964 Believe it or not, the Toronto Maple Leafs were once the dominant team in the NHL. Today, they won their third Stanley Cup in a row, defeating the Detroit Red Wings. The Leafs would win one more Stanley Cup in 1967, but they haven't done it since.

1965 The Boston Celtics outscored the Los Angeles Lakers, 129–96, to take the NBA championship series, four games to one. Despite the loss, Los Angeles' Jerry West scored 33 points in the final game, to set a playoff record of 447 points—or an average of 40.6 points per game.

1977 For the Atlanta Braves it was the kind of inning that gives the manager a headache. Atlanta gave up a major league record 12 runs in the fifth inning and lost 23–9 to the Cincinnati Reds. The Braves used three pitchers in that inning alone. Cincinnati's George Foster had seven runs batted in, five runs scored, two homers, a double and a single in the game.

1986 Brad Davis of the Dallas Mavericks hit every one of his five three-point shots in a playoff game against the Utah Jazz. That performance earned him a place in the NBA record books. Eight players have gone four-for-four but no one else has hit five without a miss.

1931 Lou Gehrig should have known better. Usually one of the smartest players in baseball, he committed a silly mistake that cost him the home run crown. The Yankees first baseman hit a home run, but then passed teammate Lyn Lary while rounding the base paths. Instead of getting credit for a home run, Gehrig was called out.

1933 *En garde!* The U.S. men's saber fencing title was won for the third year in a row by John Huffman of New York after a thrilling finish. With Huffman and his opponent tied at two victories each, Huffman won in the last minute of the fence-off.

1959 It was one of those days for Willard Schmidt. The Cincinnati Reds pitcher became the first major league player to be hit by a pitch twice in the same inning. Schmidt later had to leave the game when he was hit by a line drive. Some days it just doesn't pay to get out of bed.

1985 Utah's big man, Mark Eaton, set an NBA playoff record by blocking 10 shots in a game against the Houston Rockets. Eaton broke a mark of nine blocks held by the Lakers' Kareem Abdul-Jabbar and Washington's Manute Bol.

Jackie Robinson, the first black player in Modern Major League baseball, with Branch Rickey, the Brooklyn Dodgers president who signed him. (See April 15, 1947)

1938 For the first time, a yellow baseball was used in a game. A regular ball was dyed yellow with the stitches in red as an experiment to try to make the ball easier for hitters to see. It was used in a college baseball game between Columbia University and Fordham University in New York City. A yellow ball was tried in the pros just a few months later. (See August 2, 1938.) The experiment wasn't a big success.

1944 In his previous start, Boston Brave pitcher Jim Tobin was just one out shy of throwing a no-hitter before giving up a hit in the ninth inning. Today, he actually did it. Tobin pitched a no-hitter in a win over the Brooklyn Dodgers.

1963 Oscar Obert, a 32-year-old New Yorker, won his second consecutive U.S. Handball Assocation singles championship. For the second year, Obert defeated John Sloan of Chicago, Illinois. It was a bad day for Sloan. In the doubles competition, he and teammate Phil Elbert lost to a pair of New Yorkers, Jim Jacobs and Marty Decatur.

1968 Since the day eight months earlier that Muhammad Ali had been stripped of the championship for refusing to serve in the Vietnam War, the World Boxing Association's heavyweight title had been empty. During those eight months, the WBA had held an unusual runoff tournament to decide who would be the new champ. Today, Jimmy Ellis claimed the title by winning a 15-round decision over Jerry Quarry.

1973 Here's one basketball game that had most Americans seeing red. The Soviet national team opened a tour of the United States by beating a team of college all-stars from Utah, 72–63. A total of 80 personal fouls were committed in the sloppy game.

1983 Number 3,508 at last! Houston pitching ace Nolan Ryan struck out Brad Mills of the Montreal Expos to break Walter Johnson's career strikeout record. Johnson had set the mark of 3,507 strikeouts way back in 1927.

1934 In a game he'd like to forget, Leon Allen "Goose" Goslin of the Detroit Tigers hit into four double plays in a row. It's a good thing the Tigers beat the Cleveland Indians anyway, 4–1, or Goslin's goose might have been cooked.

1961 At age 40, pitcher Warren Spahn of the Milwaukee Braves threw the second no-hitter of his career. Against the San Francisco Giants, he allowed only two men to reach base in the 1–0 victory. It was his 290th career win.

1966 No team has more NBA Championships than the Boston Celtics. This year they went the limit before beating the Los Angeles Lakers four games to three in the final series to win their eighth league championship in a row. The Celtics are the only team in history to take the NBA crown at least once in every decade since the 1950s.

1988
SAD SACKS
OF SPORTS

What a way to start the season! The Baltimore Orioles today played their 21st game in a row without a win when the Minnesota Twins beat them, 4–2. A local radio disc jockey vowed to stay on the air until the O's won a game. Baltimore finally won, but they still finished the season in last place. The very next year, though, they nearly won their division.

1961 The thrill of victory! The agony of defeat! ABC's *Wide World of Sports* premiered as a 20-week summer replacement series. The show is now one of the longest running sports programs in the history of television.

1981 Steve Carlton of the Philadelphia Phillies became the first left-handed pitcher to strike out 3,000 batters. Carlton fanned Tim Wallach of the Montreal Expos in the first inning for number 3,000.

1986 "STUUUUUUR-IKE!" That's what the Seattle Mariners hitters heard most of the night when they faced Boston Red Sox pitching ace Roger Clemens. Roger struck out eight batters in a row, mostly with his wicked fastball, to tie an American League record. But that's not all. In the top of the ninth, Clemens fanned Phil Bradley for the fourth time, and for his 20th strikeout of the game—a new major league record.

1933

THE GOOD, THE BAD AND THE WEIRD

In one of the weirdest moments in the history of baseball, two New York Yankee baserunners were tagged out at home plate—on the same play. Lou Gehrig had started running home but then held up, thinking the hitter's fly ball would be caught. Dixie Walker headed toward the plate right behind him. When the ball fell fair, Goose Goslin made the catch and fired it home to Washington Senators catcher Luke Sewell, who tagged out both Gehrig and Walker.

1940 Belle Martell of Van Nuys, California, became the first woman boxing referee when she was licensed by the state of California today. Two days later, Martell refereed her first card of eight fights. She retired after only a month. It was a short career, but an historic one.

1961 A-MAYS-ing. That's what you could call San Francisco Giants slugger Willie Mays' performance in today's game against the Milwaukee Braves. Willie hit four home runs to tie a major league record. And he had been so sick with a stomachache the night before that he almost missed the game. By the end of the game, it was the Braves who were feeling sick.

1969 Pitcher Jim Maloney of the Cincinnati Reds struck out 13 Houston Astros batters and allowed no hits to lead the Reds to a 1–0 victory. It was the third no-hitter of Maloney's career.

1986 The somersaulters are coming! The somersaulters are coming! Ashrita Furman of Queens, New York, set a record by somersaulting along the entire route of Paul Revere's historic ride in 1775. It took more than 10 hours and 8,341 somersaults, but Ashrita did all 12 miles and 390 yards. By the way, Ashrita also made it into the *Guinness Book of World Records* for the longest time juggling while running. (See July 4, 1988.)

MAY

1884 Quick, name the first black player in major league baseball. Jackie Robinson? Wrong. Sixty-three years before Robinson made history, a black catcher named Moses Fleetwood Walker played his first game for Toledo in the American Association. Since the American Association was then a major league, he actually beat out Jackie Robinson—but since blacks were later banned from the major leagues for many years, Robinson gets credit for breaking the color barrier.

1897 Charles G. Bothner became the first fencer to win all three amateur titles: foil, épée and saber, in the same year. What's the difference between these three fencing divisions? The foil is a long, thin sword with which fencers try to touch the trunk (the upper part, not counting the head and arms) of their opponents' body. The épée is a heavier sword which can be used on the entire body. And the saber is used when you really mean business—it's a thick sword with two cutting edges. Ouch!

1920 After six innings, the score of the Boston Braves–Brooklyn Dodgers baseball game was 1–1. And that's where the score stood 20 innings later, when the game was finally called because of darkness. Dodgers pitcher Leon Cadore and Braves hurler Joe Oeschger both went the full 26 innings. The game, which was suspended after 3 hours and 50 minutes, was the longest, in terms of innings, in the history of major league baseball at that time.

1969 Some days you're hot, some days you're not. Pitcher Don Wilson of the Houston Astros threw a no-hitter to beat the Cincinnati Reds, 4–0. Nine days earlier, also against the Reds, Wilson was bombed, 14–0.

Jesse Owens, the track-and-field star who broke five world records and tied a sixth in a single day.
(See May 25, 1935)

←

1917 In what some regard as the best baseball game ever played, Fred Toney of the Cincinnati Reds and Hippo Vaughn of the Chicago Cubs both pitched nine innings without giving up a single hit. It was the first double no-hitter in major league history. Finally, in the 10th inning Vaughn gave up two hits, including the game winner to the Reds' Jim Thorpe. That's a painful loss.

1939 The great Lou Gehrig made news by *not* playing in a ball game. It was the first time the New York Yankees first baseman missed a game since June 6, 1925. Gehrig's major league record of 2,130 games played in a row still stands. Even without Gehrig in the lineup, the Yankees clobbered the Detroit Tigers, 22–2.

1967 The Toronto Maple Leafs were not supposed to make the playoffs, much less get as far as the Stanley Cup finals. Once one of the best teams in hockey, the Leafs had gotten old, with four of their top players over 38 years old. But today, the Maple Leafs played as if they were youngsters, and defeated the powerful Montreal Canadiens, 3–1, to win the championship series, four games to two.

1951 Gil McDougald, a rookie for the New York Yankees, tied a major league record by driving in six runs in one inning. In a game against the St. Louis Browns, he hit a grand slam and a two-run triple in the ninth inning. In all, the Yanks scored 11 times that inning. The final score: New York 17, St. Louis 3.

1952 Eddie Arcaro became the first jockey to win the Kentucky Derby five times. He rode Hill Gail to victory in the 78th annual "Run for the Roses," and was just a fraction of a second short of setting a Derby record. Arcaro couldn't have been too disappointed about missing the speed record. He had also ridden Whirlaway, the horse that set the record in 1941.

1980 Pitcher Ferguson Jenkins of the Texas Rangers won his 100th game in the AL by beating the Baltimore Orioles, 3–2, at Arlington Stadium in Texas. That made Jenkins the fourth player in major league history to win 100 or more games in both leagues. (He had won 139 pitching for the Chicago Cubs and the Philadelphia Phillies in the NL.)

1986 First baseman Don Mattingly of the New York Yankees is one of the greatest hitters around. But he's not selfish. Today Mattingly hit three sacrifice flies to become the sixth player to have that many sacrifice flies in one game. New York beat the Texas Rangers, 9–4.

1986 A horse named Ferdinand won the 112th Kentucky Derby, making his jockey, 54-year-old Bill Shoemaker, the oldest man to win the first leg of horse racing's Triple Crown. It was Shoemaker's fourth Derby win.

1929 The Detroit Tigers probably would have liked to nail Lou Gehrig to the New York Yankees bench. Three times in a row Gehrig came up to the batter's box, and three times in a row he hit a home run. New York needed every one of those homers. They beat Detroit, 11–9, in a wild game.

1968 Dancer's Image won the 94th Kentucky Derby today, but three days later, a painkilling drug was found in his blood and he was stripped of his Derby crown. That was the first time a Derby winner had ever been recalled. Seven months later, though, the Kentucky Racing Commission changed its mind and declared Dancer's Image the winner after all.

1968 The first ABA championships were held. The Pittsburgh Pipers beat the New Orleans Buccaneers four games to three. The league folded in 1977, but four of its teams joined the NBA. They were the Denver Nuggets, New Jersey Nets, Indiana Pacers and San Antonio Spurs.

1975 Elementary, my dear Watson. Bob Watson of the Houston Astros made baseball history by scoring the major leagues' one-millionth run. Actually, it's his teammate Milt May who deserves the credit. May hit the home run that scored Watson, who was already on base.

1904 Cy Young of the Boston Red Sox pitched the first perfect game under modern baseball rules. In Boston's 3–0 victory over the Philadelphia Athletics, Young did not allow a single Philadelphia batter to reach base. No hits, no walks, no nothing! That's about as perfect as a pitcher can get.

1969 For the seventh time in 11 years, the Los Angeles Lakers lost the NBA championship to the Boston Celtics. Their tough 108–106 loss in the seventh game was the second time the Lakers had come within two points of the final series. (The first loss came in 1959, when the Lakers played in Minneapolis.) In those 11 years, the Celts would win every world championship but one.

1973 Secretariat, perhaps the greatest racehorse of the century, set a record for speed at the Kentucky Derby. The horse's jockey, Ron Turcotte, became only the fourth man in history to win the Derby two years in a row. A year earlier, he had ridden Riva Ridge to victory. In the next few weeks, Secretariat would win the Preakness and Belmont Stakes to take the Triple Crown. (See June 9, 1973.)

1978 Pete Rose of the Cincinnati Reds hit the 3,000th base hit of his career to become the 13th player in major league history to reach that milestone. At age 37, Rose was also the youngest to do it. By the time he retired, Rose would have an incredible 4,256 hits—more than any other player ever.

1915 A new pitcher for the Boston Red Sox named Babe Ruth faced the New York Yankees, and hit the first home run of his career. For Ruth, it was the first of many homers—714 to be exact. This home run record stood almost six decades before Hank Aaron broke it in 1974. No one else has surpassed Ruth. Of course, Ruth was later sold to, and spent most of his career with, the Yankees.

1941 Indoor soccer is a newfangled invention, right? Wrong. An indoor soccer doubleheader was held in New York City's Madison Square Garden today. Instead of Astroturf, sand was spread on the floor. Several months earlier, another indoor soccer contest was held at the Garden, on a concrete floor. Dandy idea. A number of players were injured in falls.

1953 Oh-oh, Bobo. St. Louis Browns pitcher Bobo Holloman made his major league debut today by pitching a no-hitter to beat the Philadelphia Athletics, 6–0. Bobo would never throw a no-hitter again. In fact, this was the last complete game of his career.

1954 For more than 35 years, athletes had been trying to run a mile in less than four minutes. Today, Roger Bannister finally did it. It was a cold, windy afternoon at Iffley Stadium in Oxford, England—so terrible, in fact, that until 15 minutes before the race, Bannister wasn't going to run. It's a good thing he did. With a sudden sprint at the end of the race, Bannister broke the tape at 3 minutes, 59.4 seconds, to break one of the most intimidating barriers in sports.

1906 Pitcher Bill Donovan of the Detroit Tigers did something you don't see too often in baseball. He stole three bases on one trip around the bases. Donovan hit a single in the fifth inning, then stole second and third while one batter was up, and stole home during another batter's turn. He also had a triple later—which didn't leave many bases to steal. The Tigers beat Cleveland, 8–3.

1925 Shortstop Glenn Wright of the Pittsburgh Pirates made an unassisted triple play in the ninth inning against the St. Louis Cardinals. Wright caught a line drive, stepped on second to get the runner who had started toward third, and then tagged another player on his way from first. Only seven other men have made unassisted triple plays in the major leagues.

1972 It had to happen sooner or later. After losing eight NBA championship finals, the Los Angeles Lakers finally won one! And they made it look easy. They defeated the New York Knicks in just five games.

1983 CBS carried the first indoor soccer game televised on a major television network. An estimated four million viewers tuned in to watch the MISL playoff game between the Baltimore Blast and the Cleveland Force.

1933 SPORTS PROFILE Johnny Unitas was born in Pittsburgh, Pennsylvania. Although he became one of the greatest quarterbacks in football, he almost didn't even get a shot at pro ball. Unitas was considered too small to play the game, and he was cut by his hometown Steelers soon after he was drafted in 1955. He played semi-pro ball until the Baltimore Colts decided to take a chance on him in 1956. It was a smart move. In 1957 Unitas was named the NFL's Most Valuable Player and in 1958 he led the Colts to a league championship. A member of the Football Hall of Fame, Unitas still holds the record for throwing at least one touchdown pass in 47 games in a row.

1954 Imagine spinning around in a circle and throwing a 16-pound ball from under your chin 60 feet into the air. That's the idea in the shot-put competition. William Parry O'Brien became the first man to "put" a shot 60 feet, 5$^1/_4$ inches. Between 1953 and 1955, O'Brien broke the world shot-put record 14 more times. His greatest throw was 64 feet, 7$^1/_2$ inches.

1966 Outfielder Frank Robinson of the Baltimore Orioles hit a towering 451-foot shot over the left field wall of Baltimore's Memorial Stadium in the O's 8–3 win over the Cleveland Indians. It was the first time any player had hit a homer out of Memorial Stadium. The Indians must have been impressed. They later hired Robinson to manage their team, making him the first black manager in major league history.

1968 Jim "Catfish" Hunter of the Oakland A's pitched a perfect game and beat the Minnesota Twins, 4–0. Not a single Twins player reached base, even on a walk. It was the first perfect game thrown during the regular season in the AL in 46 years.

1970 The New York Knicks won their first NBA championship in 24 years by defeating the Los Angeles Lakers in seven games. Guard Walt Frazier was named the series Most Valuable Player after he scored 36 points in the final game. The Knicks won the championship again three years later. They haven't done it since.

1984 The Olympic Games are supposed to be about sportsmanship, not politics. But that's not always the case. In 1980, the United States withdrew from the Summer Olympics in Moscow, the capital of the Soviet Union, to protest the Soviet invasion of Afghanistan. Today, the Soviet Union decided to get even and announced it would not be attending the 1984 Games in Los Angeles, California. With the Soviets and some other countries missing, the Americans won the most medals (83) in Los Angeles.

1918 Babe Ruth, a talented young pitcher for the Boston Red Sox, was an even better hitter than he was a pitcher. In the Sox's 4–3 loss to the Washington Senators, he had five hits, but gave up four runs. Ruth was soon traded to the New York Yankees who used him as an outfielder, rather than as a pitcher, so that he could hit in every game. The Yanks knew what they were doing. The Babe turned out to be one of the greatest hitters ever.

1961 With just two swings of the bat, Jim Gentile of the Baltimore Orioles added eight runs to the O's score. Gentile hit two grand slams in consecutive innings to set a major league record, and powered Baltimore past the Minnesota Twins, 13–5.

BASEBALL QUIZ Everyone called him "Babe," but that wasn't Mr. Ruth's real first name. Can you find his real name on this list? While you're at it, see how many other nicknames you can match up with the real and full first names:

1. Babe Ruth	a. Denton
2. Ty Cobb	b. Reginald
3. Wee Willie Keeler	c. Lawrence
4. Cy Young	d. Henry
5. Lee Lacy	e. Edward
6. Whitey Ford	f. William
7. Reggie Jackson	g. Tyrus
8. Yogi Bera	h. Lynn
9. Lou Gehrig	i. Leondaus
10. Nolan Ryan	j. George

ANSWERS:
1.j 2.g 3.f 4.a 5.i 6.e 7.b 8.c 9.d 10.h

1969 The NFL as we now know it was born when two separate leagues—the old National Football League and the American Football League—joined together. Each league became its own conference—the National Football Conference (NFC) and the American Football Conference (AFC).

1970 Every once in a while, a pitcher sets a record and still loses the game. That's what happened to Hoyt Wilhelm, a relief pitcher for the Atlanta Braves. When Wilhelm was called in to pitch against the St. Louis Cardinals, he became the first—and only—pitcher in major league history to appear in 1,000 games. Unfortunately, Wilhelm gave up three runs, and the Braves lost, 6–5. Before he retired just short of his 50th birthday in 1972, Wilhelm had made 1,070 appearances.

1970 The Boston Bruins won their first Stanley Cup in 29 years, when they swept the final series against the St. Louis Blues with a 4–3 victory. Bobby Orr scored the game winner early in the overtime period. Like Wayne Gretzky, Orr broke many records and drew thousands of fans to hockey arenas wherever he played.

1987 His nickname is "Sleepy," but Golden State Warriors forward Eric Floyd was wide awake during his team's 129–121 playoff victory over the Los Angeles Lakers. Ford scored 51 points—more than any other person in the playoffs that year. The Warriors' victory was the only loss the Lakers suffered leading up to the final series.

1904 Boston's Cy Young set a major league record by pitching 23 innings without giving up a single hit. The streak started on April 25, and didn't end until today's seventh inning.

1955 The Brooklyn Dodgers had won 11 games in a row. Then Ernie Banks of the Chicago Cubs came to bat. Banks hit his first grand slam of the year to help Chicago end Brooklyn's streak with a 10–8 victory. By the end of the season, Banks had five grand slams.

1957 Here's a story of a man named Brady. Bobby Brady (no relation to the son on *The Brady Bunch*) staged one of the greatest comebacks in the history of handball today. In the National Amateur Athletic Union (NAAU) championship, he was trailing 19–12 in the final game, when he scored the next 9 points to win, 21–19.

1971 Pitcher Steve Dunning of the Cleveland Indians sure knew how to help his own cause. He hit a grand slam off the Oakland A's to give his team a 5–0 lead. Dunning will probably be remembered as the last AL pitcher to hit a grand slam. How come? Well, the AL now uses a designated hitter, so pitchers almost never bat.

1980 SPORTS QUIZ Max Anderson and his son, Kris, became the first men to fly a hot-air balloon nonstop from coast to coast. It took four days, but the two men made it from California on the West Coast to Quebec, Canada, on the East Coast. The name of their balloon was the *Kitty Hawk*. Where else have you heard that name?

A: Kitty Hawk was the name of the town in North Carolina where Orville and Wilbur Wright made the first powered airplane flight.

1969 Sharon Sites Adams set sail from Japan on her quest to become the first woman to sail across the Pacific Ocean by herself. Did she make it? You bet. Adams and her 31-foot boat, *The Sea Sharp*, arrived in San Diego, California, 74 days later.

1979 It was the end of "The Streak." Chris Evert had not lost on a clay tennis court in 125 matches over six years. Until today. Evert was defeated by Tracy Austin, 6–4, 2–6, 7–6, in the semifinals of the Italian Open.

1982 The USFL was founded today with 12 teams, Although the league was clearly competing with the NFL, they purposely played their games in the spring, so they wouldn't overlap with the NFL's schedule. It didn't help. The USFL folded four years later.

1931 Do over! At a thoroughbred horse race in Jamaica, New York, all the horses went around the track, completed the race...and then found out it didn't count. One of the animals had a false start. So back they went to do it all over again. The horse that came in first in the race that didn't count came in second in the one that did. And the horse that won the real race had placed second in the first race.

1952 There's a record that will be hard to beat. Ron Necciai, a young pitcher for the Pittsburgh Pirates farm club in Bristol, Connecticut, set a professional baseball record by striking out 27 batters. You can't strike out any more than that in a nine-inning game! Necciai struck out every single batter he faced in today's game except for three. No major league pitcher has ever come close to accomplishing that feat.

1955 New York Yankees slugger Mickey Mantle was a switch-hitter. That means he was able to bat equally well from both sides of the plate. Today, he proved that, when he hit three home runs in New York's 5–2 win over over Detroit. He hit two of the homers as a lefty, and one batting right. Exactly 12 years later to the day—on May 13, 1967—Mantle hit his 500th homer in the Yanks 6–5 win over Baltimore.

1967 "And in this corner...And this corner...And this corner ..." As an experiment, a boxing match took place in West Orange, New Jersey, in which the normal, four-sided ring was replaced by an eight-sided one. Boxing officials hoped the fighters wouldn't get hurt if they weren't always being pinned in the corner. The idea never caught on.

1874 It was a simple twist of fate that shaped the way Americans play football today. When the game was originally invented, football had 15 players on a side, rather than 11, and players were only allowed to kick the ball. But today, a team from McGill University in Montreal, Canada, traveled south to meet Harvard University. Since the game was played in Massachusetts, it was played under the "Boston Rules," which allowed players to run with the ball as well as kick it. Unfortunately, four of the McGill players became ill and couldn't make the game, so both squads played with 11. It must have been a good game. Both the Boston Rules and using 11 players on a side soon took hold.

1972 The day Willie came home. The great Willie Mays started his career in New York, playing with the Giants baseball team. When the Giants moved to San Francisco in 1958, New York said good-bye to Mays—but not for good. Today, the "Say Hey Kid" returned to the Big Apple to finish his career with the Mets. In his first game, against his old Giants teammates, the 41-year-old Mays hit a home run to give the Mets a 5–4 win.

1988 Lee Chin Yong set the record for the most chin-ups from a hanging position. He did 370 of them without stopping, at Backyon Gymnasium in Seoul, South Korea. Chin up, Lee Chin. You're in the record books.

1862 The first enclosed baseball park opened at the Union Grounds in Brooklyn, New York, on this date. The site had been a skating rink.

1919 What, me superstitious? Brooklyn Dodgers pitcher Al Mamaux was having a beauty of a game. For 12 innings, he had kept the Cincinnati Reds off the scoreboard. Then came the unlucky 13th inning. Mamaux gave up 10 runs to lose the game.

1952 Virgil "Fire" Trucks threw the Detroit Tigers' first no-hitter in 40 years when he beat the Washington Senators 1–0. Three months later—on August 25—Trucks threw his second no-hitter of the season, another 1–0 win against the powerful New York Yankees. Most of the time, though, there wasn't any fire when Virgil pitched. He finished the season with a 5–19 record for the last-place Tigers. For one strange season, Trucks was the best worst pitcher in baseball.

1968 The National and American football leagues both ruled that all stadiums had to be able to seat at least 50,000 fans. Any team playing in a smaller arena had to promise to add extra seats, build new stadiums or move by 1970.

1984 Do you believe in Magic? You do if you're a Los Angeles Lakers fan. In a playoff game against the Phoenix Suns, superstar Earvin "Magic" Johnson showed how he got his nickname by setting an NBA playoff record for assists. He had 24 assists to lead the Lakers to a 118–102 victory.

1903 George A. Wyman hopped on his motorcycle in San Francisco, California, today to take a little trip. OK, it was a *big* trip. He wanted to become the first man to ride cross-country on a motorbike. On July 6, he arrived in New York City, tired, happy and probably walking a little funny.

1914 The Grand League of the American Horseshoe Pitchers Association was formed today. They immediately began to plan the sport's first championship, to be held October 23, 1915, in Kellerton, Iowa.

1981 If you look at the percentages, triples are the least likely kind of base hit in baseball. So what are the chances of hitting *three* triples in the same game? Not great. But that's what Craig Reynolds of the Houston Astros did. His three three-base hits led the Astros to a 6–1 victory over the Chicago Cubs.

1988 In an exhibition of shooting skill, Ted St. Martin set a basketball record by hitting 169 free throws in 10 minutes. St. Martin's record-breaking display was the halftime feature at a game in Jacksonville. Florida. In all, he only missed six shots—for an amazing 98.7 average. Eleven years earlier, St. Martin had set another record by hitting 2,036 free throws in a row.

1875 The first Kentucky Derby was run at Churchill Downs in Louisville, Kentucky. The Derby is the youngest of the three races that make up the Triple Crown for horses. (The other two events are the Preakness and the Belmont Stakes.) In the first Derby, 15 horses entered the $1\frac{1}{2}$-mile contest—14 of which were ridden by black jockeys. The winner was Aristides, ridden by Oliver Lewis.

1970 Hank Aaron made his 3,000th career hit in a game against the San Francisco Giants. In his next at-bat, the Atlanta Braves rightfielder slammed a home run, number 500 in his career, making him the only player to have 3,000 hits and 500 home runs.

1983 The New York Islanders today swept the Edmonton Oilers in four games, and won their fourth Stanley Cup in a row. But the Oilers got their revenge the next year, when they beat the Islanders, four games to one, to capture the Cup.

1988 John Stockton of the Utah Jazz made 24 assists in a play-off game against the Los Angeles Lakers to tie a playoff mark for most assists. The record had been set only four years earlier by one of Stockton's opponents on this night—Magic Johnson of the Los Angeles Lakers.

1912 Pity the manager of the Detroit Tigers. His players were on strike and refused to take the field against Philadelphia. So he threw together a squad made up of college students from a local school. The pitcher, Aloysius Travers, gave up 24 runs on 25 hits in a 24–2 loss. That's more runs than any pitcher had ever given up in one game.

1929 It was quite a day for Johnny Frederick of the Brooklyn Dodgers. Frederick set a league record for most runs scored in two consecutive games. Against the Philadelphia Phillies, he scored five times in the first game, played May 17, and then three times in the second game.

1969 The Minnesota Twins pair of Cesar Tovar and Rod Carew did so much stealing today, it's a miracle someone didn't call the police. The two stole five bases in one inning, working a double steal before Tovar stole home and Carew stole third. Well, Detroit Tigers catcher Bill Freehan must have been napping, because Carew then stole home, too. These were the only two runs Minnesota scored in their 8–2 loss.

Babe Ruth, the player who was sold by the Boston Red Sox to the New York Yankees and went on to be one of baseball's greatest hitters. (See May 6, 1915)

1942 Take that, all you sexists. The first golfer to have two official holes in one in one round was a woman. Mrs. W. Driver got aces on the third and eighth holes at the Balgowlah Golf Club in Australia. Another woman would later become the first golfer to have two holes in one in a row. (See May 29, 1977.)

1974 It would be an exaggeration to say that singer Kate Smith won the Stanley Cup for the Philadelphia Flyers. But she may have had something to do with Philadelphia's first Cup ever. Smith was most famous for singing "God Bless America." When she sang it at the Spectrum in Philadelphia before the start of important hockey games, the Flyers had a record of 36 wins, 1 tie and only 3 losses. So for today's game, the crucial seventh of the series between Philadelphia and the Boston Bruins, a red carpet was rolled out on the ice and Kate walked out to sing. The Flyers won, 1–0.

1989 Tennis player Andre Agassi won two separate singles matches today...in just four hours. At the Italian Open Men's Tennis Championships in Rome, he defeated Leonardo Lavelle of Mexico in straight sets. Then, in the afternoon, Agassi beat Guillermo Perez-Roldan of Argentina, also in straight sets. Agassi ended up advancing to the finals, where he lost to Alberto Mancini.

1956 Jim Jacobs, a 26-year-old student at UCLA, won the NAAU tournament in New York City to become the first man to take the three major handball singles championships in the same year. The other two titles were the National YMCA and the USHA crowns.

1989 It was the closest Preakness Stakes horse race ever run. Sunday Silence won the second leg of racing's Triple Crown by a nose, inching past Easy Goer down the home-stretch. Sunday Silence had also upset Easy Goer two weeks before in the Kentucky Derby. It was the first time since 1978 that the Preakness had ended in a photo finish.

1989 For the second time in three weeks, a major league base-ball team scored 17 runs or more in one game. Today, the Minnesota Twins routed the Texas Rangers, 19–3. Randy Bush tied a team record by driving in eight runs, including two homers, in the game. On May 1, the Cincinnati Reds had scored 17 runs against the Montreal Expos.

Earvin "Magic" Johnson, the superstar who set the NBA record for most assists in a playoff. (See May 15, 1984)

1819 One of the very first bicycles in the United States was seen on the streets of New York City today. Originally called a velocipede (from the word *velocity*, or speed), or a "swift walker," these big, ugly bikes weren't too swift at all. They had huge front wheels, and were uncomfortable and very hard to control.

1881 The United States Lawn Tennis Association (USLTA) was created in a hotel in New York City. Made up of 34 local clubs, the USLTA became the nation's first national tennis society. Rules were made about the height of the net, the size of the ball, and the length of the court. In 1975, the group dropped the "Lawn" from its name, becoming simply the United States Tennis Association (USTA).

1891 For the first time in boxing history, an automatic timer was used with a gong that went off at the end of each three-minute round. Since the fight in question, between Peter Jackson and James John Corbett, went 61 rounds, it certainly came in handy.

1968 Two major bowling records are set at the same event in Garden City, New York. Wayne Zahn of Atlanta, Georgia, rolled his way to a new mark for 18 games with a total of 4,043. That's an average of 224.6 a game. Ray Bluth of St. Louis sets a six-game record of 1,473, or 245.5 points per game.

1977 "Gentlemen—and Janet—start your engines...." On the last weekend of qualifying, Janet Guthrie became the first woman to qualify for the Indianapolis 500 car race. She drove an average speed of more than 188 miles per hour, and she had the fastest car in the final weekend of qualifying. Unfortunately, her luck didn't hold out in the big race seven days later. After only 27 laps Guthrie's car broke a valve seal and she had to drop out.

1977 The Boston Red Sox beat the Milwaukee Brewers, 14–10, in a battle of home runs. The two clubs hit 11 homers between them to tie a major league record. The Sox had six homers and the Brewers had five.

1922
THE GOOD,
THE BAD
AND THE
WEIRD
Hub "Shucks" Pruett was a mediocre rookie pitcher for the St. Louis Browns with a 7–7 record. The only reason he was playing baseball was to earn money for medical school. So, of course, he was the only man in the AL who could handcuff the great slugger, Babe Ruth. Today, Pruett struck out the Babe, beginning an incredible streak against the New York Yankees outfielder. Over the next four months, Pruett struck Ruth out nine times, and got him to bounce out once. Babe finally broke the spell with a giant home run on September 17. By the way, Pruett did go to medical school and became a doctor.

1876 The first no-hitter in NL history was pitched by Boston's Joe Borden. There was bad news for poor Borden, however. The official scorer incorrectly counted two walks given up by Borden as base hits, so his no-hitter isn't in any record books. But that was the least of Borden's problems. Soon after hurling his no-hitter, he developed pitching problems. By the end of the season, he was bounced from the club and became their groundskeeper.

1910 John Ennis wasn't the first man to walk from one end of the country to the other. But he was the only man to swim part of the way. Ennis took a plunge in the Atlantic Ocean today before starting his walk from New York to San Francisco. Along the way, he also swam across Lake Erie, the Mississippi River and seven other lakes. It took Ennis 80 days to make it to San Francisco, California.

1922 Boxer Harry Greb won a 15-round decision over the great Gene Tunney. It would be the only loss ever suffered by Tunney, who later became the heavyweight champion of the world.

1935 Let there be lights! Baseball's first major league night game was played at Crosley Field in Cincinnati, Ohio. President Franklin D. Roosevelt turned on eight giant towers of 363 lights by pushing a button in the White House. The 25,000 blinking fans at the game saw the Reds beat the Philadelphia Phillies, 2–1.

1936 New York Yankees slugger Tony Lazzeri set an AL record when he drove in 11 runs, including two grand slams, in one game. He wasn't the only Yankee with a sizzling bat, as New York flattened the Philadelphia Phillies, 25–2.

1981 Bobby Unser won the 65th Indianapolis 500. Or did he? Unser crossed the finish line first, but the next day Mario Andretti was declared the winner. The U.S. Auto Club said Unser had illegally passed another car after the yellow flag was put up following an accident. Drivers are not allowed to pass during the yellow. But wait—on October 8 the Auto Club changed its mind and gave the victory back to Unser.

1987 Canadian jockey Herve Filion set a harness-racing record by winning his 10,000th race at Yonkers Raceway in New York. In harness racing, the jockey doesn't sit on the horse, as in thoroughbred racing. He sits in a light, wheeled cart behind the horse. Also, the horses trot or "pace" rather than gallop.

1923 In 23 years in the majors (1905–28), Ty Cobb set a number of records that still stand. Among those records are the most times stealing home (50) and highest career batting average (.367). But no mark is more important than the one he set today, when he scored his 1,741st career run. After all, you can't win if you don't score. By the time he retired, Cobb scored 2,245 runs.

1935 At the Big Ten college track and field championships in Ann Arbor, Michigan, it took Jesse Owens only 45 minutes to set three world records and to tie a 4th. At 3:15, he tied the mark for the 100-yard dash. Ten minutes later, he long-jumped 26 feet, 8¼ inches, breaking the existing record by 6 inches. By 4:00, he had also set marks in the 220-meter dash, and the 220-yard hurdles.

1974 Want to make your mom laugh? Tell her you think anyone over 40 is really old. Well, sorry, Mom, but when it comes to most sports, that *is* old. On this day, a 41-year-old West German woman named Gerhard Weidner became the oldest person to break a world record, when she set a mark in a 20-mile walk.

1975 The Golden State Warriors dodged the Washington Bullets, 96–95, to sweep the NBA championship in four games. It was only the third sweep in NBA championship history. Golden State's Rick Barry was named Most Valuable Player of the series.

1928 Andrew Payne of Claremore, Oklahoma, must have been in great payne...er, pain... when he crossed the finish line at New York City's Madison Square Garden. Some 573 hours earlier, he had left Los Angeles, California, by foot. Payne was declared the winner of the country's first coast-to-coast walking race. He beat 273 other entrants in the 3,422-mile race.

1959 Pitcher Harvey Haddix of the Pittsburgh Pirates was working on a perfect game. Through 12 innings, he hadn't allowed a single Milwaukee Braves batter to reach first base. Unfortunately, his teammates weren't spending much time crossing home plate either, and the score was still 0–0. Then came the unlucky 13th. Milwaukee first baseman Joe Adcock hit a home run. Not only didn't Haddix get his perfect game, he ended up with the loss.

1975 The longest tennis game in history was played today at a tournament in England. Keith Glass of Great Britain and Anthony Fawcett of the African nation of Rhodesia (now Zimbabwe) played a single game that lasted 31 minutes. That was just one game in the match!

1976 If you've ever tried to prove you were better than your brother, you'll love what happened when two famous baseball brothers pitched against each other. Joe Niekro was a pitcher for the Houston Astros. His older brother, Phil, pitched for the Atlanta Braves. Today, Joe beat Phil, 4–1, and hit a home run off his brother.

1896 Columbia University was the easy winner of the first inter-collegiate bicycle meet. Five races, ranging from one-quarter mile to five miles, were held at a track in Brooklyn, New York. In addition to Columbia, teams from Yale, Pennsylvania and Harvard also participated.

1985 Whoever named the horse "Spend a Buck" knew what they were talking about. The Kentucky Derby winner had $2.6 million to spend after winning the Jersey Derby at Garden State Park in Cherry Hill, New Jersey. To this day, the $2.6 million is the largest purse in horse-racing history.

1985 No one expected the Los Angeles Lakers to be blown away in an NBA championship game—not even by the mighty Boston Celtics. So when the Celts manhandled their California rivals 148–114 in the opener, people took notice. Boston swingman Scott Wedman went 11 for 11 from the floor, including four three-pointers, to set a record for the most consecutive field goals in a championship series. And it was the first time in playoff history that any NBA player who took more than eight shots made all of them.

1912

SPORTS PROFILE

Golf great Sam Snead was born in Hot Springs, Virginia. Known as "Slamming Sammy Snead," he won his first major tournament, the PGA, in 1942. After fighting in World War II, he won the event twice more. Before he retired in the 1960s, Snead won more than 100 tournaments, including the British Open and the Masters (twice). The one major tournament that eluded him was the U.S. Open. The popular golfer was named to the PGA Hall of Fame in 1963.

1956 Pittsburgh Pirate first baseman Dale Long lived up to his last name. Today he hit his eighth "long" home run in eight consecutive games—a baseball record that Don Mattingly of the New York Yankees tied on July 18, 1987. The streak, which began on May 19 against the Chicago Cubs, ended 10 days later when Brooklyn Dodgers pitcher Don Newcombe foiled Long.

1976 Ron LeFlore's 30-game hitting streak came to an end today. When the Detroit Tigers slugger failed to get a hit against the New York Yankees, it was the first time since April 17 he had gone hitless. During that period LeFlore had batted .392 with 51 hits in 130 at bats.

1922
THE GOOD,
THE BAD
AND THE
WEIRD
The New York Yankees defeated the St. Louis Browns, 2–1. Or so everyone thought. Both teams had already headed back to their clubhouses when the umpires held a conference. They ruled the Yankees first baseman, who had caught the last out, had actually bobbled the ball. The batter was safe. The game wasn't over after all. Both teams were called back onto the field, and the fans returned to their seats. The Browns ended up scoring seven more runs and won the game they had just lost, 8–2.

1977 Race-car driver A. J. Foyt became the first man in history to win the Indianapolis 500 auto race four times. Foyt had previously won in 1961, 1964 and 1967, but it took him 10 years to get the 4th title and set the record. This year's race also made history for having the first woman participant— Janet Guthrie. (See May 22, 1977.)

1977 Golfer Sue Prell made not one, but two holes in one at a golf course in Sydney, Australia. In fact, she hit the two aces back-to-back. Prell became the first woman golfer ever to do that.

1988 Syracuse University held off Cornell University to take the NCAA lacrosse championships. There were 20,220 fans at Syracuse's Carrier Dome—the largest crowd to ever watch a lacrosse match. Lacrosse is somewhat like soccer, except instead of kicking a large ball, players toss and catch a smaller, harder ball in a small net attached to a long stick.

1953 SPORTS QUIZ Mountain climbers Edmund Hillary and Tenzing Norgay became the first men to climb the 29,028 feet to the top of the world's tallest mountain. Can you name the mountain and tell where it is?

A: Mount Everest. It is located in the Himalayan Mountains of south Asia, between Nepal and Tibet.

1911 More than 80,000 fans came out to watch the first Indianapolis 500 auto race. Ray Harroun beat 43 other cars in winning a very close race. He ran the 500-mile course in almost 7 hours at an average speed of 74.59 miles per hour, and won $10,000. Now the Indy is run in less than half that time. Almost 80 years after it began, the Indy 500 is still the most important auto race in the United States.

1922 The Chicago Cubs took on the St. Louis Cardinals in a doubleheader that had a strange twist. In the first game Max Flack played for the Cubs, and Cliff Heathcote played for the Cards. Then, between the games, the two players were traded. Each played the second game for the other team.

1923 Tommy Milton won the 11th Indianapolis 500 with an average speed of 90.95 miles per hour. It was his second Indy victory in three years. In 1921 he became the first man to win the 500 in an eight-cylinder car. Milton was the first man to win the famous race twice.

1982 Poor Rick Mears. With the finish line of the Indianapolis 500 in sight, he was dead-even with fellow race-car driver Gordon Johncock. At the finish, Johncock's auto inched ahead to take the checkered flag in what was the closest Indy race in history. Amazingly, only 0.16 seconds separated the two cars after 500 miles of driving.

1988 Christian Hosoi tied a skateboarding record when he reached a height of 9.5 feet above the top of the ramp in the highest air competition. In this event, contestants go up and down a high, curved wall on their boards until they pick up enough speed to go into the air. Hosoi tied a world record set on September 14, 1987, by Tony Magnuson.

1868 The first known bicycle race was held in a park in Paris, France. An Englishman named Dr. James Moore won the two-kilometer (1.24 mile) race, although there is no record of his winning time. The first bicycle race in the United States was also held in May, 10 years later, in Boston, Massachusetts. C.A. Parker of Harvard University won the 3-mile race in 12 minutes and 27 seconds.

1927 An unassisted triple play—in which a fielder makes all three outs by himself—is one of the rarest plays in baseball. Only eight major league fielders have ever done it. But two of those unassisted triple plays occurred two days in a row! On May 30, Chicago Cubs shortstop Jim Cooney turned one against the Pittsburgh Pirates. Then, today, first baseman Johnny Neun of the Detroit Tigers did it against the Cleveland Indians.

1975 Fred L. Newman began his quest to become the greatest basketball shooter in history. He began shooting baskets, and didn't stop for 24 hours. During that time, Newman scored 12,874 baskets in 13,116 attempts. That's a .982 percentage. Wow!

1986 Auto racer Bobby Rahal set a record for the fastest Indianapolis 500. Rahal averaged almost 171 miles per hour and finished the race in 2 hours, 55 minutes and 42 seconds. It was the first time in the 75-year history of the Indy 500 that anyone finished in under 3 hours.

1925 Lou Gehrig played first base for the New York Yankees in today's game. And the next game. And the next game. And for every single game for the next 13 years. His streak of 2,130 games at first base set a major league record that still stands today. It didn't come to an end until May 2, 1939.

1946 Only eleven horses have ever won horse racing's Triple Crown. So why did this rare sweep happen three times in six years? Today, Assault became the seventh Triple Crown winner. In 1943, a horse named Count Fleet won the Kentucky Derby, Preakness and Belmont. And two years before that Whirlaway was the Triple Crown winner.

1952 Boxing referee Max Pippow was used to counting out fighters who had been knocked out. But today, *he* was knocked to the canvas by one of the boxers. Middleweight Champion Pete Muller became so angry with the calls Pippow made during a match in Germany that he slugged him. Muller was disqualified and banned from boxing in Germany.

1975 Nolan Ryan of the California Angels blanked the Baltimore Orioles 1–0 to record his fourth career no-hitter and tie Sandy Koufax's record. It was also Ryan's 100th major league victory. Ryan has now pitched six no-hitters, something no one has ever done.

1986 When golfer Pat Bradley won the Ladies' Professional Golf Association (LPGA) golf championship, she did more than just win another golf match. She became the first woman to win all four of the top women's tournaments: the du Maurier Classic, the U.S. Open, the Dinah Shore and the LPGA. If that weren't enough, on May 18, she had also become the first woman to earn more than $2 million in her career.

Lou Gehrig, the reliable New York Yankee's first baseman who played more games in a row than any other player. (See June 1, 1925)

1880 The first perfect game in NL history was pitched by John Richmond of Worcester, Massachusetts. Five days later, John Montgomery Ward of Providence, Rhode Island, hurled the league's second perfect game. The third one took a little longer—it came 84 years after the first two.

1883 Two amateur teams from Fort Wayne, Indiana, played baseball's first night game. Fort Wayne outscored Quincy, 19–11. The major leagues would be a long time in coming around. Their first night contest didn't take place for another 42 years—a game between Philadelphia and Cincinnati. (See May 24, 1935.)

1922 His name was Stuffy McInnis, and on this day, he set a major league record for handling his 1,700th play at first base without committing an error. Stuffy's streak, which began almost exactly a year earlier, continued even while he switched teams during that time. He played for the Boston Red Sox and the Cleveland Indians.

1951 A minor league team from Tarboro, North Carolina, had one of the biggest innings in baseball history. In the fifth inning of a game against Wilson, North Carolina, the first 25 batters Tarboro sent to the plate reached base. Tarboro scored 24 runs on its way to a 31–4 blowout.

1851 The New York Knickerbockers became the first baseball team to wear uniforms. Their outfits weren't quite as practical as the ones today. The players wore straw hats, white button-down shirts and baggy blue trousers.

1956 Ouch! White Sox batter Nellie Fox survived one of the most painful at bats in baseball history. He became the first man to be hit by two pitches in a row. Fox was hit in the rear end by Baltimore pitcher Johnny Schmitz, but the umpire ruled that Fox hadn't tried hard enough to get out of the way of the pitch. On the next pitch, Fox was hit in the very same spot. This time the umpire let him take first base.

1975 The world's highest-paid athlete agreed to sign a three-year, $7 million contract today. Guess what sport he played. Baseball? Football? Basketball? Would you believe soccer? Brazilian superstar Pelé (pronounced *pay-LAY*) announced he would play for the New York Cosmos of the NASL. His contract was the biggest ever given to any athlete in any sport. Was it worth it? With Pelé, the Cosmos won their second NASL championship in 1977.

1977 Dennis Eckersley of the Cleveland Indians had pitched $22^1/3$ innings without giving up a hit. Then the Seattle Mariners' Ruppert Jones came to bat. Jones broke Eckersley's streak in a big way—with a homer in the sixth inning. Had Eckersley been able to get Jones and the next batter out, he would have tied Cy Young's major league record for hitless innings.

1989 Judi St. Hillaire set an American record at the 11th Annual Freihoffer's Run for Women in Albany, New York. St. Hillaire won the 5-kilometer (3-mile) road race in 15 minutes, 25.3 seconds—nearly 6 seconds faster than the previous American mark. The 29-year-old runner from Hingham, Massachusetts, came within six seconds of setting a world record.

1976 Today's NBA championship game between the Boston Celtics and the Phoenix Suns is considered one of the greatest basketball games ever played. It certainly was one of the longest. The heavily favored Celts survived three exhausting overtime periods to shake off the pesky Suns, 128–126. Despite being huge underdogs, Phoenix held on for two wins before finally losing the series, four games to two.

1983 Mike Ashman, a minor league baseball player for the Albany-Colonie (New York) A's, became the first man in pro baseball to play all 10 positions in one game. In addition to pitching, catching and playing all the positions in the outfield and infield, Ashman also took a turn as his team's designated hitter. Two major league players—Bert Campaneris and Cesar Tovar—played in all nine positions in one game, but their teams didn't have a DH. (See September 8, 1965, and September 22, 1968.)

1987 Holy Moses! Track star Edwin Moses lost the 400-meter hurdles at a meet in Spain to another American, Danny Harris. It was Moses' first loss in almost 10 years. His 122 wins in a row set a track and field record.

1988 Ever play with a footbag—those little sandbags you have to keep in the air using your feet and knees? Well, believe it or not, they keep records in that sport, too. Today, Ted Martin of Park Ridge, Illinois, set the mark for the most successful kicks without dropping the footbag. He kept it in the air for 48,825 kicks. It took him more than eight hours.

1935 "IIIIIII'M out!" In a rather unusual baseball twist, an umpire in the Pacific Coast League (PCL) was called on to be a pinch hitter—during the game. Wee Willie Ludolph was a player for the Oakland Oaks. He was serving as substitute umpire in a game against Los Angeles because the real ump was sick. Then Ludolph was called on to pinch hit. He struck out.

1964 Seventeen-year-old Jim Ryun of Los Angeles became the first high school student to run a mile in less than four minutes. Ryun's time was exactly 3 minutes, 59 seconds. Ten years earlier Englishman Roger Bannister had become the first man to run a mile in less than four minutes (see May 6, 1954). Ryun went on to become one of the greatest runners of the 1960s and 1970s.

1977 The Portland Trail Blazers nipped the Philadelphia 76ers, 109–107, to win their only NBA championship. The Blazers became the first team in the history of the championships to win four games in a row after losing the first two.

1896 Row, row, row your boat...George Harbo and Frank Samuelson set out from New York City to become the first people to row a boat across the Atlantic Ocean. Some 61 days—and 100 pounds of food—later, they arrived in Le Havre, France. Along the way they hit a storm, and a giant wave knocked the two men overboard. They just climbed back in and kept going.

1946 Today the first major basketball league, the BAA, was formed in New York. In 1950, the BAA merged with an older league that had teams in the Midwest, called the National Basketball League (NBL). Together, they became the NBA—the league still in existence today.

1973 Runner Kip Keino defeated his arch-rival Jim Ryun in the mile race to bring to an end the first *professional* track season. A record crowd of 15,502 turned up to watch the two famous runners at New York City's Madison Square Garden.

1988 Of all the motorcycle races in the world, the oldest—and most important—is on the Isle of Man, a tiny island in Great Britain. The long, exhausting course has 264 curves and corners. A speed record for one lap was set today by Joey Dunlop, who pushed his Honda to more than 118 miles per hour.

1892 Jack Doyle of the Cleveland Spiders became the first baseball player ever to get a pinch hit. He reached first while batting for pitcher George Davies in a game against the Brooklyn Dodgers. Doyles hit safely in two of his next four at bats as a pinch hitter, but despite his impressive average in that role (.600) he never pinch hit again.

1909 How long can a hot-air balloon stay in the air? Funny you should ask. The balloon *Indiana* today broke a record for staying in the air 44 hours. Hot-air balloons have no engines and stay afloat due to wind and the hot gases that fill the balloon. There must have been a lot of gas!

1913 Hudson Stuck. Sounds like what happens when New York's Hudson River gets clogged with garbage. It's not. It's the name of the first man to climb Mount McKinley in Alaska. At 20,320 feet, McKinley is the highest mountain in North America. Stuck, an Episcopal clergyman, led a party of four men to scale the peak.

1938 If you ever go to the Baseball Hall of Fame in Cooperstown, New York, you'll see a sweatshirt that was once worn by pitcher Johnny Allen of the Cleveland Indians. Allen was wearing it on the mound in a game against the Red Sox when the umpire said the sleeve was too long and had to be cut. Allen thought this was ridiculous, and refused. When the umpire insisted, Johnny walked off the mound and left the game. Allen was fined $250 by his own manager. But it was worth it—how many players have their clothes in the Hall of Fame?

1950 When the Boston Red Sox decide to score some runs, they don't kid around. Between yesterday's game against the St. Louis Browns and today's, the Sox scored 49 runs. That's a major league record for two games. They broke six major league marks in today's 29–4 win at Fenway Park. Among the records: the most runs scored by one team, the most extra-base hits (17), the most total bases (60), and the most hits in two games (51).

1950 Lee Mackey, a little-known golfer who barely qualified for the U.S. Open Championship, shocked golf fans around the country today. He shot an Open record score of 64 in the first round. The next day, with the world now watching him, Mackey shot a dismal 81. He ended up tied for 25th place.

1961 The Milwaukee Braves hit four home runs in a row in the seventh inning and *still* lost to the Cincinnati Reds, 10–8. The homers were hit by Eddie Matthews, Hank Aaron, Joe Adcock and Frank Thomas.

1968 Don Drysdale of the Los Angeles Dodgers pitched his way into the record books by going 58²/₃ innings without giving up a single run. That's more than six games! Drysdale's streak, which began on May 14 with a two-hit, 1–0 win over the Chicago Cubs, ended almost a month later when a Philadelphia Phillies outfielder named Howie Bedell hit a sacrifice fly to drive in a run.

1959   Relief pitcher Steve Kraly of the Southern Baseball Association's (SBA) Nashville team faced only two batters in two separate games—and won them both. In the first game, Kraly came in during the top of the ninth inning, got the third out, then watched as his team rallied to win. Three days later, the same thing happened.

1973   Secretariat won the 105th annual Belmont Stakes today and became the first horse in 25 years to win the Triple Crown. Secretariat also set a record on a dirt track for the biggest victory in Belmont history, 31 lengths. Secretariat was the ninth thoroughbred to win the Kentucky Derby, the Preakness and the Belmont Stakes, which make up the Triple Crown.

1976   Playing at a golf course in Phoenix, Arizona, the Reverend Harold Snider made three holes in one. Two of them came in a row, on the 13th and 14th holes. Only one other golfer in history had three aces in one round. Dr. Joseph Boydstone did it on October 10, 1962.

1946
SAD SACKS
OF SPORTS

Billy Martin used to get thrown out of a lot of ball games by umpires, but he had nothing on Mel Ott, the manager of the New York Giants in the 1940s. During a doubleheader against the Pittsburgh Pirates, Ott was tossed out of the first game for arguing with umpire Tom Dunn. Then he was ejected in the fifth inning of the second game when he protested a decision by umpire George Magerkurth. Ott became the first major league manager or player to be thrown out of both ends of a doubleheader.

1892 Baltimore Oriole catcher Wilbert Robinson wasn't much of a hitter, but you couldn't tell from this game. Against St. Louis, Robinson became the first major league player in the history of baseball to get seven hits in seven times at the plate. Robinson, who later managed the Brooklyn Dodgers, cranked out six singles and a double. Only two other hitters have gone seven for seven since. Cesar Gutierrez did it in 1967, and Rennie Stennett did it in 1975.

1938 Ray Ainsley had the most embarrassing hole in the history of professional golf today. At the 16th hole of the U.S. Open championship, he shot the ball into a stream. Not one to give up, Ray jumped right in and took 11 more shots trying to get the ball out of the water. He finally did it...but the ball went into the bushes. In all, Ainsley took 19 strokes on the hole.

1944 Joe Nuxhall of the Cincinnati Reds became the youngest pitcher to play in the majors. Joe hadn't turned 16 yet when he pitched ⅔ of an inning in the Reds' 18–0 loss to the St. Louis Cardinals. Unfortunately, he gave up five runs, and five walks, and threw a wild pitch. Nuxhall still went on to have a very good career, with a record of 135–117.

1978 For the first time in history, there are Triple Crown winners two years in a row. In 1977, Seattle Slew became the 10th horse to win the Kentucky Derby, the Preakness Stakes and the Belmont Stakes. Not to be outdone, the thoroughbred Affirmed won all three races, completing the sweep by winning the Belmont today. There hasn't been a Triple Crown winner since.

1902 Ahoy, checkmates! For the first time, a chess match was held between players on two different ships at sea. The ships, the *Philadelphia* and the *Campania,* were 70 miles apart at sea with passengers broadcasting their moves over wireless radios. The game was interrupted when the radios were needed to guide the ships.

1919 Sir Barton won the 51st annual Belmont Stakes to become the first horse to win thoroughbred racing's Triple Crown. Earlier, in May, he had won both the Kentucky Derby and Preakness Stakes.

1967 The Chicago Cubs and the New York Mets tied a major league record for the most home runs in one game today. The Cubs hit 7 and the Mets 4, tying the 2-team total of 11 set by the New York Yankees and the Detroit Tigers in 1950.

1985 Von Hayes of the Philadelphia Phillies led off a game against the New York Mets with a homer. Then he hit a grand slam later in the same inning. Hayes became the 21st player to hit 2 homers in 1 inning, and the first player ever to do it in the first inning. As you may have guessed, the Phillies won the game, 26–7.

1987 A team from the United States won the women's World Bowling Championships in Helsinki, Finland, for the third time in a row. The women set a record for the most points in a game—1,063. The average score of the 5 women on the team was 212.6.

1930 In a title bout held in New York City, boxer Max Schmeling of Germany became Heavyweight Champion of the World in a rather unusual way. Opponent Jack Sharkey was disqualified in the fourth round for a low blow. Schmeling became the only man to win the heavyweight title on a foul.

1939 The National Baseball Hall of Fame was dedicated today in Cooperstown, New York. Ty Cobb and Babe Ruth headed a list of 26 greats who were officially inducted. The opening of the Hall was designed to mark the 100th anniversary of the reputed invention of baseball by Abner Doubleday. To be elected to the Hall, a player must have played at least 10 years, have been retired for 5, and must get 75% of the vote of a select group of members of the Baseball Writers' Association of America.

1957 Olympic weightlifting champion Paul Anderson set an odd record today. In a demonstration in Toccoa, Georgia, he lifted 6,270 pounds in a back lift. That is the most weight any human being has ever lifted. The crazy thing was that Anderson wasn't lifting standard weights. He hoisted a steel safe filled with lead and heavy auto parts on a special table. It weighed more than 17 times his own weight of 364 pounds.

1974 Little League baseball announced girls will be allowed to play for the first time. Until today, only boys were allowed to take part. A number of girls and their parents had sued the Little League, forcing them to change their policy.

1980 Golf great Jack Nicklaus set a record for the lowest 72-hole score in any U.S. Open championship, with a total of 272. It was also Nicklaus's fourth Open win since 1962.

1912   June 13 must have been New York Giants pitcher Christy Mathewson's lucky day. Mathewson, one of the greatest hurlers of the early 1900s, won his 300th game today with a 3–2 victory over the Chicago Cubs. Exactly seven years earlier, on June 13, 1905, Mathewson pitched a no-hitter, also against Chicago.

1957   The Boston Red Sox beat the Cleveland Indians 9–3, thanks to three home runs and five runs batted in by Ted Williams. It was the second time in the season that Williams had hit three homers in one game. He was the first player in the history of the AL to do that.

1985   What do you call the little wooden stick that golfers put the ball on when they swing at it? It's called a tee. Golfers in the tiny democratic Chinese nation of Taiwan may want to change the name to a Tze, after their fellow countryman Tze-Chung Chen. On this day, Chen made history by becoming the first man to get a double eagle in the 84-year history of the U.S. Open championship. A double eagle means the golfer used three strokes fewer than "par"— what is expected on a hole. Chen made two on a par-five hole.

1904
SPORTS
PROFILE   Harold Edward "Red" Grange was born in Forksville, Pennsylvania. Known as "The Galloping Ghost of the Gridiron," he was by far the greatest football player of the 1920s. As a halfback at the University of Illinois, Grange was named All-America three times, and once scored six touchdowns in one game. By the time he played professional ball for the Chicago Bears and New York (football) Yankees, he was a national hero. Grange scored a total of 1,058 points in his pro career, and was one of the first players inducted into the Pro Football Hall of Fame.

1876 The Boston Reds clobbered the St. Louis Browns 17–6 in baseball today. But both teams were probably just as anxious to forget the game ever took place. Between the two of them, they set a major league record by committing a pathetic 40 errors.

1924 The New York Giants might as well have changed their name to the Kellys today. George "Highpockets" Kelly drove in all eight of the Giants' runs and had three homers in the team's 8–4 win over Cincinnati.

1954 George Ballick of Old Forge, Pennsylvania, became the first man to be recognized by the ABC for rolling 12 perfect games. Ballick's first 300 game had come 17 years earlier, in 1937.

1965 Talk about tough breaks. Pitcher Jim Maloney of the Cincinnati Reds struck out 18 New York Mets and held the team hitless through 10 innings. Then, with one pitch, his great performance was gone. Johnny Lewis's leadoff homer in the 11th inning gave New York a 1–0 victory.

1987 Golfer Chi Chi Rodriguez saw his record winning streak come to an end when Gary Player beat him by one stroke in the Senior Tournament Players Championship. Rodriguez had won four tournaments in a row, and six in as many months—both of which set records. Even with his streak ended, Chi Chi still had the neatest name in golf!

1902 Corsicana embarrassed Texarkana 51–3 in a Texas League baseball blowout. Nig Clarke set a pro baseball record by hitting eight home runs in eight at-bats. When the score of the game was sent out to newspapers over the telegraph wires, some telegraph operators thought the huge score must have been a mistake. Instead of 51–3, they made it 5–3.

1938 Johnny Vander Meer of the Cincinnati Reds became the first player to pitch two no-hitters in the same season. In fact, he threw two in a row. No one else has ever done that. Today, he beat the Brooklyn Dodgers 6–0 for the second one. Four days earlier, he had held the Boston Braves hitless.

1955 Would you believe that the first sports event between the United States and the Soviet Union was a weightlifting competition? American Paul Anderson amazed 15,000 people in Moscow, the capital of the Soviet Union, today by setting two world records. He lifted 425.5 pounds in the clean and jerk, and 402.4 pounds in the 2-handed press.

1971 Cheryl White rode a horse named Ace Reward at the Thistledown Race Track in Cleveland, Ohio, to become the first black woman jockey. Unfortunately, the 17-year-old jockey finished last.

1913
THE GOOD,
THE BAD
AND THE
WEIRD
What do you get when you play baseball in a swimming pool? An idea that's all wet. Strange as it sounds, a number of "water baseball" games were played in the early 1900s. The first took place in a New York swimming pool, with all the players in the water at once. The hitter, standing in water over his knees, hit the ball and swam to first base, which floated because it was made out of cork. The sport never really caught on. You might say it was a washout.

1894 The squeeze play was used in a baseball game for the first time today by two Yale University players in a game against Princeton University. In a squeeze play, the batter bunts the ball slowly to the infield so that the runner on third base can attempt to come home safely.

1938 Red Sox slugger Jimmy Foxx had a great day at the plate against the St. Louis Browns. He scored two runs, reached base on each of his six at bats . . . but he never hit the ball. How did he do it? The Boston first baseman drew a walk each time he came to the plate. His six walks in one game set a major league record.

1946 Golfer Byron Nelson must have been really mad. Here he was, in the lead of the U.S. Open championship, when his caddy accidently kicked the ball. The kick counted as a stroke, and that was enough to cost Nelson the tournament title.

1976 For the first and only time, a baseball game in an indoor stadium was called on account of rain. No, the roof at the Astrodome didn't leak. It was raining so hard in Houston, that the area outside the stadium was flooded and no one could get into the building. So the game, between the Astros and the Pittsburgh Pirates, was called.

1921 Sixty-two colleges and universities competed in the first NCAA Track and Field Championships. The University of Illinois was crowned the winner, followed by Notre Dame and Iowa. The event was held at the University of Chicago in Illinois.

1962 One of the most popular players for the newly formed New York Mets was "Marvelous" Marv Throneberry. Marv was a nice guy, but he wasn't much of a baseball player. He was sort of the Bob Uecker of his time. Take today, for example. Throneberry hit a rare triple in a game against the Chicago Cubs—only he forget to touch first and second base. Not-so marvelous Marv was called out.

1978 New York Yankee pitcher Ron Guidry set an AL record for lefthanded pitchers when he struck out 18 California Angels batters. Guidry fanned 15 in the first six innings alone. The Yanks won, 4–0.

1989 It isn't every day a volleyball tournament begins with an Indian sun dance. But that's what happened during the opening ceremonies of a pro volleyball tournament held in Boulder, Colorado today. Sudden rainstorms had caused lots of delays and cancellations during the past two years. So this year, the organizers weren't taking any chances. They called in eight Indians from the state of Montana to perform their native sun dance.

Joey Dunlop, the motorcycle racer who held the one-lap speed record at Great Britain's Isle of Man course. (See June 6, 1988)

1621 America's first recorded fencing duel took place in Massachusetts. Edward Leister and Edward Dotey, two servants of one of the Plymouth Colony leaders, wounded each other in the hand and thigh. Neither man was declared the winner.

1897 Wee Willie Keeler made big baseball news today. The Baltimore Oriole outfielder hit safely in his 44th game in a row, a new major league record. In 201 at bats during the streak, Keeler had 82 hits, 53 runs and a .408 average.

1953 The Boston Red Sox walloped the Detroit Tigers, 23–3. The Sox scored an amazing 17 runs in the 7th inning, thanks in part to Gene Stephens's 3 hits. No other player has ever had that many hits in one inning. Catcher Sammy White also set a record in the seventh by scoring three runs.

1960 Golfer Arnold Palmer battled back from a horrible start to win the U.S. Open championship in Denver, Colorado. Palmer was seven shots down going into today's final round. Then he tied a record by shooting 30 for 9 holes. Palmer went on to beat Jack Nicklaus by two strokes.

1924
SPORTS
PROFILE
Basketball legend George Mikan was born in Joliet, Illinois. Considered the game's first superstar, Mikan played for Chicago and Minneapolis of the NBL in the 1940s and 1950s, and continued with the Minneapolis Lakers when they joined the new NBA. He scored 11,764 points during his ten-year career, including a then-record 61 points in one game. In all, Mikan played in nine playoffs and four All-Star Games. He later coached the Lakers briefly in 1957, and became the first commissioner of the ABA in 1968. In 1959 he was elected to the Basketball Hall of Fame.

1846 Play ball! The very first formal baseball game was played at Elysian Fields in Hoboken, New Jersey. In a game that wasn't quite a nail-biter, the New York Nine squeaked by the Knickerbockers, 23–1, in a four-inning contest. Alexander Cartwright, the man who is now believed by some to have invented the game, served as umpire. At one point he gave out a six-cent fine to one of the New York Nine players for swearing.

1867 The first Belmont Stakes were held in Jerome Park, New York. A horse named Ruthless won with a time of three minutes, five seconds. In 1906, the famous race was moved to a newer track in Belmont, New York, where it is still held. The Belmont has become the final race of horse racing's important Triple Crown.

1938 After pitching two no-hitters in a row, Johnny Vander Meer of the Cincinnati Reds threw a three-hitter against the Boston Bees. Vander Meer gave up a single with one out in the fourth, to end his hitless streak at 21 2/3 innings. The Reds stung the Bees, 14–1.

1988 On the one hand, Isiah Thomas of the Detroit Pistons had reason to celebrate after Game Six of the championship series with the Los Angeles Lakers. Thomas set an NBA finals record by scoring 25 points in the third period. But it wasn't much consolation. His team still lost a thriller, 103–102. Los Angeles went on to take the championship, four games to three.

1912 Every year, soccer clubs from around the country participate in a competition to see who will win the National Challenge Cup, the most important award in U.S. soccer. Today, the silver trophy that is still awarded to the winners was donated to the American Amateur Football Association (AAFA) by Sir Thomas Dewar of Britain. It was worth about $500. The competition was soon opened up to include professional teams.

1943 Runner Greg Rice must have been simmering after the 5,000-meter race at the national AAU track and field championships in New York City. Rice not only lost for the first time in 66 races, but he did so by a full 35 yards, to Sweden's Gunder Hagg.

1960 Boxer Floyd Patterson became the first man to lose and then regain the heavyweight championship of the world. Today he knocked out Ingemar Johansson in the fifth round to regain his title. A year earlier he had lost the title to Johansson by a knockout on June 26, 1959.

1968 Jim Hines became the first man to run the 100-meter dash in less than 10 seconds. He was timed at 9.9 seconds at the AAU track-and-field championships in Sacramento, California.

1947 Two world records fell in one track meet at the NCAA Championships in Salt Lake City, Utah. Harrison Dillard won the 220-yard low hurdles in 22.3 seconds, and Herb McKenley took the 440-yard dash in 46.2 seconds.

1964 Jim Bunning of the Philadelphia Phillies didn't allow a single New York Mets batter to reach base as he blanked New York at Shea Stadium, 6–0. It was the first regular-season perfect game in major league baseball in 42 years.

1970 Cesar Gutierrez, a little known baseball player from Venezuela, got seven hits in seven times at bat for the Detroit Tigers in a 12-inning game against the Cleveland Indians. He became the first player in the 20th century to go seven for seven. It was his one moment of glory: The next year, Gutierrez batted .189 and was cut by the Tigers.

1986 Red Sox pitcher Roger Clemens defeated the Baltimore Orioles, 7–2, in Boston for his 13th straight win of the season. Clemens became the 7th pitcher in major league history to start the season with 13 wins.

1988 The Los Angeles Lakers became the first basketball team since 1969 to win back-to-back NBA titles. They defeated the Detroit Pistons, 108–105, to take the championship series in seven games. The last team to win two in a row was the Boston Celtics in 1968 and 1969. The Pistons would get their revenge a year later by sweeping the Lakers in the finals.

1909 Bert Scott and James Smith, driving a Model-T Ford, arrived in Seattle, Washington, today to win the first cross-country automobile race. Six cars set out from New York City, exactly three weeks earlier, but one of them refused to start. Where's a mechanic when you need one?

1930 New York Yankees slugger Babe Ruth hit two homers in the first game of a doubleheader against the Philadelphia Athletics. Then, he hit another in the nightcap. Ruth, who had hit three homers the day before, set new major league marks for most home runs in two and three games. Not to be outdone by his teammate, Lou Gehrig hit three homers off Philadelphia pitching in the nightcap. New York easily won both games, 10–1 and 20–13.

1962 Boog Powell of the Baltimore Orioles hit a towering 469-foot homer in a game against the Boston Red Sox. He became the first batter ever to hit one over the centerfield hedge at Baltimore's Memorial Stadium.

1889
SAD SACKS
OF SPORTS
The Louisville Colonels were bad. *Really* bad. Today, they set an embarrassing major league baseball record by losing their 26th game in a row. By the end of the season, their record would be 27–111. By the way, their manager was named Chicken Wolf.

1904 The first motorboat race was held in New York's Hudson River. *Standard* won the Gold Cup for the 32-mile race. It averaged 19.67 nautical miles per hour.

1917 Here's a strange one. In a game between the Boston Red Sox and Washington Senators, Boston pitcher Babe Ruth walked the first batter, protested the call and was thrown out of the game. The runner was thrown out while stealing and reliever Ernie Shore came in and retired the next 26 batters. Even though he didn't exactly pitch the entire game, Shore was credited with pitching a perfect game.

1931 Lili de Alvarez may be the first tennis player to make Wimbledon history not for winning, but for what she wore. Alvarez appeared on the court at the famous English tournament in an outfit she had made herself, which included—yikes!—shorts. At that time, all women playing tennis wore bloomers—baggy trousers, which made it hard for them to move. Alvarez was the first woman ever to appear at Wimbledon in shorts. Unfortunately, it did her little good: She didn't win the tournament. But she looked great.

1951 Imagine throwing a 16-pound ball more than 50 feet? That's what Henry Dryer did at the national AAU track and field championships in Berkeley, California. In the shot-put event, he "put" that 16-pound shot 41 feet, 6³/₄ inches. That toss gave Jim Fuchs, the world shot-put record-holder, his first loss in nearly three years.

1987 Abel Kiviat, the oldest living Olympic medalist, celebrated his 95th birthday today by going out and jogging. Kiviat won the silver medal in the 1,500-meter race back in the 1912 Olympics.

1922 The American Professional Football Association (APFA) changed its name to the NFL. Curly Lambeau bought the rights to the Green Bay Packers for a whopping $50. The team would go on to become one of the most successful in the history of the NFL. In case you've ever wondered why they're called the Packers, it's because the original owners were a packing company in Wisconsin.

1929 The 32nd annual International Rowing Association Regatta, the most important rowing competition in the United States, was also one of the strangest this year. The race on the Hudson River in upstate New York began in total darkness. Without any way for the rowers to see, four of the nine boats sank almost immediately. The rest of the boats finished with very slow times.

1952 Horse-racing great Eddie Arcaro became the first American-born jockey to win 3,000 races. By the time he retired in 1962, after 31 years of riding horses, he had increased his total to an astounding 4,779 winners!

1956 Chris von Slatza broke a women's world record by swimming the 500-yard freestyle in 5 minutes, 52.5 seconds today at a swimming meet in Santa Clara, California. So what? She was only 12 years old, that's what!

1972 Bernice Gera became the first woman umpire in baseball today. Then she became the first woman to quit. Gera resigned just hours after umpiring her first game, a minor league contest between Auburn and Geneva, New York, in the Class A New York–Pennsylvania Baseball League.

1952 Ruby Goldstein may have been the first boxing referee ever to throw in the towel. Goldstein was refereeing the world light heavyweight title match between Joey Maxim and Sugar Ray Robinson. It was a horribly muggy, 104-degree night in New York, and Goldstein got so tired that he couldn't go on. He left the fight after the tenth round. Sugar Ray Robinson didn't do much better. He was too exhausted to answer the bell for the 14th round. It was the only time in his professional career that Sugar Ray didn't finish a fight.

1953 Tennis elbow, anyone? It took five hours, but Jaroslav Drobny finally beat Budge Patty of Los Angeles, California, at Wimbledon. It was, at the time, the longest match in tennis history. When was the record broken? Read two entries on.

1968 Rookie Bobby Bonds of the San Francisco Giants hit a grand slam home run in his very first major league game. He became the second player to do that in the history of major league baseball. A grand slam homer, by the way, is a home run hit when the bases are loaded.

1969 What is it about June 25 and endless tennis matches? This match, the longest in history, took two *days* to complete. Pancho Gonzales defeated Charles Pasarell. The 112-game match took 5 hours and 12 minutes to complete. Play had to be called due to darkness on June 24, and then continued on the 25th.

1944 In the battle of New York, the Brooklyn Dodgers beat the New York Yankees and the New York Giants today—all in one game. This special exhibition game was held to raise money for the World War II effort. Each of the three teams took a turn sitting out in each inning. The final score of this six-inning exercise in confusion: the Dodgers, 5; the Yankees, 1; the Giants, 0. Aren't you glad there are only two teams in New York these days?

1987 Track and field superstar Carl Lewis won the long-jump competition and the 200-meter dash at the USA/Mobil Outdoor Track and Field Championships in San Jose, California. It was his 50th straight long-jump win in more than 6 years.

1914 SPORTS PROFILE: Her full name was Mildred Ella Didrikson Zaharias, but to the world she was just "Babe." Born today in Port Arthur, Texas, Babe grew into one of the greatest all-around women athletes ever. She won two gold medals and a silver in track and field in the 1932 Olympics. Then she took up golf, winning an incredible 17 tournaments in a row, including the U.S. Women's Amateur championship. As if that wasn't enough, Babe often took on professional baseball and basketball players in exhibitions. In 1949, she and her husband, a wrestler named George Zaharias, and two friends founded the LPGA. Babe died of cancer in 1956, at the age of 42.

1884   Larry Corcoran of the Chicago Nationals became the first baseball pitcher to throw three no-hit games. He blanked Boston (Massachusetts) on August 19, 1880, Worcester (Massachusetts) on September 20, 1882 and Providence (Rhode Island) today.

1898   A Canadian named Joshua Slocum became the first man to sail around the world by himself. Slocum left Boston on April 24, 1895, in a 37-foot boat named *Spray*. He saw plenty of sea spray on his three-year, 46,000-mile journey. He arrived in Newport, Rhode Island, today.

1906   Franz Szisz, a Hungarian race-car driver in a Renault, won the first Grand Prix auto race. The two-day event covered 770 miles and was run over the streets of the city of Le Mans, France. Szisz completed the course in 12 hours and 14 minutes. The Grand Prix—one of the world's most famous auto races—is still held in Le Mans.

1972   Most people would agree that it isn't good for brothers to fight each other. In the case of professional boxers Jerry and Mike Quarry, some days it isn't so great for them to fight other people either. Both boxers were knocked out in separate bouts on the same program tonight in Las Vegas, Nevada. Jerry was knocked out by Muhammad Ali in the seventh round of their heavyweight bout. Brother Mike hit the canvas in the fourth round of his light heavyweight title bout with Bob Foster.

1907 Catcher Branch Rickey of the New York Yankees didn't exactly have the best day of his career behind the plate. In a game against the Washington Senators, 13 base runners were able to steal on him. No wonder the Senators won 16–5. Forty years later, Rickey would again make history. As president of the Brooklyn Dodgers, Rickey signed Jackie Robinson, the first black player to play in the major leagues and one of the legends of the game.

1972 Bobby Hull was one of the biggest stars in the NHL, and he had more goals than any other player in the league. So when the Chicago Blackhawks left wing jumped to the Winnipeg Jets in the upstart (WHA), it made big news. Hull, known as the Golden Jet, received $2.75 million to play for the Winnipeg Jets. The Jets later joined the NHL.

1973 The Black Sports Hall of Fame was formed by *Black Sports* magazine today. Thirty-eight athletes were inducted, including football great Jim Brown, Olympic champion Jesse Owens, basketball star Elgin Baylor, boxer Joe Louis, runner Wilma Rudolph and tennis star Althea Gibson.

1980 Wouldn't it be great if your *teachers* had to write papers called, "What I did over my summer vacation"? John Marino, a 32-year-old gym teacher from Santa Monica, California, would have a lot to write about. He set a record by riding his bicycle from Santa Monica to New York City in 12 days, 3 hours and 41 minutes. In all, Marino rode for 2853.9 miles.

1923 The Brooklyn Dodgers whipped the Philadelphia Phillies, 14–5. Brooklyn's Jacques Fournier certainly did his part. He had six hits in six at bats, including a home run, two doubles and three singles.

1941 Way to go, Joltin' Joe! Centerfielder Joe DiMaggio of the New York Yankees hit safely in both games of a double-header against the Washington Senators to tie, and then break, an AL batting record. With a double in the first game and a single in the nightcap, DiMaggio had gotten a hit in 41 consecutive games, breaking Georges Sisler's record. But DiMaggio was only getting started. By the time his streak ended on July 17, he had hit safely in an amazing 56 games in a row.

1957 Here's another good reason to pay attention in math class. Jacqueline Pung was disqualified from winning the U.S. Women's Open Championships because she put down the wrong score on one hole. Besty Rawls was named the winner.

1984 Pete Rose of the Cincinnati Reds set a major league record today by playing in his 3,309th baseball game. By the time Rose retired in 1986, he had increased his record to 3,562 games. He also took a mind-boggling 14,053 trips to the plate.

1859 Charles Blondin of France became the first man to cross Niagara Falls on a tightrope. It took 5 minutes for him to walk the 1,100 feet of cable that stretched 160 feet above the giant falls that separate New York State and Canada. On later occasions, Blondin crossed Niagara Falls blindfolded, pushing a wheelbarrow, walking on stilts and with another man on his back. Didn't the guy ever hear of a boat?

1899 Charles Murphy of New York became the first man to pedal a bicycle as fast as a speeding train. Murphy waited on his bicycle until a special Long Island Railroad train in New York traveling 60 miles per hour sped by. Murphy not only kept up with the train, but he actually passed it. This made him the first man to pedal faster than a mile a minute, at least as far as anyone can figure.

1929 If it's possible to have a blowout in a golf tournament, Bobby Jones recorded one today. Jones, one of the greatest golfers of all time, won the important U.S. Open championship in an 18-hole playoff by an incredible 23 shots, at the Winged Foot Golf Course in Mamaroneck, New York.

1962 Pitcher Sandy Koufax of the Los Angeles Dodgers struck out 13 New York Mets batters without allowing a hit. He beat New York, 5–0. It was the first of Koufax's four no-hitters (one was a perfect game). He threw one every year between 1962 and 1965. Only Nolan Ryan has thrown more no-hitters.

1984 The longest professional football game on record wasn't played in the NFL. It was a USFL playoff game. The Los Angeles Express outlasted the Michigan Panthers to win, 27–21, in the third overtime period. The game took 93 minutes and 33 seconds of official game time.

1859 In the first college game ever played in this sport, Amherst College defeated Williams College, 73–32. Can you guess the sport? No, it wasn't basketball. It was baseball. In this particular game, there were 13 men to a side, and the game lasted 26 innings.

1928 One of the biggest crazes of the late 1920s and 1930s was the dance marathon. Couples would dance for days on end until they became too exhausted to go on. The last couple standing won. The first major dance marathon ended today in New York City's Madison Square Garden after 481 hours. Actually, no one won. The police were called in to stop the contest because the city's health department thought it was too dangerous for the nine teams still dancing to continue.

1989 Davey Allison won his first Daytona 400 car race in Daytona Beach, Florida, thanks to a little luck. With only five laps to go, leader Mark Martin's car ran out of gas, allowing Allison's Ford to pass him. In all, the lead changed hands 28 times during the race.

1961
SPORTS
PROFILE

Track star Frederick Carlton (Carl) Lewis was born today in Birmingham, Alabama. His father had been the captain of his college football team, and his mother competed in the hurdles at the 1951 Pan American Games. Lewis's younger sister, Carol, also represented the United States in track and field in the 1984 Olympics, and one of his brothers had been the first black to play in the North American Soccer League. But Lewis is the star of the family. In the 1984 Olympics in Los Angeles, California, he won gold medals in the 100-meter dash, 200-meter dash, 4 x 100-meter relay and the long jump. That made him the first athlete since his idol, Jesse Owens, to win four gold medals in track and field events. (Owens did it in 1936.) Lewis won two more gold medals in the 1988 Olympics.

Bruce Jenner, holder of the record for most points in the Olympic decathlon. (See July 30, 1976)

1938 In a battle of the Helens, Helen Wills Moody defeated Helen Hull Jacobs, 6–4, 6–0, to win the women's singles championship at the prestigious English tennis event called Wimbledon. It was the eighth time Moody had won the title. Only one other player in history has won as many. Martina Navratilova won her eighth Wimbledon title in 1987.

1941 Only 8,682 fans showed up at Yankee Stadium to watch New York play the Boston Red Sox. But what a treat they got! Yankees outfielder Joe DiMaggio broke Wee Willie Keeler's record for hitting safely in 44 games in a row. DiMaggio hit a homer in the fifth inning off rookie pitcher Dick Newsome. Joe's streak ended 2 weeks later at 56 games.

1988 Steffi Graf of West Germany defeated Martina Navratilova to win the women's singles tennis championship at Wimbledon. It ended a record streak of six straight Wimbledon titles for Navratilova. (She's won eight Wimbledon crowns in all.) For Graf, on the other hand, it was her first Wimbledon title.

1921
THE GOOD,
THE BAD
AND THE
WEIRD
If you showed up for the doubleheader between Newark and Jersey City of the International Baseball League (IBL), you would have been a little confused. You see, no one else showed up. No fans, no players, not even the umpires. The doubleheader was scheduled for the same time as a heavyweight championship fight between Jack Dempsey and Georges Carpentier, which was also held in Jersey City. And everyone, it seemed, went to the fight instead.

1912 Pitcher Rube Marquard of the New York Giants tied a major league record set before 1900 by winning his 19th game in a row. The Giants edged the Brooklyn Dodgers, 2–1. Marquard's streak would come to an end in his next start. On July 8, he lost a 7–2 decision to the Chicago Cubs.

1927 Tennis pro Henry Cochet of France staged one of the greatest comebacks in Wimbledon history. He had defeated Frank Hunter of the United States in the quarterfinals after losing the first two sets. Then he did the same thing against Bill Tilden, also of the United States. Finally came today's championship match, and Cochet once again fell behind in the fifth and final set with the score, 5–2. All his opponent, Jean Borotra of France, had to do was win one more game to capture the men's singles title. Borotra had six match points, but failed to win. Cochet pulled off another miracle comeback, winning the next five games.

1931 Twenty-year-old Sidney B. Wood, Jr., won the men's singles tennis championship at Wimbledon to become the youngest winner in the event's history. But compared to Boris Becker, who won the title in 1985 when he was 17 years old, Wood was practically an old man.

1989 Peter Koech of Kenya set a world track and field record when he ran the 3,000-meter steeplechase in 8 minutes, 5.35 seconds. In the steeplechase, runners must make their way around a course that includes 28 hurdles and 7 water jumps. Koech had been the silver medalist in the 1988 Olympics in Seoul, South Korea.

1883 Rodeos have been around for a long time although they first were known simply as "Cowboy Tournaments." The first cowboy tournament with cash prizes was held today in Pecos, Texas. Winners of the riding and roping contests received $25, and $15 went to the runners-up.

1939 Fans at a packed Yankee Stadium witnessed a tearful good-bye tribute to one of their heroes, Lou Gehrig. In his brilliant 17-year career with the New York Yankees, Gehrig set a record for playing in the most consecutive games (2,130). Today, though, the star first baseman, who was dying of a rare disease that attacked his muscle joints, was retiring. (Gehrig's illness is now known as "Lou Gehrig's disease.") Two years later, he died. No one who was at Yankee Stadium will ever forget this emotional farewell. And no baseball fan will ever forget Lou Gehrig.

1962 "Rowski, rowski, rowski your boat...." For the first time, Soviet rowing teams competed in an American race. They did more than just participate in the 2,000-meter international Independence Day Regatta in Philadelphia, Pennsylvania. They won all three events!

1982 In one of the longest tennis finals in the history of Wimbledon, Jimmy Connors finally beat John McEnroe for the title. The match took 4 hours and 16 minutes. McEnroe, who had won Wimbledon the year before, would come back to reclaim his title in 1983. What was *the* longest match in Wimbledon history? (See June 25, 1969.)

1988 What do you get when you combine running with juggling? Joggling, of course. And it's a sport, of sorts. Ashrita Furman holds the record for the longest time running while juggling three balls. She competed in a marathon run in Salmon, Idaho, and kept her balls in the air for more than three hours.

1947 Larry Doby became the first black player in the American League when he joined the Cleveland Indians lineup as a pinch hitter in a game against the Chicago White Sox. Only three months earlier, Jackie Robinson of the Brooklyn Dodgers had become the first black to play in the modern major leagues. (See April 15, 1947.)

1975 Another great moment in black sports history. Today, Arthur Ashe became the first American black player to win the men's singles tennis title at Wimbledon. He defeated Jimmy Connors in four sets. A few years earlier, when South Africa had refused to let Ashe play in its country because he was black, he didn't give in. After taking his fight to the United Nations, Ashe was finally allowed to play in South Africa in 1973.

1980 Sweden's Bjorn Borg set a Wimbledon record by winning his fifth singles tennis title in a row. Borg defeated John McEnroe in five exciting sets: 1–6, 7–5, 6–3, 6–7, 8–6. The most thrilling moment came when McEnroe won a fourth-set tiebreaker, 18–16.

1986 The first Goodwill Games opened in Moscow, the capital of the Soviet Union. Some 3,000 athletes from 70 countries participated in a competition similar to the Olympics. You won't find some of these 18 sports in the actual Olympics, however. The Goodwill Games included motoball—a Soviet game of soccer played on motorcycles.

1987 Australian tennis player Pat Cash defeated Ivan Lendl, originally of Czechoslovakia, to win the men's singles finals at Wimbledon, 7–6, 6–2, 7–5. For this day, at least, it was better to take Cash than a Czech.

1929 It was the second game of a doubleheader, but the St. Louis Cardinals weren't the least bit tired. They scored 10 runs in the first inning and 10 runs in the fifth to beat the Philadelphia Phillies, 28–6, to set a National League record for the most runs in a game.

1933 The first baseball All-Star Game was played in Chicago, Illinois, as part of the World's Fair. Babe Ruth of the Yankees hit a two-run homer to lead the American League to a 4–2 victory. The game was a huge hit with fans, and has been played every year since—except for one. In 1945, the All-Star Game was called off because of World War II. Between 1959 and 1962, there were two All-Star Games played each year.

1957 Althea Gibson of the United States becomes the first black player to win a tennis title at Wimbledon. The New Yorker took the women's singles championships. Later that year, on September 8, she became the first black woman to win the U.S. Open.

1979 Here's a King who is queen of the courts. Billie Jean King and Martina Navratilova won the women's doubles tennis competition at Wimbledon. With the win, King set a Wimbledon record. It was her 20th Wimbledon title, breaking Elizabeth Ryan's record of 19. Ryan had died of a heart attack at the age of 87 only the day before. She had said she never wanted to live to see her record broken.

1983 After losing to the NL team every year since 1972, the AL finally won an All-Star Game. And did they win! The final score was 13–3. Fred Lynn of the California Angels hit the first grand slam in the 50 years of All-Star Games.

1884 Hugh Daily, a pitcher for Chicago of the Union Association League, became only the second man in baseball history to strike out 19 batters in one game. Daily's record is especially impressive since he was missing his left arm. His nickname was "One Arm" Daily. Despite his handicap, Daily led the league in strikeouts that year.

1923 It was not one of your better pitching outings. Red Sox hurler Lefty O'Doul gave up 13 runs in one inning in Boston's, 27–3, loss to the Cleveland Indians. Later, Lefty got smart and switched from pitching to the outfield. In 1929, he set an NL record with 254 hits in one season. That record still stands.

1936 Nowadays, it's rare for the AL to win the All-Star Game. But when the game first began, the AL won the first three games. Today's fourth All-Star Game was the first one won by the NL, 4–3.

1985 Speaking of young, 17-year-old Boris Becker of West Germany became the youngest tennis player ever to win a Wimbledon championship. He defeated Kevin Curren, three sets to one. Becker was not expected to even come close to winning Wimbledon that year. He would be back to win again in both 1986 and 1989, though.

1889 If you've ever watched a boxing match on TV, you know the kind of damage a punch can do. Now imagine a boxing match *without* gloves. That's what fighters did in the 1800s—and they used to go on until there was a knockout. Today, in the last bare-knuckle fight ever held, John L. Sullivan knocked out Jake Kilrain in the 75th round to win the heavyweight championship. Rules requiring gloves—called the Marquis of Queensberry rules—were soon standard.

1912 New York Giants pitcher Rube Marquard gave up six runs in six innings in a 6–2 loss to the Cubs. It was his first loss since the season started on April 11, and ended Marquard's major league record streak of 19 straight wins in one season. In eight decades since, no pitcher has come close to breaking that record.

1935 Pitcher Lefty Gomez of the New York Yankees powered the AL to its third consecutive All-Star-Game victory, 4–1. The NL thought it was unfair that one pitcher had pitched so much, and pushed for a rule change that allowed no man to pitch more than three innings (not counting extra innings). That rule still exists.

1947 In the 14-year history of the All-Star Game, no rookie pitcher had ever gotten the victory. Until today. Rookie Frank Shea of the New York Yankees, pitched three sizzling innings, as the AL beat the National squad, 2–1, at Chicago's Wrigley Field.

1946 Ted Williams of the Boston Red Sox set a major league record by hitting two home runs, driving in five runs and scoring four times, all in one All-Star Game. It's no wonder his AL squad smashed the National Leaguers, 12–0. To this day, it's still the most lopsided All-Star Game in history. And Williams is still remembered as one of the greatest sluggers to ever play the game.

1949 Fortune Gordien of San Francisco, California, set a world record in the discus throw in an American-Portuguese track and field meet in Lisbon, Portugal. Gordien threw the heavy disk 185 feet, 3 inches.

1977 Golfer Tom Watson of the United States set a record for the lowest 72-hole score (268) in the history of the British Open championship. It was Watson's second win in jolly old England in three years. He would also take the tournament title in 1982 and 1983.

1984 In a special exhibition basketball game, the U.S. Olympic squad embarrassed a team of NBA All-Stars, 97–82. A record crowd of 67,596 at the Hoosier Dome in Indianapolis, Indiana, watched. The NBA players didn't have to feel too badly, however. The Olympic team included such future NBA stars as Patrick Ewing, Michael Jordan and Chris Mullin, and went on to win the gold medal in Los Angeles, California.

1920 Man o' War, one of the greatest horses in racing history, today ran in what may have been the most exciting horse race ever. Man o' War defeated John P. Grier in the Dwyer Stakes to set a world record time for the 1 1/8 mile of 1 minute, 49 1/5 seconds.

1932 The game is over, Johnny, you can go home now. In an incredible 18-inning game, Johnny Burnett of the Cleveland Indians set a record for most hits in a game—nine. Even so, the Indians lost to the Philadelphia Athletics, 18–17. The marathon contest also set another record: A's pitcher Ed Rommel broke an AL mark by working 17 innings *in relief*. He gave up 21 hits and 14 runs ... and still won the game.

1934 The AL won the second annual baseball All-Star Game, 9–7. The highlight of the game was when pitcher Carl Hubbell of the New York Giants, struck out five of the greatest hitters of all time in a row: Babe Ruth, Lou Gehrig, Jimmie Foxx, Al Simmons and Joe Cronin.

1989 Lloyd Daniels, a former high school basketball star, was lucky to be alive. Six weeks earlier, he had been shot three times on the streets of New York City, and had almost died. Today, though, the 21-year-old Daniels was back playing basketball again, and announcing plans to join a pro team in the Netherlands. Doctors removed two bullets, but Daniels continues to play with another bullet in his arm.

1989 Rumanian runner Paula Ivan set a world record in the women's mile at a track and field competition in Nice (pronounced Neece), France. Ivan, who won the gold medal in the Olympic 1,500-meter race in Seoul, South Korea, today ran the mile in 4 minutes, 15.61 seconds. It was more than a second faster than the mark set by Mary Decker Slaney in 1985.

1924 Eric Liddell of Great Britain ran an electrifying 400-meter race to win the gold medal at the Olympics in Paris, France. In setting an Olympic record, Liddell was so fast that two of his opponents fell trying to keep up. His story became the basis for the movie *Chariots of Fire*.

1950 It was perhaps the greatest All-Star Game in baseball history. It was also the first game in 17 All-Star contests to go into extra innings, and the first to be broadcast on television. Red Schoendienst of the St. Louis Cardinals hit a home run in the top of the 14th inning to win it for the NL, 4–3.

1985 On this day, pitching ace Nolan Ryan of the Houston Astros struck out Danny Heep of the New York Mets on three pitches to become the first pitcher to strike out 4,000 batters. Ryan has broken more records than a radio deejay with a bad case of the shakes. He holds records for strikeouts, no-hitters and throwing the fastest pitch in baseball.

1886
THE GOOD,
THE BAD
AND THE
WEIRD
Maybe you have heard about the many daredevils who have gone over Niagara Falls in a barrel. Well, meet the man who started it all: Carlisle Graham, a Philadelphia barrel-maker (what else?) became the first man to ride the rapids below the giant, dangerous falls. Graham repeated his remarkable ride twice. A month after this first run, with his head sticking out of the barrel, he suffered permanent hearing loss from the noise of the water. In 1901, Graham nearly drowned. There's got to be an easier way to have fun.

1931 The Chicago Cubs and St. Louis Cardinals must have been seeing double after their doubleheader today. The two teams set a major league record with 9 doubles between them in the opener and an incredible 23 doubles in the second game. That's 32 doubles in the doubleheader.

1949 The owners of all the major league baseball clubs agreed to install warning tracks in the area just in front of the outfield walls at their stadiums. The smooth dirt paths let ball-watching outfielders know when they are near the wall or fence, so they can avoid ramming into it and hurting themselves. This was even more dangerous in the 1940s, since many stadiums had brick walls as their outfield fence. Ouch.

1964 Golfer Mickey Wright won a dramatic playoff over Ruth Jessen in the U.S. Women's Open golf tournament. Wright had already won the Open in 1958, 1959 and 1961, and became only the second woman in history to win four times. Betsy Rawls won her fourth in 1960.

1964 Twenty-year-old Joel Robert of Belgium became the youngest motocross champion ever by winning a 250-cc race today. In motocross, motorcycles are raced through sand and mud, over hills and drops, and around sharp turns. Robert would become one of the greatest motocross racers ever, and would win a record 50 races.

1912 It was the longest amateur wrestling bout in history. Martin Klein of Russia and Alfred Asikainen of Finland wrestled for 11 hours and 40 minutes in the 1912 Olympics in Stockholm, Sweden. Klein finally pinned his opponent, but he was so exhausted he was unable to continue the competition. He settled for a silver medal. Under modern rules, such long bouts are no longer allowed.

1934 New York Yankees slugger Babe Ruth became the first man in baseball ever to hit 700 homers. The record-breaker was as dramatic as anything else the Babe did. He hit a towering homer off Tom Bridges of the Detroit Tigers. After zooming over the rightfield wall, the ball rolled several hundred feet down a street.

1971 It had to happen sooner or later. After losing eight All-Star Games in a row, the AL finally won one. Reggie Jackson of Oakland, Frank Robinson of Baltimore, and Harmon Killebrew of Minnesota all contributed homers in the AL's, 6–4, victory. Jackson's homer is remembered because it hit a power generator on the rightfield roof.

Steffi Graf, the young tennis player who put an end to Martina Navratilova's Wimbledon winning streak. (See July 2, 1988)

1951 What do you think was the first sporting event to be televised in color? The World Series? The Super Bowl? The Olympics? How about the Molly Pitcher Handicap at Monmouth Park, a horse-racing track in Oceanport, New Jersey? CBS broadcast the event live and in color. On the same day across the country, another horse was making history. Citation became the first horse to win more than $1 million in career earnings by winning the Hollywood Gold Cup in California.

1970 The NL All-Stars scored three runs in the 9th inning and one in the 12th to beat the AL, 5–4. Boston's Carl Yastrzemski became only the third player to have four hits in an All-Star Game. The other two were St. Louis's Joseph Medwick in 1937 and Ted Williams in 1946. "Yaz" hit three singles and a double to earn the game's Most Valuable Player award and a place in the record books.

1930

THE GOOD, THE BAD AND THE WEIRD

Alvin "Shipwreck" Kelly set a record by sitting on top of a flagpole in Atlantic City, New Jersey, for 23 days in a row. In the 1920s and 1930s, people used to climb flagpoles and sit there for hours and hours. They did it for money or just to set records. Kelly did, in fact, set a record today. But then he refused to come down. In fact, he stayed up on the flagpole 1,177 hours—more than 49 days. He finally came down on August 9, after a young woman was pulled up the rope to give him a shave and a haircut.

1969 Perhaps the most exciting play in baseball is when a base runner steals home. Well, in 1969, Minnesota Twins second baseman Rod Carew caused a lot of excitement. He stole home seven times in four months! His steal today tied a record set in 1946 by Pete Reiser of the Brooklyn Dodgers. With Carew's help, the Twins won the game, 6–2.

1973 Nolan Ryan of the California Angels recorded his second no-hitter in two months. The righthanded pitcher fanned 17 batters as California zipped the Detroit Tigers, 6–0. The 15th is obviously a lucky day for Ryan. On May 15, he pitched his *first* career no-hitter, 3–0, over the Kansas City Royals.

1979 Jerilyn Britz was an unlikely woman to set a record at the U.S. Women's Open golf championship. In six years as a professional, she had never won a tournament. As it turned out, she never won the Open again. But this was her year. Britz not only won the title, but her score of 284 tied the lowest in U.S. Open history. Since then, her record has been broken six times, most recently by Betsy King who shot a 278 in 1989.

1989 Virginia Wade was the Number One tennis player in Britain for nine years in a row in the 1970s and 1980s. Today, she was inducted into the International Tennis Hall of Fame in Newport, Rhode Island. She is the last Englishwoman to have won the singles title at England's famous tournament, Wimbledon.

1900 American track star Ray Ewry won gold medals in the standing high jump, standing long jump and standing triple jump events in the Olympics in Paris, France. In the next two Olympics, Ewry went on to win seven more gold medals. His achievements are especially impressive because he had polio as a child. Polio is a disease that once killed many people and left many others crippled. By the way, all three of the standing jump events—in which participants jump without taking a running start—were discontinued after 1912.

1909 The Washington Senators and Detroit Tigers played the longest scoreless game in AL history. The game was called after 18 innings with the score still knotted at 0–0. Pitcher Ed Summers of Detroit allowed only seven hits in the entire game.

1950 Picture the Rose Bowl—one of the largest football stadiums in America—with all of its seats filled. Now double that. That's the size of the largest crowd to ever watch a soccer game. Some 205,000 fans crammed into a stadium in Rio de Janeiro, Brazil, in South America, to watch Brazil take on Uruguay in the World Cup, soccer's most important event.

1989 Just when it looked like race-car driver Emerson Fittipaldi couldn't lose a race, along came Bobby Rahal. After winning three auto races in a row, Fittipaldi was finally beaten by Rahal in the Marlboro Grand Prix in East Rutherford, New Jersey, today. The 150-lap race was cut short by 5 laps because of rain.

1914 There was good news and bad news for Pittsburgh pitcher Babe Adams today. The good news was that he didn't walk a single batter in 21 innings of a game against the New York Giants. The bad news is he gave up a 2-run homer to Larry Doyle in the 21st inning and lost the game, 3–1. Tough break. Babe.

1941 Joe DiMaggio's famous hitting streak came to an end on this date. A day after setting a record for hitting safely in 56 consecutive games, the New York Yankees center-fielder had no hits in four at bats, and a walk. Pitchers Al Smith and Jim Bagby of the Cleveland Indians shut down DiMaggio before 67,000 fans in Cleveland, Ohio. During his streak—which dated back to May 15—the "Yankee Clipper" as DiMaggio was called, had 91 hits, including 15 home runs. What most people don't remember is that the streak was really part of an even longer one, in which Joe got on base in 84 games in a row.

1965 It is a good day for runners. In a track meet held in Kingston, on the Caribbean island of Jamaica, Wyomia Tyus of the United States tied the women's 100-yard dash record. On this day in 1966, Jim Ryun of the United States set a mark in the mile in Berkeley, California. His time was 3 minutes, 51.3 seconds.

1987 Don Mattingly's homer helped the New York Yankees topple the Texas Rangers, 8–4. So? So, it was the seventh game in a row in which the Yankees first baseman had hit at least one home run. No AL player had ever done that before.

1882 Louisville pitcher Tony Mullane became the first major leaguer to pitch righthanded and lefthanded in the same game. Mullane began by throwing with his right hand, and switched over to his left in the fourth inning. Unfortunately, Mullane didn't do too well either way. He lost to Baltimore, 9–8.

1908 It's hard to believe, but the Tug of War event created the biggest controversy of this year's Olympics in London, England. In the first round, the Liverpool, England, police department, one of several teams representing Great Britain, pulled the American team over the line in a matter of seconds. The Americans protested that their competitors had used illegal boots with spikes on them to dig into the ground. When the protest was denied, the United States dropped out of the competition, and Britain took all three medals. The event was discontinued after 1920.

Greg LeMond, the first American to win bicycling's Tour de France. (See July 27, 1986)

1877 The first Wimbledon tennis tournament finals were held in England today. Two hundred spectators showed up to watch Spencer Gore win the men's competition. Wimbledon's first sore winner, years later Gore complained he found lawn tennis boring. The first women's singles champion was Maud Watson.

1911 It happened in the minor leagues, but it was a pretty major accomplishment. Walter Carlisle, an outfielder for Vernon (Los Angeles) of the Pacific Coast League became the only outfielder in baseball history to make an unassisted triple play. Carlisle was playing so shallow in centerfield that he was practically on second base when the ball was hit to him. He caught the ball in the air (out number one), somersaulted, tagged second base (out number two) and then ran to first base before the base runner could get back (out number three). The fact that Carlisle was a former circus acrobat came in handy.

1859 For the first time, fans had to pay to watch a baseball game. About 1,500 people spent 50 cents to watch a game between Brooklyn and New York at a racetrack on Long Island. New York won the game, 22–18. Admission prices have increased just a wee bit since.

1924 Sybil Bauer of the United States outswam her competition in the women's 100-meter backstroke at the Olympics in Paris, France. Bauer set an Olympic record with her time of 1 minute, 23.2 seconds. Her winning margin of more than four seconds is still the biggest ever in this Olympic event. At the time of her Olympic win, Bauer held every backstroke record for women. She never lost a race in her career.

1937 Many tennis experts consider this the greatest match ever played. Don Budge of the United States was a huge favorite to beat Baron Gottfried von Cramm of Germany in Davis Cup action. But Budge was not up to his game, and Cramm played brilliantly. It looked like Cramm was on the verge of a major upset when he took the first two hard-fought sets, 8–6, 7–5. But then Budge came alive, winning the third 6–4, the fourth 6–2, and taking the brilliantly played final set, 8–6. The United States went on to win the Davis Cup, and few people would ever forget this exciting match.

1973 Wilbur Wood of the Chicago White Sox pitched both ends of a doubleheader today. No one has done it since. Unfortunately, he lost both games to the New York Yankees.

1985 Today former Olympic cyclist John Howard set a speed record on a very odd bicycle. He rode a special 46-pound bike with motorcycle wheels 152 mph.

1921 Double trouble. An AL record was set for most doubles in a game when the Cleveland Indians beat the New York Yankees, 17–8. Cleveland had nine two-base hits and the Yanks had seven.

1956 Roberto Clemente of the Pittsburgh Pirates hit a three-run homer to power the Pirates to a, 4–3, come-from-behind victory over the Cincinnati Reds. The loss snapped Cincinnati pitcher Brooks Lawrence's 13-game winning streak.

1976 At the Olympics in Montreal, Canada, weightlifter Zbigniew Kaczmarek blew his chance of becoming one of Poland's few gold-medal winners. After winning the lightweight competition by snatching 135 pounds and jerking 172.5 pounds, he had to give up his medal when he tested positive for illegal steroids. These dangerous body-building drugs have become a major problem for the sport. At the Montreal Olympics, at least one weightlifter in each of the weightlifting classes was disqualified for using steroids.

1989 Chick who? Golfer Chick Evans was not even supposed to be in the 72-player Ameritech Senior Golf Open in Cleveland, Ohio. He was rushed in at the last minute when another golfer had to drop out. Yet there he was, not only tied for the lead after the first round, but with a Seniors record. Evans birdied six straight holes on the back nine—for the longest string of birdies on the tour that season.

1876 In his major league debut, Louisville pitcher Johnny Ryan threw a record 10 wild pitches. But that was the least of his problems. Louisville was embarrassed by Chicago, 30–7. Not surprisingly, it was also's Ryan's *last* game.

1894 One of the world's first auto races was held in France—and it was a strange one. In addition to the typical gasoline-powered autos, there were cars run by electricity, steam, and one which was run by its passengers, who shifted their weight from one side to the other. Sounds like something out of *The Flintstones*. The winner of the 80-mile, one-day race was a Peugeot, powered by good, old-fashioned gasoline.

1952 The Reverend Bob Richards, a theology professor in California, had an interesting second job. He was a world-class pole vaulter. Known as "The Vaulting Vicar," he set an Olympic record today by clearing 14 feet, 11 inches at the Games in Helsinki, Finland.

1976 With the world watching, a tiny 14-year-old gymnast from Rumania named Nadia Comaneci earned a place in history. At the Olympics in Montreal, Canada, she received her first of seven perfect scores. They were the first "10s" ever given out in Olympic gymnastics. Nadia recently left Rumania to live in the United States.

1984 Golfer Kathy Whitworth finished first at the Rochester (New York) Open for her 85th career win. The victory made Whitworth the winningest golfer of all time—male or female. Sam Snead had held the record with 84 PGA wins.

1989 Race-car driver Emerson Fittipaldi was so hot, you almost had to call the fire department when he raced. A week after setting a track record at the Meadowlands in New Jersey, Fittipaldi did the same in Toronto, Canada. In winning the top qualifying spot, he smashed the previous record with a speed of 107.69 miles per hour.

1925 Lou Gehrig's grand slam powered the New York Yankees to an 11–7 victory over the Washington Senators. It was the first of Gehrig's 23 career grandslam—a major league record.

1930 Pie Traynor of the Pittsburgh Pirates was a two-time hero today. His ninth-inning homer in the first game of a doubleheader was the game winner. Then he turned around and hit a homer in the 13th inning to win the nightcap. Sound tough? For Pie, it was a piece of cake.

1955 They said he was crazy. Several men had already died trying to be the first to drive a speedboat 200 miles per hour. Yet David Campbell of England decided to give it a shot. He piloted his speedboat *Bluebird* 202.32 mph on a lake in England, breaking the record by almost 25 mph. In 1959, he set a record of 275 mph. And then his luck ran out. On January 4, while Campbell was trying to break the 300-mph barrier, the *Bluebird* flew into the air and crashed. Campbell was killed.

1989 In one of the most stunning comebacks in sports history, Greg LeMond of the United States won cycling's Tour de France for the second time. (See July 27, 1986.) The grueling 2,025-mile race is the world's most important bicycle competition and goes on for three weeks. Going into the final day of the race, LeMond was trailing. But he rallied to win by the smallest margin in Tour de France history— eight seconds. Two years earlier, LeMond had been seriously injured in a hunting accident. Most people thought he would never race again.

1908 Dorando Pietri of Italy was about to win the Olympic marathon, when disaster struck. Dazed and exhausted, he entered the stadium in London, England, and began to run the wrong way. Officials pointed him in the right direction, but Pietri fell to the ground once, twice, three times, and again a fourth time. British officials finally ran to help him across the finish line, but he was disqualified because of their help. The next man to cross the line, John Hayes of the United States, was declared the winner.

1973 The popular Willie Mays—the "Say Hey Kid"—wasn't supposed to play in this year's All-Star Game. He had not been selected. It would have been the first time he missed the game in 24 years. But baseball commissioner Bowie Kuhn increased the player limit so Mays could play after all. Thanks to Kuhn, Willie brought his number of All-Star records up to 7; most at bats (75), most games played (24), most games played for the winning team (17), most runs (20), most hits (23), most triples (3), and most total bases (40).

1882 Cleveland pitcher Dave Rowe had an outing that can **SAD SACKS** only be described as a nightmare. He gave up 29 hits, **OF SPORTS** 7 walks and 35 runs in Cleveland's, 35–4, loss to Chicago. While we're on the subject of bad pitchers, the record for the worst earned run average (ERA) in history is shared by two men: Joe Scheible of the 1893 Cleveland Spiders, and Joe Cleary of the 1945 Washington Senators. Both had ERAs of 189.00. That means that if either man ever completed a game, he would have given up about 189 runs in nine innings. Obviously, they both got pulled from the mound early, and forever.

1918 It's impressive when a pitcher records a 15-inning complete game. It's even more amazing when it's a five-hitter. Walter Johnson of the Washington Senators blanked the St. Louis Browns, 1–0, today in 15 innings. He only gave up a single hit through the first 11 innings.

1939 The New York Yankees defeated the St. Louis Browns, 5–1, behind the arm of pitcher Atley Donald. It was Donald's 12th straight victory—an AL record for a rookie starting pitcher.

1976 In his very first international meet—the Olympics in Montreal, Canada—Edwin Moses of the United States set a world record of 47.64 seconds in the 400-meter hurdles. Moses is one of the greatest track and field stars of modern times, but you never would have expected that from his background. A 20-year-old engineering and physics major, Moses was attending Morehouse College in Atlanta, Georgia, on an academic, not athletic, scholarship. In fact, his school didn't even have a track. But he not only set a world record today, he won the gold medal in the process.

Bjorn Borg, the only man to win five Wimbledon singles titles in a row. (See July 5, 1980)

1859 The first college rowing regatta was held in Worcester, Massachusetts. In a battle of Ivy League schools, Harvard defeated Yale and Brown. Actually, the regatta was supposed to be held the year before, but one of the members of the Yale team drowned.

1942 July 26 is a good day for the Chicago Cubs Clyde McCullough, but not for his team. Today, McCullough hit three home runs in a row as Chicago lost to Philadelphia, 4–3. Exactly nine years later, on July 26, 1951, McCullough again hit three homers and drove in six runs, and his team lost again, to the Red Sox, 13–10.

1952 No Olympic event is more demanding than the decathlon. Made up of 10 separate track and field events spread over two days, it is a true test of strength, speed and endurance. Today, Robert Mathias of the United States became the first man in history to win his second decathlon gold medal in as many Olympics.

1954 It's a lucky thing the Welch, West Virginia, minor league team had great fielders, because their pitchers were just awful. In a game against Johnson City, the Welch infielders helped their pitcher by completing a rare triple play to get out of an inning. The very next inning, they had another triple play. It's the only time in professional baseball history when there's been a triple play by the same team two innings in a row.

1918 Brooklyn's Henry Heitman may be the only pitcher in history who never got a man out in his entire career. Of course, his career wasn't very long. After giving up four hits in a row to St. Louis batters, Heitman was pulled from the game and never pitched again.

1984 Superstar Pete Rose broke Ty Cobb's record for most singles in a career. Rose, then with the Montreal Expos, hit his 3,053rd single against the Philadelphia Phillies. Poor Cobb. Rose would later break Cobb's record for most hits in a career, with 4,256.

1985 In a game against the New York Mets, the Houston Astros gave up 16 runs—and not one of them was earned. The Astros committed five errors, which allowed most of the Mets runs to score. The final score was 16–4.

1985 British runner Steve Cram may have set a world record for setting world records. He broke three of them in a 20-day period. Today, he shattered the mark in the mile run. Eleven days earlier, he had set a new record in the 1,500-meter race, and on August 4, he would set yet another world mark in the 2,000-meter race. He almost had a fourth. On August 10, Cram finished with the world's second-best time in the 1,000 meters. Had there not been a strong wind with him, he might have broken that record, too.

1986 The Tour de France—a 23 day-long bicycle journey through France—is the best-known bicycle event in the world. Today, Greg LeMond became the first American ever to win it. He covered the 2,500-mile route in 110 hours, 35 minutes, 19 seconds. The race began on July 4. He would win another Tour de France in 1989. (See July 23, 1989.)

1931 It was the eighth inning. The Yankees were pounding the Chicago White Sox, 12–3. How could New York possibly lose? Easy: They could give up 11 runs in one inning. And that's just what they did. Chicago's Bob Fothergill led the attack with a homer and a triple in the inning.

1952 The basketball team from France had just defeated Uruguay at the Olympics in Helsinki, Finland, when referee Vincent Farrell was attacked and injured. The people responsible were two Uruguayan players who were upset about the officiating. Next time, they should consider the boxing competition.

1943
SPORTS
PROFILE

Basketball great Bill Bradley was born in Crystal City, Missouri. Named a college All-America at Princeton University in 1964 and 1965, Bradley's greatest days were still to come. After leading the U.S. Olympic team to a gold medal in 1964, he was drafted by the New York Knicks. But Bradley decided to attend England's Oxford University as a Rhodes Scholar instead. (Rhodes Scholarships are given to the smartest and most talented college students in the world.) He finally returned to the United States and played with the Knicks for 10 seasons. Bradley's leadership abilities and his excellent defensive skills helped them win NBA championships in 1970 and 1973. Known for being thrifty, he was given the nickname "Dollar Bill" by his teammates. Today, Dollar Bill is also Senator Bill. He has served as a U.S. Senator from New Jersey since 1979. Many people believe he may one day run for President.

1928 Finland's Paavo Nurmi finished his brilliant Olympic career by winning his ninth gold medal in the running events. At age 31, Nurmi set an Olympic record in the 10,000-meter race, the same event in which he had won his first gold medal eight years earlier. In his career, "The Flying Finn" set a total of 29 world records in distances ranging from 1,500 to 20,000 meters.

1940 John Sigmund of St. Louis turned the Mississippi River into the world's longest swimming pool. He swam 292 miles nonstop from St. Louis to Caruthersville, Missouri, in 89 hours and 40 minutes.

1968 Ron Hansen, the Washington Senators shortstop, became the eighth man in major league history to complete an unassisted triple play. Unfortunately, everything else didn't go so brilliantly for Hansen in today's game against the Cleveland Indians. He struck out four times—one short of another less happy record.

1973 Italy's Giacomo Agostini easily outdistanced Phil Read of Great Britain to win the Finnish Motorcycling Grand Prix in Tinatra, Finland. It was his sixth straight world 350-cc motorcycling title.

1978 The official speed record for crossing the English Channel was set by Penny Dean of California. She swam the 21-mile stretch from England to France in just 7 hours and 40 minutes. As of early 1990, no one has yet beaten that record.

1983 What a way to end a streak! First baseman Steve Garvey of the Los Angeles Dodgers had set an NL record on April 6 for consecutive games played. The streak got to 1,207, but it ended with this game, though, because he dislocated his thumb during a home-plate collision. Ouch.

1962 Guess the age of the youngest person ever to get a hole-in-one in the game of golf? Eighteen? Fourteen? Twelve? Would you believe four years old? That's how old Scott Statler of Greensburg, Pennsylvania, was when he got a hole in one at a golf course in Pennsylvania.

1976 At the Olympics in Montreal, Canada, Bruce Jenner of the United States became an instant hero when he won the gold medal in the decathlon and established a world record for most points in the event. Four years earlier, Jenner had also participated in the Olympic decathlon, and come in 10th. He used his sudden popularity to make a movie and commercials, and later became a TV sports commentator.

1947
SPORTS
PROFILE
The Terminator is born. O.K., so it's not *really* the Terminator, but Arnold Schwarzenegger. He was born in Graz, Austria, on this day. The world's most famous bodybuilder, he won the Mr. Olympia title seven times between 1970 and 1980. Schwarzenegger used his fame and his body to start a successful acting career, starring in such movies as *The Terminator* and *Twins*. In 1990, President Bush named him chairman of the President's Council on Physical Fitness and Sports.

1932 Canadian athlete Duncan McNaughton won the gold medal in the high jump at the Olympics in Los Angeles, California, but he almost didn't get to compete at all. The Canadians wouldn't allow him on their team. McNaughton kept begging. Finally, only a few days before the match, the Canadian coach agreed, probably just to shut this guy up. Bet the coach was happy Duncan had a big mouth.

1954 Milwaukee Braves first baseman Joe Adcock set a major league record with 18 total bases by hitting four home runs and a double in five at bats. The Braves beat the Brooklyn Dodgers, 15–7.

1961 For the first time in history, the All-Star Game ended in a tie. With the score 1–1 at the end of nine innings, it began to rain at Boston's Fenway Park. After a half-hour delay, the game was finally postponed, never to be completed. The following year, the AL won a completed contest in one of the All-Star games held that year. It would be their last victory until 1971.

1984 It was a great upset—and a great day for American gymnastics. With the Soviets boycotting the Olympics in Los Angeles, the powerful Chinese were expected to take most of the men's gymnastics medals. But the Americans proved they had more guts and talent than anyone ever imagined. Not only did they take seven medals, but they also shocked the Chinese in the team competition, taking the gold. The American gymnasts were Peter Vidmar, Bart Conner, Mitch Gaylord, Timothy Daggett, James Hartung and Scott Johnson.

1715 The first recorded rowing competition of modern times was held in Ireland. The event was sponsored by an Irish actor named Thomas Doggett, who so loved the sport he left money in his will so that his boat race would continue forever. It still does, making it the oldest rowing competition in the world—and one of the oldest races of any kind.

1957 Glen Gorbous, a former major leaguer playing for Omaha (Nebraska) of the American Association, had one heck of an arm. Today, his team set up a special exhibition to show off his throwing skills. One of his throws went 445 feet, 10 inches. That's the farthest any man has officially thrown a baseball.

1972 First baseman Nate Colbert of the San Diego Padres treated fans in Atlanta to a home-run festival. He hit 5 homers, including a grand slam, and drove in 13 runs in a doubleheader between the Padres and Braves. In so doing, Colbert set a record for the most RBIs in a day and tied the mark for the most homers. He also set a record for total bases, with 22. Not a bad day, Colbert.

1982 Greg Louganis of the United States is considered the greatest diver of our time. No wonder. In a competition in the Central American nation of Ecuador, Louganis received a perfect "10" from all seven judges for his inward 1 1/2 somersault in the pike position today. He became one of only two men in the history of the sport to receive perfect scores from all the judges.

Carl Lewis, winner of four gold medals in the 1984 Olympics. (See August 4, 1984)
←——————

1938 Imagine a bright yellow baseball coming at you at 85 mph. Yellow? That's what happened today. As an experiment, the Brooklyn Dodgers and St. Louis Cardinals used a yellow ball in a game won by the Dodgers, 6–2. They hoped the ball would be easier for batters to see. Did it work? Do you see many yellow baseballs these days? Four months earlier, a yellow ball was used in a college game. (See April 27, 1938.)

1984 Greco-Roman wrestler Jeff Blatnick of the United States won the gold medal in the super heavyweight division. Then the big guy dropped to his knees, looked up toward the sky and began to cry. Only two years earlier, Blatnick had been diagnosed with cancer. His doctors told him he'd be lucky to live, much less wrestle again. Blatnick proved them wrong. And when the cancer came back in 1985, he fought it off again. Now, *there's* a champion.

1987 Eric Davis of the Cincinnati Reds was not the first player to hit 30 home runs and steal 30 bases in the same season. Six men had done so before him. But no one had ever joined the 30-30 club so early in the season. With almost 2 months still to do, Davis got home run number 30 today in the Reds', 5–4, victory over the San Francisco Giants.

1989 Swimming champion Janet Evans, the sweetheart of the 1988 Olympics, won the women's 400-meter freestyle at the U.S. Championships in Los Angeles. She posted the fastest time in the world for that year. The big winner for the men was David Wharton, who broke his previous American record in the 400-meter individual medley.

1932 Poor Jules Noël. In the 1932 Olympics, the Frenchman would have won the gold medal in the discus throw but the officials had been watching another event, and never saw his throw. Noël had to try again, but this throw was much weaker. He came in fourth place.

1975 The Superdome in New Orleans, Louisiana opened today. It truly *is* super—the world's largest indoor arena. The building covers 13 acres, holds 69,573 spectators in the regular season and more for the Super Bowl, and cost $163 million to build.

1984 Sixteen-year-old gymnast Mary Lou Retton struck Olympic gold in the All-Around by getting perfect scores in the floor exercise and vault. Believe it or not, the tiny athlete from West Virginia had never before competed in a major competition.

1989 It's the Cincinnati baseball club that's known as the Reds, but the Houston Astros were the ones who were red in the face at the end of this game. In scoring 14 runs in the bottom of the first inning, Cincinnati set the major league record for most hits in the first inning. In a half-inning that lasted 38 minutes, the Reds pounded out an incredible 16 hits. They won the game, 18–1.

1956 Wilhelm Herz became the first man to ride a motorcycle more than 200 miles per hour. He rode his bike exactly one mile at the Bonneville Salt Flats in Utah at a speed of 210 miles per hour.

1984 Carl Lewis of the United States won his first gold medal of the Los Angeles Olympics in the 100-meter dash. The flashy, confident runner would add three more medals before the Olympics closed—the 200-meter run, the long jump and the 4 x 100 meter relay. He became only the second person in history to win four gold medals in track and field in one Olympics. The only other man to do it was his idol, Jesse Owens, in 1936.

1985 Forty years old and still terrific. At an age when most pitchers are retired, Tom "Terrific" Seaver became the 17th player in the history of the major leagues to win 300 games. Seaver hurled a six-hitter against the New York Yankees to help his Chicago White Sox win, 4–1.

1982

THE GOOD, THE BAD AND THE WEIRD

Joel Youngblood started off the day playing for the New York Mets. He drove in the winning run in their 7–4 victory over the Cubs. After the game, he was traded to the Montreal Expos. He flew to Philadelphia, where the Expos were playing, and got a single for his new club. Youngblood—who by then must have had tired blood—became the first player in major league history to get a base hit for two different teams in two different cities in the same day.

1921 Pittsburgh radio station KDKA broadcast the first major league baseball contest today. In a game played in Pittsburgh, the Pittsburgh Pirates beat the Phillies, 8–5. Later that year, WJZ of Newark, New Jersey also became the first radio station to issue reports from the World Series, broadcasting phoned-in plays as the New York Giants beat the New York Yankees, 5–3.

1936 Despite a light rain, Jesse Owens of the United States set an Olympic record of 20.7 to take the gold medal in the 200-meter dash. It was Owens's third gold of the Olympics in Berlin, Germany. His magnificent performance angered German dictator Adolf Hitler, host of the events. Owens was black, and Hitler believed blacks weren't as good as whites, particularly German whites. One interesting side note about this race: The silver medal winner was another black American, Matthew "Mack" Robinson. Robinson's brother was also a famous athlete. Can you guess who? Jackie Robinson, the first black man to play major league baseball.

1967 The Denver Broncos were the first AFL team to defeat an NFL team. They beat the Detroit Lions, 13–7, in an exhibition game. The AFL is now one conference of the NFL. But before the two leagues merged, the AFL was the newer, and weaker, of the two leagues.

1984 Cliff Johnson of the Toronto Blue Jays hit his 19th career home run as a pinch hitter, setting a new major league record. Johnson scored the big blast against the Orioles in Baltimore's Memorial Stadium. Later in his career Johnson would add to his record by hitting his 20th home run as a pinch hitter. By the way, today's record-breaker helped the Blue Jays win, 4–3.

1926 Gertrude Ederle became the first American woman to swim the English Channel. She crossed the 21-mile stretch between England and France in 14 hours and 34 minutes.

1969 Willie Stargell of the Pittsburgh Pirates today became the only player to hit a ball out of Dodger Stadium in Los Angeles. Stargell's homer, off Los Angeles pitcher Alan Foster, went over the rightfield seats and landed 512 feet from home plate. Four years later, on May 8, 1973, Stargell almost did the same thing, but this time the ball landed on the rightfield roof.

1972 Hank Aaron of the Braves hit his 660th and 661st home runs against the Cincinnati Reds. The blasts broke Babe Ruth's record for the most home runs with one club. Later, Aaron would break another Ruth record—for the most home runs in a lifetime. (See April 8, 1974.)

1981 Because of a strike that lasted 50 days, major league baseball players approved a special split-season. The New York Yankees, Oakland A's, Philadelphia Phillies and Los Angeles Dodgers were declared champs for the first half of the season. They played in a special division series against the second-half winners. When it was all over, the Yankees and Dodgers remained, and met in the World Series.

1986 It was a battle of grand slams. Toby Harrah of the Texas Rangers hit one in the second inning, but Larry Sheets and Jim Dwyer of the Baltimore Orioles did even better than that: They *both* hit grand slams in the same inning. Three grand slams in one game is a major league record.

1932 Track star Babe Didrikson had tied Jean Shiley, also of the United States, in the high-jump competition in the Los Angeles Olympics. After the first jump-off the judges decided to disqualify Didrikson, saying she had used an illegal jump. Babe cleared the bar with her head first, and then her body. At the time, the rules required jumpers to go feet first or sideways. Because of the uproar over Babe's disqualification, the rules were soon changed to allow her move. But it was too late for Didrikson. She was denied her third gold medal.

1932 The swimmers in the 100-meter freestyle at the Los Angeles Olympics had quite a surprise. As they were preparing for the event, a German sportswriter, still wearing his business suit, suddenly jumped into the pool. Someone had bet the man $100 he wouldn't have the nerve to do it. Bad bet.

1985 Lou Scripa, Jr., entered the *Guiness Book of Sports Records* by doing 100,003 sit-ups without stopping. Scripa, who had begun on August 5, didn't stop for 50 hours. By that time his stomach must have been as hard as a three-week-old meat loaf.

1928 At the 1928 Olympics in Amsterdam, the Netherlands, Ulise "Pete" DesJardins of Miami Beach, Florida, won the springboard competition. Three days later he got two perfect "10s" in the platform-diving competition. They were the first perfect scores given in the modern Olympics. DesJardins also became the first man to win both the springboard and platform diving events. Who was the most recent man to do that? He's three entries down.

1976 The Chicago White Sox made history today, but it was because of their knees, not their hitting. They became the first major league team to wear shorts as part of their uniform. The cool Sox beat the Kansas City Royals, 5–2.

1982 When Doug DeCinces of the California Angels decided he wanted to hit some home runs, he didn't kid around. The California slugger hit two solo homers and a two-run shot to help his team clobber the Seattle Mariners, 9–5. It was the second time in six days he had hit three homers in the same game.

1984 Greg Louganis won both the springboard and highboard Olympic diving competitions in Los Angeles, California. Louganis set world records in both events. Four years later, Louganis provided one of the most dramatic moments in the Olympics at Seoul, South Korea. He again captured both gold medals, this time after hitting his head on a diving board during the qualifying round.

1939 Third baseman Red Rolfe of the New York Yankees scored a run today to begin an 18-game scoring streak. It's the first—and last—time in the 20th century that any player has scored at least one run in that many games. Red was truly red-hot. He scored a total of 30 runs in those 18 games.

1939 New York television station W2XBS became the first station anywhere to broadcast a tennis tournament. Their cameras were actually able to show viewers close-ups (wow!) from the Eastern Grass Court championships in Rye, New York.

1957 So much for romance. Lee Calhoun, gold medal winner in the 1956 Olympic 110-meter hurdles, was disqualified as an amateur by the AAU. The AAU learned he had gotten married on the television show *Bride and Groom* and had accepted gifts from the show. The AAU claimed that this made him a professional. Baaah, humbug!

1975 The record had stood for 53 years. But with one quick dash, Davey Lopes of the Los Angeles Dodgers stole his 32nd base in a row without being thrown out, to set a major league stealing record in a 2–0 win over the New York Mets. Lopes would steal six more bases before being thrown out on August 24.

1976 With his election to the Baseball Hall of Fame today, Robert "Cal" Hubbard became the first athlete to be enshrined in two Halls of Fame. Hubbard was voted into the Professional Football Hall of Fame on April 4, 1963.

1969 Cesar Tovar of the Minnesota Twins singled in the ninth inning to spoil Baltimore Orioles pitcher Mike Cueller's no-hit game. Earlier in the year, Tovar had spoiled a no-hit bid with a single in the ninth against Dave McNally of the, you guessed it, Baltimore Orioles.

1974 Jorge Lebron, a 14-year-old shortstop from Puerto Rico, holds the honor of being the youngest person ever to play professional baseball. His first game for Auburn, a Philadelphia Phillies farm club, had to be rescheduled from 7:30 p.m. to 6:00 p.m., so that Lebron could finish the game by his bedtime. The young Puerto Rican slugger played in only three games, then returned to his homeland to go to junior high school.

1981 With a swing of his bat, baseball great Pete Rose entered the record books—again. He rapped out his 3,631st career base hit against St. Louis Cardinals pitcher Mark Littell. That broke Stan Musial's NL record.

1984 It was the event everyone had been waiting for in the Los Angeles Olympics. The two best runners in the 3,000-meter race were finally going to face off—Mary Decker, the popular favorite from the United States, and Zola Budd, a South African running for Great Britain. Halfway through the race, the crowd watched in horror as the two bumped legs, got tangled, and Decker fell to the ground. She stayed there, crying in frustration and pain from a pulled gluteus muscle. The crowd of 85,000 began to boo Zola, who continued the race, also in tears. Maricica Puica of Romania won the race. Budd was competing for Great Britain because South African athletes are not allowed to participate in international competitions due to South Africa's racist policies.

1926 Tris Speaker of the Cleveland Indians hit the 700th double of his career in a 7–2 loss to the Chicago White Sox. By the time Speaker retired, in 1928—after 22 seasons in baseball—he set a mark by hitting 793 doubles.

1928 Swimmer Johnny Weissmuller of the United States won two gold medals today in the Olympics in Amsterdam, the Netherlands. He had already won three golds in the 1924 games. Weissmuller would go on to gain even more fame—playing Tarzan in the movies.

1959 When Gil Carter says, "Going, going, gone," he means *gone*. The pitcher for Carlsbad, New Mexico, of the Sophomore Baseball League, blasted a shot over the leftfield fence, over a light tower, across the street, past two alleys and across two lots before it landed near a house some 730 feet from home plate. It may be the longest home run ever hit.

1973 Jean Balukas, a 14-year-old girl from Brooklyn, New York, won her second U.S. Open Pocket Billiards women's championship in Chicago, Illinois. The year before, she had become one of the youngest champions of any sport.

1984 One of two new events was added to the Olympics in Los Angeles: rhythmic gymnastics (the other was synchronized swimming). In rhythmic gymnastics, female gymnasts do floor exercises using ribbons, balls, Indian clubs and hoops.

1984 The favored Brazilian men's volleyball team embarrassed the United States in straight sets: 15–12, 15–11, 15–2. It was the American squad's only loss at the Los Angeles Olympics. Five nights later, the Americans got their revenge. They defeated the Brazilians in straight sets to win the gold medal.

1900 Ever tried to see how long you could hold your breath under water? Would you believe that in 1900, an underwater swimming event was held in the Olympics? A Frenchman named Charles de Vendeville won the gold medal by swimming 60 meters (almost 200 feet) in 1 minute and 8 seconds, without having to come up for air.

1936 Thirteen-year-old Marjorie Gestring of the United States became the youngest woman to win a gold medal in the Olympics. She took the springboard diving event, beating out two other Americans at the Games in Berlin, Germany. In the 1900 games, a boy who was even younger—no more than 10 years old—won a gold medal as the coxswain (he steers the boat) of the Dutch rowing team. However, his name is not known since he was a last-minute substitute.

1889
THE GOOD,
THE BAD
AND THE
WEIRD
How long is 2 hours and 41 minutes? Longer than most movies. Longer than just about any TV show. Almost as long as an entire afternoon of school. But that's how long two teams in India participated in a tug-of-war! Yes, it is a world's record. And the members of one team only had to yank the other team 12 feet. That works out to an average speed of .00084 miles per hour. Not quite the Indy 500.

1906 Jack Taylor had been completely perfect. Until tonight. The Chicago Cubs pitcher had tossed 1727 complete innings in a row and had also completed 15 games in relief. Then along came the Superbas. They knocked him out in the third inning of today's game, ending Taylor's record streak.

1910 If a baseball game could have an echo, this would be it. Everything the Brooklyn Dodgers did today, the Pittsburgh Pirates did, too. The Dodgers had 13 hits. The Pirates had 13 hits. The Dodgers had 12 assists and 2 errors. The Pirates had 12 assists and 2 errors. Both teams had 38 at bats, 5 strikeouts, 3 walks, 1 man hit by a pitch and 1 passed ball. What was the final score? It was an 8–8 tie. Of course.

1932 The most exciting rowing race ever was held at the Olympics in Long Beach, California, outside of Los Angeles. Coming on strong with only a few feet to go before the finish line, the American team inched past the Italians to capture the gold medal. It was the fourth time in as many games that the Americans had won the event in the Olympics, and would be their fourth of eight straight Olympic golds.

1935 Ouch! The first Roller Derby games were held in Chicago, Illinois. Both men's and women's teams slugged it out to see who could keep skating the longest. In the 1940s, Roller Derby became quite popular, as professional wrestling is now. In 1948, CBS even showed Roller Derby matches live on TV.

1936 Does dribbling in the sand sound like fun? The Olympic basketball final was played on a sand-and-clay tennis court. Unfortunately it rained that day, and the sand turned to mud. It's little wonder the game didn't have a lot of scoring. The United States beat Canada 19–8 and took the gold medal.

1976 A record crowd of 77,691 fans crammed Giants Stadium in New Jersey to watch a quarter final playoff game of the North American Soccer League. The New York Cosmos beat the Ft. Lauderdale Strikers 8–3.

1987 Mark McGwire of the Oakland A's slammed a two-run homer off California Angels pitcher Don Sutton to help the A's to a 7–6 win in 12 innings. It was McGwire's 39th shot over the fence in his rookie season.

Babe Didrikson, the track star who was denied her third Olympic gold medal on a technicality. (See August 7, 1932)

1941 What a way to lose a ball game—on an error from the grounds crew. The Washington Senators were beating the Boston Red Sox, 6–3, in the eighth inning when it began to rain in the nation's capital. The grounds crew was slow in covering the field, and the umpires ruled that the crew did it on purpose, hoping the game would have to be called and Washington would win. It didn't work—the Senators were forced to forfeit instead.

1970 Patricia Palinkas of Tampa, Florida, became the first woman to play in a professional football game. She held the ball for a point after a touchdown attempt by her husband, Steve, who was the placekicker for the Orlando Panthers of the Atlantic Coast League (ACL). But the snap was off-target, and Palinkas—who weighed all of 122 pounds—started to run with it. A 235-pound lineman quickly knocked her to the ground. She stood up, and trotted off the field into the history books.

1926

**THE GOOD,
THE BAD
AND THE
WEIRD**

This had to be one of the weirdest moments in baseball history. The bases were loaded as Brooklyn Dodgers star Babe Herman came to bat. He hit a solid double and the man on third scored. The man on second rounded third, but went back to third just as the man who was on first got there. Soon Herman also slid into third, making it one very crowded base. What should have been a three-run hit ended up being the final two outs of the inning.

1921   Tennis star Suzanne Lenglen lost only one match in the seven years between 1919 and her retirement in 1926—and in that match her opponent was illness. Lenglen was trailing Molla Mallory in the second round of the U.S. Open Tennis Tournament when she forfeited because she wasn't feeling well. She never lost again.

1954   The first edition of *Sports Illustrated* magazine was issued. Published by the same company as the news magazine *Time*, the magazine was designed to be the first complete weekly sports magazine in the country. Milwaukee slugger Ed Mathews was shown taking a swing during a night baseball game on the first cover.

1967   A hole in the ground did to Jim Maloney what 19 Pittsburgh Pirates couldn't. It broke up Maloney's no-hitter. The Cincinnati Reds pitcher had retired 19 Pirates batters in a row when he stepped in a hole in Pittsburgh's Forbes Field and injured his ankle. He had to leave the game only $2^{2}/_{3}$ innings short of a complete no-hitter. Reliever Billy McCool (is that a great name, or what?) allowed just two hits as the Reds went on to win, 4–0.

1976   The St. Louis Cardinals defeated the San Diego Chargers, 20–10, in a pre-season football game played in Tokyo, Japan. More than 30,000 fans watched the first NFL game played outside of North America. Today, NFL pre-season games are played in a lot of different countries.

1894 It wasn't one of John Wadsworth's better days on the mound. The pitcher for the NL's old Louisville team set two professional baseball records by giving up 28 singles and a total of 36 hits in a, 29–4, loss to Philadelphia. Both records still stand.

1917 Twelve-year-old Gertrude Caroline Ederle set a world record in the women's 880-yard freestyle swim at a meet in Indianapolis, Indiana. Her time was 13 minutes, 19 seconds. She is the youngest person ever to set a world record.

1933 These days, most players for the New York Yankees are lucky if they stay with the team for a season or two. But on this day, New York Yankees great Lou Gehrig set a major league record by playing in his 1,308th game in a row. Lou wasn't nearly done. On May 2, 1939, he played in his 2,130th consecutive game as Yankee first baseman—a record that still stands.

1938 Henry Armstrong's arm wasn't the only thing that was strong. Armstrong today became the only boxer in history to hold three titles in three different weight classes at the same time. Armstrong won the lightweight title from Lou Ambers on a 15-round decision. He already held the welterweight and featherweight titles.

1946 Mildred Dietz of St. Louis, Missouri, won the women's championships of the National Amateur Bicycle Association (NABA) in Columbus, Ohio. She became the first woman to win the race twice in a row. A year earlier, on August 19, 1945, she had cycled to victory when the contest was held in Chicago, Illinois.

1951 Gil Heron, a native of Detroit, Michigan, became the first American to play soccer for a European team. Heron scored a goal for the Celtics of Glasgow, Scotland, in their 2–0 win over another Scottish team, from Morton. Although Americans now have a better appreciation of "football" (as soccer is known in Europe), the game is still much more popular with many Europeans and South Americans.

1956 In a real home run marathon, the Cincinnati Reds hit eight balls over the fence and the Milwaukee Braves sent another two downtown. Together, they set an NL record for most home runs by two clubs in a nine-inning game. The Reds ended up scalping the Braves, 13–4.

1965 Everyone who watches TV knows that Bob Uecker wasn't much of a baseball player. But today he *did* save the St. Louis Cardinals a home run. He did it with his brains, not his glove. After Hank Aaron of the Milwaukee Braves hit a towering home run, Uecker, the Cardinals catcher, pointed out that Aaron had been partly out of the batter's box. The home run was taken back. Milwaukee won anyway, 6–2.

1989 It's not easy being Green. Dallas Green became the 17th manager to be fired by New York Yankees owner George Steinbrenner. Bucky Dent, a former Yankees hero who helped New York win a playoff game against the Boston Red Sox with a home run, was brought in as the 18th manager in 17 years. The Yankees lost his first game as manager to the Detroit Tigers, 7–3. (For Dent's historic home run, see October 2, 1978.) Bucky Dent was fired June 6, 1990 and was replaced by Stump Merrill.

1917 You've heard of baseball managers being thrown out of a game, but have you ever heard of them being arrested? Today, New York Giants manager John McGraw and manager Christy Mathewson of the Cincinnati Reds were locked up for playing a game on a Sunday. In those days, many states had laws making it illegal to play sports on Sunday, for religious reasons.

1921 Ty-ing one on. Detroit's Ty Cobb, one of the greatest hitters in the history of baseball, got the 3,000th hit of his career. At age 34, he was the youngest player ever to enter the 3,000-hit club.

1951 But where's the strike zone? Eddie Gaedel, all 3' 7" of him, became the smallest man ever to play professional baseball. The 65-pound player pinch hit for the St. Louis Browns in a game against the Detroit Tigers. Gaedel wore number $\frac{1}{8}$. Tiger pitcher Bob Cain, who was used to a bigger, higher strike zone, kept throwing the ball over Gaedel's head, and walked him on four pitches. Two days later, the president of the AL banned the Browns from ever using Gaedel again.

1967 Here are the scores, guess the sport: 26–24, 17–19, 30–28. Sounds like football, right? Well, try tennis. Those were the scores for three sets in the doubles competition at the U.S. Tennis Open when Mark Cox and Robert Wilson defeated Charles Pasarell and Ron Holmburg. The match lasted 6 hours and 23 minutes.

1945 Tommy Brown of the Brooklyn Dodgers became the youngest player ever to hit a home run. He was 17 years, 8 months and 14 days old when he hit the ball over the fence against pitcher Preacher Roe of the Pittsburgh Pirates. Brown was a 16-year-old high school student when he first began playing for Brooklyn.

1967 When swimmer Debbie Meyer breaks a record, she doesn't fool around. Meyer improved the mark for the 1,500-meter freestyle by 22.9 seconds at a swimming meet in Philadelphia, Pennsylvania, today. Her time was 17 minutes, 50.2 seconds.

1973 The thrill of victory, the agony of defeat. Fourteen-year-old James Gronen had won the All-American Soap Box Derby on August 18. Today, though, he was stripped of the championship because he had used an illegal magnetic system on his homemade racer. Soapbox cars are homemade cars that do not have pedals or motors.

1974 California Angels pitcher Nolan Ryan threw the fastest pitch ever clocked in major league baseball. The pitch, thrown in a game at Anaheim Stadium, zoomed across the plate at 100.9 miles per hour. Now *that's* a fastball.

Mary Lou Retton, the Olympic gymnast who won a gold medal with perfect scores. (See August 3, 1984)

1902 His nickname was "Iron Man." In this case, Iron Foot would have been more like it. Joe "Iron Man" McGinnity of the Baltimore Orioles was thrown out of the NL (yes, the NL) for stepping on an umpire's toes, spitting in his face and punching him. Talk about unsportsmanlike conduct. McGinnity's suspension didn't last long, however. He was a popular player and the fans begged the League to let him back in the game. The League finally gave in.

1908 Look out below! Gabby Street, a catcher with the Washington Senators, had a funny name and a dangerous sense of adventure. As a stunt, one of the Street's teammates went up to the top of the Washington Monument in Washington, D.C. From a window 555 feet up, the teammate began to throw balls down to see if Street could catch them. Gabby caught the third ball. Scientists have estimated that by the time the ball reached him, it had a force of between 200 and 300 pounds.

**1936
SPORTS
PROFILE** Wilt "the Stilt" Chamberlain was born in Philadelphia, Pennsylvania. It seems only fitting, then, that he should spend much of his brilliant career playing in Philadelphia. At 7′ 1″, Chamberlain was one of the tallest men ever to play basketball—and one of the best. In 1973, when he retired after 14 seasons, he had set six different scoring records: most points in a game (100), highest career scoring average (30.1), highest season average (50.4) most seasons leading league in scoring (7), most points in a pro season (4,029) and most points in a rookie season (2,707), and three rebounding records: most rebounds in a career (23,924), most rebounds in one game (55) and most seasons leading the league in rebounds (11). Chamberlain was the only man ever to score 100 points in an NBA game. (See March 2, 1962.)

1886 This was a baseball game for the dogs—and chickens and wolves. In a contest between Cincinnati and Louisville, Louisville batter Chicken Wolf hit the ball into the out-field. Outfielder Abner Powell ran back to get it, but while doing that he woke up a dog sleeping near the fence. The dog bit Powell's leg. By the time Powell could shake him off, Wolf had an inside-the-park home run—the game winner.

1917 The Pittsburgh Pirates' Carson Bigbee went to the plate 11 times in a 22-inning game against the Brooklyn Dodgers. The 11 at-bats tied a major league record. It was the third game in a row in which the Pirates had gone into extra innings. The total of 59 innings in four games also set an NL record.

1951 More than 72,000 fans turned up to watch the Harlem Globetrotters in an exhibition game at Olympic Stadium in Berlin, Germany. It was the largest crowd ever to attend a basketball game. Hey, it was free!

1971 A volleyball team from the United States became only the second U.S. squad to travel to Cuba since Communist leader Fidel Castro took power in 1959. Cuba beat the United States and earned a place in the 1972 Olympic vol-leyball competition.

1989 Nolan Ryan, the Texas Rangers pitcher, collected the 5,000th strikeout of his career—more than any other man in the history of baseball. Rickey Henderson of the Oak-land A's was done in by a Ryan fastball traveling 96 miles per hour. Ryan still lost the game, 2–0.

1930 American tennis star Mary Sutton Bundy became the first person ever to play a match while using a crutch. Bundy had slipped and fractured her leg during the action at the U.S. Open. Rather than give up, she found a crutch and finished the match. It shouldn't come as any great surprise that she lost.

1952 Two batters, two ejections, one out? In a game against the St. Louis Cardinals, New York Giants batter Bob Elliot was thrown out of the game for complaining about a strike-two call and kicking dirt at the umpire. Teammate Bobby Hoffman was called in to finish the at bat, but he protested the strike-three call, and he, too, was thrown out of the game.

1961 Five San Francisco players hit homers in one inning as the Giants bombed the Cincinnati Reds, 14–0. The homers by Orlando Cepeda, Felipe Alou, Jim Davenport, Willie Mays and Johnny Orsino tied a major league record for the most homers by a team in one inning.

1985 Who says men are better athletes than women? Well, Bobby Riggs did, but he was forced to eat his words. Today Riggs, age 67, and his partner, Vitas Gerulaitis, lost to Martina Navratilova and Pam Shriver: 6–2, 6–3, 6–4.

1989 Victoria Brucker became the first girl from the United States to play in the Little League World Series. She scored three runs in leading her squad from San Pedro, California, past a team from Tampa, Florida, 12–5.

1989 In the worst baseball scandal in decades, Cincinnati Reds Manager Pete Rose agreed to a lifetime suspension from the game. Baseball commissioner A. Bartlett Giamatti said that he believed Rose had bet on baseball games, including those of his own team.

1875 For more than a century, swimmers had tried to cross the 21-mile stretch between England and France known as the English Channel. Matthew Webb of Great Britain became the first man to do it, setting out from Dover, England on this day. Some 21 hours and 45 minutes later, he arrived in France.

1951 St. Louis Browns owner Bill Veeck [pronounced VECK] found a way to get the fans involved in the game. He passed out cards saying "yes" and "no" to 1,000 fans behind his dugout. Whenever the coach had to make a decision, he turned to the crowd and let them vote on what do do. The fans did a great job. St. Louis beat Philadelphia, 5–3.

1985 Don Baylor of the New York Yankees tied an AL record by getting hit by a pitch for the 189th time in his career. Hey, Baylor, there's a less painful way to get to first base.

1973 Cyclist Allan Abbott set a special record by traveling 140.5 miles per hour on a bicycle. Abbott set the record at the Bonneville Salt Flats in Utah. It would be broken there 12 years later when John Howard pedaled at more than 152 miles per hour. (See July 20, 1985.)

1985 When you're talking about the New York Mets pitching sensation Dwight Gooden, 20/20 doesn't necessarily refer to his vision. At age 20, Gooden became the youngest major league pitcher to win 20 games in a season. The record-breaker came in a 9–3 win over the San Diego Padres. A year earlier he broke the record for the most strikeouts for a rookie. (See September 12, 1984.)

1988 Here's a record that will make you dizzy. Jeff Schwartz jumped up and down on a trampoline for 266 hours and 9 minutes without stopping. He had begun his bounce-athon 11 days earlier on August 14.

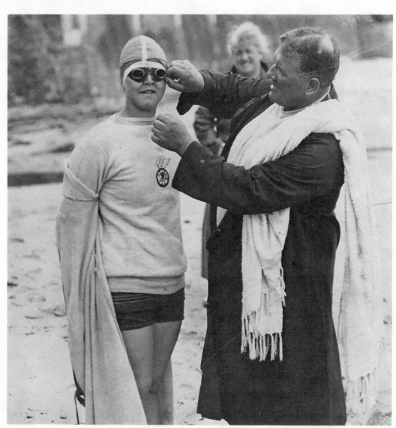

Gertrude Ederle, the first woman to swim the English Channel. (See August 6, 1926)

1939 Can you imagine not being able to watch baseball on television? Well, that was the case until this historic day. The first major league games (a double header) were covered by station W2XBS New York, as the Cincinnati Reds took on the Brooklyn Dodgers at Brooklyn's Ebbets Field.

1947 He should have stuck to hitting. Brooklyn Dodger pitcher Dan Bankhead hit a home run in his very first major league game. Unfortunately, he also gave up 10 hits and 6 earned runs in $3\frac{1}{3}$ innings of relief. The Pittsburgh Pirates beat the Dodgers, 16–3.

1960 In one of the most controversial calls in Olympic history, Australian swimmer John Devitt was declared the winner of the 100-meter freestyle race in Rome, Italy. The finish was close, and most people thought an American named Lance Larson was the real winner. Even Devitt thought he had lost.

1987 Paul Molitor of the Milwaukee Brewers entered today's game against the Cleveland Indians with a league-record 39-game hitting streak on the line. As he waited in the on-deck circle with the game still scoreless in the bottom of the 10th, his streak was in jeopardy. After four at bats, he was still hitless. And that was the way it would stay. The hitter before Molitor, Rick Manning, singled in the winning run, and Paul never got his fifth try. The streak was over at 39.

1874 The Boston Red Stockings and the Philadelphia Blue Stockings packed up their colorful socks and headed back to the United States. The two clubs had just completed a 28-day tour of England and Ireland, playing 15 exhibition games for the British. They became the first American teams ever to play baseball outside the United States. By the way, back in the late 1800s it was common to give nicknames to baseball teams based on the color of their socks. In addition to the Red Stockings and Blue Stockings there were the Cincinnati Red Legs (now the Reds), the Chicago White Stockings (White Sox) and the Providence Grays.

1987 Race-car driver A.J. Foyt, Jr., set a record for the highest average speed for one lap, at the Fort Stockton Test Center in Texas. Foyt zoomed along at more than 257 miles per hour in a test run of a car with a special turbo-charged engine. Surprise! An engine based on the same design was later used in a 1988 Oldsmobile.

1989 Cyclist Greg LeMond of the United States won the World Cycling Championships in France, only a month after his dramatic win of the Tour de France. He became the fifth man in history to win both races in the same year. He won both races with exciting, come-from-behind victories.

1955 The first sudden-death overtime football game was played today. In a pre-season match played in Portland, Oregon, the Los Angeles Rams defeated the New York Giants, 23–17. The Rams scored the winning touchdown three minutes into overtime. Before the sudden-death rule went into effect, any game that ended in a tie stayed that way.

1960 Here's another entry in the "Life Just Isn't Fair" department. Ted Kluszewski of the Chicago White Sox hit a three-run homer in the eighth inning to give his team a 4–3 lead over the Baltimore Orioles. But what's this? The third base umpire had called time because two White Sox players were warming up on the sideline. The home run didn't count, and Chicago lost, 3–1.

1977 The New York Cosmos defeated the Seattle Sounders, 2–1, to capture the North American Soccer League Championship. More than 35,000 fans showed up to say good-bye to Pelé, the Cosmos' Brazilian superstar, who was playing in his final NASL game. Three seasons earlier, Pelé had signed a whopping $7 million deal with the Cosmos, making him the richest athlete in the world. (See June 3, 1975.)

1978 Donald Vesco of Loma Linda, California set a record for the fastest speed on a motorcycle. His special 21-foot-long Kawasaki traveled more than 318 miles per hour at the Bonneville Salt Flats in Utah.

1965 Willie Mays of the San Francisco Giants hits his 17th home run of the month to power the Giants past his future teammates, the New York Mets, 8–3. Mays broke the record of 16 homers in one month set by Ralph Kiner in September 1949.

1974 High school basketball sensation Moses Malone signed a two-year contract with the Utah Stars of the ABA to earn $150,000 and $200,000 a year. He became the first player to go directly from high school into professional basketball without going to college.

1977 Outfielder Lou Brock of the St. Louis Cardinals needed only two steals to break the modern baseball record of 892 stolen bases in a career, set by Ty Cobb. Leading off in a game against San Diego, he drew a walk, and on the very next pitch he tied Cobb's record. Six innings later, Brock rapped out a single, grabbed a big lead off first, dashed to second on the pitch... here's the slide... and he's SAFE!

1977 Nolan Ryan of the California Angels stuck out 11 batters, but lost to the Baltimore Orioles, 6–1. It was still a memorable game for the pitching ace because he recorded his 300th strikeout of the season—the fifth time in his career he had done that.

1987 Little League was having a big party, but the U.S. team had little to celebrate. In the 40th anniversary of the Little League World Series, a team from the Chinese Republic of Taiwan trounced an American club from Irvine, California, 21–1, in Williamsport, Pennsylvania. Teams from Taiwan, Japan and other countries in the Far East had won 17 of the last 21 World Series.

1916 Two minor league teams from the North Carolina League, Winston-Salem and Ashville, played the shortest game in baseball history. The game lasted only 31 minutes. The Winston-Salem team needed to catch an early train back home, so both teams agreed to swing at every pitch and run onto the field when changing sides.

1953 The Milwaukee Braves set a major league record by hitting eight home runs in one game. Jim Pendleton had three homers, and Eddie Mathews had two. Not surprisingly, Milwaukee beat the Pittsburgh Pirates, 19–4.

1904

THE GOOD, THE BAD AND THE WEIRD

The marathon at the Olympics in St. Louis, Missouri was a little strange. First, there was the runner from Cuba, a man named Felix Carvajal, who had never before run in a race. Carvajal had saved his money for the trip to St. Louis, but halfway there he lost it in a card game. He continued on by hitchhiking and arrived only a few minutes before the race was to begin, still wearing his street shoes and long pants. The event was delayed while discus thrower Martin Sheridan cut Felix's pants into shorts. The crowd laughed, but Felix came in fourth. And that wasn't all that was unusual. The American who was first declared the winner of the race, Fred Lorz, had to give up his gold medal when it was learned he had hitched a ride in a car for 11 of the 26 miles.

1881 The first U.S. Lawn Tennis Association Championships were held in Newport, Rhode Island. The event is now called the U.S. Open. Twenty-five men entered the first singles competition, and 13 teams entered the doubles. Women were not allowed to play. Richard D. Sears won the singles title, and Clarence W. Clark and Fred W. Taylor won the doubles. Sears would go on to win the next six men's titles. No other player in history has ever won seven in a row.

1935 Golfer Glenna Collett Vare captured her sixth women's U.S. Amateur Golf Championship. The native of Philadelphia, Pennsylvania, who had won her first amateur title in 1922, became the first woman to win six times. In more than 50 years since, no one else has won six.

1982 New York Yankees pitcher Ron Guidry earned the 100th win of his career by beating the Minnesota Twins. By the time he left major league baseball in 1988, Guidry had 170 wins, including 26 shutouts.

1983 Gott-ya! That's what the Baltimore Orioles must have said every time they scored a run off pitcher Jim Gott of the Toronto Blue Jays. The Orioles scored seven runs before Gott retired a single batter in the first inning. The O's went on to beat the Blue Jays, 10–2.

SEPTEMBER

1880 The first national tennis tournament was held on Staten Island, one of New York City's five boroughs. Twenty-three players competed for a silver cup, worth about $100. O.E. Woodhouse, an Englishman, won the men's title.

1947 The New York Giants set a major league baseball record for the most home runs by a team in a season. Three Giants players hit homers to bring the season total to 185, three more than the record set by the 1936 New York Yankees.

1949 Eugene McPherson, a 22-year-old student at Ohio State University, left Santa Monica, California, today on his way across country on a bicycle. McPherson arrived in New York City 20 days later, becoming the first man to ride from one coast to the other in less than three weeks.

1973 Jockey Braulio Baeza made horse-racing history today when he won two races—in different states. Baeza won his first race in Belmont Park on Long Island, New York, then hopped on a plane to Philadelphia, Pennsylvania, to win the Kindergarten Stakes at Liberty Bell Race Track.

1984 In one of the most lopsided games in modern college football history, Mississippi State University pulverized Kentucky State University, 86–0. Mississippi State quarterback Willie Totten piled up 536 yards with 37 completed passes. In all, his team gained 699 yards in the air.

Jose Canseco, the only baseball player to hit forty home runs and steal forty bases in the same season. (See September 23, 1988)

←

1909 Somebody should have kept an eye on New York Giants pinch runner Bill O'Hara. For the second day in a row, he stole both second and third base. O'Hara, who was a rookie, became the only pinch runner ever to steal two bases two days in a row.

1960 Like father, like son. Baseball great Ted Williams slapped one of his many home runs against Don Lee, a right-handed pitcher for the Washington Senators. Twenty-one years earlier, at the beginning of his career, Williams had hit several homers against Lee's father, Thornton.

1974 Jerry Lewis isn't the only one who stays up for hours to raise money to fight the crippling disease, muscular dystrophy. Today, two teams of women entered the record books for the sake of Jerry's kids. To raise money for muscular dystrophy, they played the longest softball game in history—620 innings.

Greg Louganis, the first man to win two diving gold medals in consecutive Olympics. (See September 27, 1988)

1895 Two teams from small towns in Pennsylvania met for the first professional football game. The team from Latrobe beat a squad from Jeanette, 12–0. This qualified as a professional game only because Latrobe quarterback John Brallier was paid $10 to cover his expenses.

1911 William A. Larned won his fifth straight singles competition at the U.S. Open Tennis Championships, and his seventh win over all. He was only the second player in the history of the game to win seven men's titles. Richard D. Sears won seven in a row through 1887. Only one other man has done it since—Bill Tilden, who won his seventh in 1929.

1968 At the U.S. Olympic Swimming Trials in Long Beach, California, Mike Burton set a world record of 16 minutes, 8.5 seconds, in the 1,500-meter freestyle. Four years later, at the Olympics in Munich, West Germany he smashed his own world record with a time of 15 minutes, 52.58 seconds.

1977 SPORTS QUIZ Here's an easy one. Or maybe it's not so easy. Can you name the professional baseball player who hit more home runs than any other?

A: No, it's not Hank Aaron. He holds the record for major league baseball. On this day, though, Japanese star Sadaharu Oh passed Aaron's mark of 755 homers. Oh retired in 1980 with 868 home runs.

1928 What a day for doubleheaders! The Boston Braves played the first of nine doubleheaders in a row which set a major league record. Exactly 22 years earlier on this date, the New York Highlanders had set a similar record by winning both ends of their 5th straight doubleheader.

1937 Doris Kopsky of Belleville, New Jersey, won the first women's bicycling championship. The one-mile race, sponsored by the National Amateur Bicycling Association, was held in Buffalo, New York. Kopsky's winning time was 4 minutes, 22.4 seconds.

1953 The New York Yankees took the AL pennant for the fifth time in five years to become the first team in major league baseball to win five league titles in a row. A month later, the Yankees would win their fifth World Series in a row, defeating the Brooklyn Dodgers, four games to two. The Yankees manager for all five years was the great Casey Stengel.

1972 Mark Spitz of the United States swam on the winning 4 x 100 meter medley relay to collect his seventh gold medal at the Olympics in Munich, West Germany. Spitz set world records in all but one of the seven events he won. No one had ever won that many gold medals before in a single Olympics, and no one has done it since.

1985 Slugger Gary Carter of the New York Mets hit two home runs in a game against the San Diego Padres. That gave him five homers in two games, which tied the major league record. By the way, the Mets beat San Diego, 9–2.

1918 Here's why it's nearly impossible to go to any sporting event these days without the national anthem being played: During the seventh-inning stretch of today's World Series game between the Red Sox and the Chicago Cubs in Chicago, Illinois, the band suddenly decided to play "The Star Spangled Banner," and the crowd began to sing along. That was the first time the song was played at a sports event. Later, around World War II, it became a tradition to play the anthem at the beginning of the game.

1972 Tragedy struck at the Olympic Games in Munich, West Germany. Eleven athletes from the country of Israel were killed when Palestinian terrorists broke into the Olympic Village and took a group of them hostage. All Olympic events were suspended for 34 hours. When they continued, much of the joy and excitement of the Games was missing.

1979 Ann Meyers became the first woman to sign with an NBA team. The former Olympic and college star at UCLA signed a one-year $50,000 contract with the Indiana Pacers. However, Meyers was cut from the team before she could play a single game.

1989 There have been few players in the history of tennis more popular than Chris Evert, and few more talented. Today, Chrissie, who had already announced her retirement, played her last match at the U.S. Open. She lost to Zina Garrison, 6–7, 2–6, and left the stadium choking back tears as the crowd gave her a standing ovation. In her 19-year career, Evert won more than 150 titles, including six U.S. Open Championships. Her final match record was 1,304 wins against only 146 losses.

1883 There are bad innings, and then there are *bad* innings. The Detroit Wolverines of the NL gave up an incredible 18 runs to the Chicago White Stockings in the bottom of the 7th inning. In fact, Chicago scored 13 runs off two Detroit pitchers before the Wolverines had a single man out. The final score was 26–6. Seventy years later, on June 18, 1953, another Detroit team, the Tigers, surrendered 17 runs, also in the 7th inning, to the Boston Red Sox. Boston sweated out a 23–3 victory.

1924 Charles Paddock was known as "The World's Fastest Human." Today he lived up to that name when he set world records in the 100- and 220-yard dash at the AAU's national senior outdoor track and field championships. Paddock defeated Loren Murchinson, the defending champion in both events.

1974 For the first time in 55 matches, tennis star Chris Evert was defeated. She lost to Evonne Goolagong of Australia in the semifinals of the U.S. Open. Three days later, Goolagong would lose the women's championship match to Billie Jean King who collected her fourth U.S. Open. Goolagong never won the competition.

1988 The youngest swimmer to cross the English Channel is Thomas Gregory, an 11-year-old English boy who swam it in 11 hours, 45 minutes today. The Channel, a 21-mile body of water that separates Britain from France, has fascinated long-distance swimmers for years. Ever since another Englishman, Matthew Webb, first swam the crossing in 1875, dozens of people have tried to do so. The oldest woman to swim the Channel was Stella Ada Rosina Taylor of England, who was nearly 46 years old on August 25, 1975, when she swam it in 18 hours, 15 minutes.

1908 Not a bad little series for Washington Senators pitcher Walter Johnson. For the third time in a four-game series against the New York Highlanders, Johnson pitched a complete game shutout. The Highlanders later changed their name to the Yankees.

1953 Oh, no, it's Little Mo. Maureen "Little Mo" Connolly became the first woman to win the Grand Slam of tennis today when she won the U.S. Open Championship. Connolly had already won the world's three other major tournaments: the Australian Open, the French Open and Wimbledon.

1970 Call it a shoe-in for the record books. Jockey Bill Shoemaker set a horse-racing record by winning his 6,033rd race. "The Shoe" has won a lot more since then. Before retiring in early 1990, he had ridden more than 8,800 winners.

1984 Ace pitcher Dwight Gooden of the New York Mets earned a place in the record books by striking out Ron Cey of the Chicago Cubs. It was Gooden's 228th strikeout, more than any other rookie in National League history. That was Gooden-uff to surpass the mark set by Grover Cleveland Alexander in 1911.

1965 Bert Campaneris of the Kansas City Athletics (now the Oakland A's) became the first player in the history of baseball to play all nine positions in one ball game. He played one inning at each position. As a pitcher in the eighth inning, he gave up one run.

1969 Only two men and three women have won the Grand Slam of tennis, which means winning Wimbledon, and the U.S., Australian and French Open Championships in one year. Only one person has done it twice in his career. Australian Rod Laver, who first won the Grand Slam in 1962, today completed his second Slam by winning the final tournament, the U.S. Open.

Florence Griffith Joyner, the runner who set an Olympic record in one event, a world record in another and won a gold medal in a third—all in one day. (See September 29, 1988)

1895 The American Bowling Congress (ABC) was formed in New York City. The group began to make rules and regulate bowling tournaments, which had, by then, already become quite popular. By 1990, the ABC had almost $3\frac{1}{2}$ million members. There is also a Women's International Bowling Congress and The Young American Bowling Alliance, which has 646,000 young members.

1965 Los Angeles Dodgers lefthander Sandy Koufax became the first pitcher in baseball history to throw four no-hitters in his career. In today's game against the Chicago Cubs, Koufax struck out 14 and didn't let a single batter get to first—making it his first perfect game. Poor Bob Hendley, the Cubs pitcher, only gave up one hit in his team's, 1–0 loss. Nolan Ryan broke Koufax's record with his fifth no-hitter in 1981 and got his sixth in 1990, but Sandy is still considered one of the best pitchers ever.

1968 Arthur Ashe of the United States became the first black champion of the U.S. Open Tennis Championships. He defeated Tom Okker of the Netherlands in the men's singles division for his only Open victory.

1987 Pitching for the Houston Astros, Nolan Ryan struck out 16 San Francisco Giants batters, including 12 of the last 13 men he faced, to set a record with 4,500 strikeouts in his career. Nolan got the win for the game, too, as Houston beat the Giants, 4–2.

1960 In a baseball game against the Tigers in Detroit, Michigan, Mickey Mantle of the New York Yankees broke his own distance record by hitting a home run 643 feet. It was the longest home run in a regular season game. It sailed over the rightfield roof and landed in a lumberyard. What do you expect? Mickey's bat *was* made of wood.

1967 Tennis great Billie Jean King today defeated Ann Haydon Jones of England to win the women's singles championships at the U.S. Open. The victory made King the first woman in 28 years to win the U.S. Open and Wimbledon singles, doubles *and* mixed doubles championships all in one year.

1972 For 62 straight games, the U.S. basketball team was undefeated in the Olympics. Until today. Playing for the gold, the Soviet Union beat the United States for the first time, 51–50, in a controversial ending. A timeout was called before the Soviets scored the winning shot. Although the U.S. said there was one second left on the clock when the timeout was called, the timekeeper gave the Soviets three seconds. The International Amateur Basketball Federation stood by the decision and the Americans took their first loss. They refused their medals.

1974 Lou Brock of the St. Louis Cardinals was one of the greatest base stealers in the history of baseball. In a game against the Philadelphia Phillies today, Brock stole his 105th base of the season to break Maury Wills's season record of 104. By the end of the season Brock had 118 stolen bases. When he retired in 1979, he had stolen a career total of 938 bases. That's 46 more than Ty Cobb had stolen when he set the record.

1971 Nine-year-old Priscilla Hill of Lexington, Massachusetts, became the youngest figure skater ever to win a gold medal at a sanctioned professional event. She placed first at a competition in Lake Placid, New York.

1974 Going, going, yawn. In what turned out to be the longest completed game in baseball history, the St. Louis Cardinals defeated the New York Mets 4–3 in 25 innings. The game lasted 7 hours and 4 minutes, and ended at 3:13 in the morning. The Mets also have the distinction of having played the longest 1–0 game—24 innings against the Houston Astros on April 25, 1968. As if that's not enough, they also played the longest doubleheader in history—9 hours 52 minutes. That twin bill against the San Francisco Giants on May 31, 1964 included a 23-inning nightcap. What's with those Mets?

1985 Another historic feat for Pete. Before 47,000 cheering fans in Cincinnati, Ohio, Pete Rose lined a single off San Diego Padres pitcher Eric Show to break a Ty Cobb record for hits that had stood for 57 years. The hit was the 4,192nd of Rose's career. By the time Rose retired in 1986, he had racked up a dizzying 4,256 hits.

1988 Yves Pol of France set a world record for running a 5-kilometer (3.1-mile) race *backward*. It took him 22 minutes and 33 seconds to finish the course, which went through the streets of New York City. He might have run even faster, but people kept telling him he was going the wrong way.

1885 Arbroath, a soccer team in Scotland, scored the most points ever recorded in one match. Arbroath beat another Scottish team 36–0 in a Scottish Cup Match. At the time, there were no nets behind the goal, so the goalie often had to waste several seconds running after the ball after each score. If it weren't for that, Arbroath might have scored 50 goals.

1975 The world's first movable stadium was dedicated in Honolulu, Hawaii. Aloha Stadium was built to seat 50,000 in six 14-story-high sections. Four of the sections can be moved as much as 185 feet in 25 minutes by forcing air through hydraulic jacks.

1976 Fifty-three-year-old Minnie Minoso of the Chicago White Sox became the oldest player in major league history to get a hit. Minoso got a single off the Angels Sid Monge. On October 5, 1980, Minoso broke his own record; he was 57-years old.

1984 He was barely out of high school, but he was already in the record books. The New York Mets' remarkable rookie pitcher, Dwight Gooden, fanned 16 Pittsburgh Pirates to set a record for the most strikeouts by a rookie, 251. In his very next start, Dr. K again struck out 16 batters, tying Nolan Ryan's and Luis Tiant's record for the most strikeouts in two games and setting a league record for the most (43) in three games.

1987 Paul Lynch of Great Britain set a record today by doing 32,573 push-ups in 24 hours. Lynch also held the record for doing 3,857 one-arm push-ups in 5 hours. Both records were set in London, England. Jolly good, Paul, but don't your arms hurt?

1965 There's nothing unlucky about September 13 for baseball hitters. Today, San Francisco Giants outfielder Willie Mays hit his 500th home run off Houston's Don Nottebart in the Giants', 5–1, victory. On this same day in 1971, Frank Robinson of the Baltimore Orioles joined the 500-homer club when he nailed a shot off Fred Scherman of the Detroit Tigers.

1970 After 73 years, the Boston Marathon finally got some competition when the first New York City Marathon was held in Central Park. Gary Muhrcke of New York won with a time of 2 hours, 31 minutes, 39 seconds. Fewer than half the 127 starters finished the race. The Marathon was moved from Central Park to the streets of New York, where it is now held.

1980 The East Carolina University football team set a rather embarrassing record today. They fumbled the ball five times on five straight possessions in one quarter. Southwestern Louisiana converted four of the fumbles for scores, and won, 27–21.

SPORTS QUIZ In addition to Boston and New York, a major city in the midwestern United States is also known for having an important international marathon. Can you name that city?

A: Chicago, Illinois.

1923 What a slugfest! In a boxing match that ended just one minute into the second round, heavyweight champion Jack Dempsey knocked Luis Firpo down 10 times, and Dempsey hit the canvas twice, himself. At one point, Firpo hit the champion so hard, Dempsey went through the ropes and landed in the laps of the sportswriters. They pushed him back into the ring. Dempsey won the fight, with a knockout (what else?) in the second round.

1929 Of all the great racehorses in history, which one was the first to win more than $100,000 in a race? That's both a question *and* an answer. A horse named Which One took the Belmont Futurity at Belmont Park in New York, winning a purse of $105,730. Now, who's on first?

1951 Outfielder Bob Nieman of the St. Louis Browns slammed two home runs off Red Sox pitcher Mickey McDermott in his first two at bats. Nieman had just been called up from the Brown's Oklahoma City minor league club. He is the only player in the majors ever to get hits in his first two at bats. The Browns still lost the game, though, 9–6.

1987 Shortstop Cal Ripken, Jr., of the Baltimore Orioles ended his streak of playing every inning of every game for six seasons. Ripken played 8,243 innings over 904 games during the streak, which began on June 5, 1982. Today, the Orioles manager—Ripken's father—Cal Ripken, Sr., pulled his son from the game.

1938 Oh, brother! Paul Waner of the Pittsburgh Pirates stepped up to bat against New York Giants pitcher Cliff Melton. Boom! The ball went over the fence. It was the second homer in a row Melton had given up. In the previous at bat, Waner's brother, Lloyd, had also slammed one home. That's the only time brothers have hit successive homers in a major league game.

1963 Here's an NFL record that's been tied at least five times, but will never be broken. Quarterback George Izo, of the Washington Redskins threw a 99-yard touchdown pass to receiver Bobby Mitchell. It was one of the day's only highlights for Washington, which lost to the Cleveland Browns, 37–14. Why can't the record be broken? Because a football field is only 100 yards long.

1969 Steve Carlton of the St. Louis Cardinals became the first pitcher in this century to strike out 19 batters. And he still lost the game. Carlton struck out each of the New York Mets at least once, but one of them, Ron Swoboda, also managed to hit two two-run homers. The Mets spoiled Carlton's day, 4–3.

1971 For the first time in 16 years, Americans won both the men's and women's titles in the U.S. Open Tennis Championships. Stan Smith took the men's singles competition, and Billie Jean King was the women's winner.

1978 Boxer Muhammad Ali won a decision over Leon Spinks in 15 rounds, in New Orleans, Louisiana, to become heavyweight champion. Again. Ali earned a place in the record books for becoming the first boxer to win the title three different times.

1950 It was the football battle of the decade. The NFL champion Philadelphia Eagles faced the Cleveland Browns, champs of the rival All-America Football Conference. Most people thought the NFL team would easily beat their foes from the weaker league, which no longer exists. But the Browns pulled a major upset, clipping the Eagles, 35–10, before a shocked crowd in Philadelphia, Pennsylvania.

1973 O.J. can stand for orange juice. Or it can stand for one of the greatest runners ever to play football—O.J. Simpson. The man who was sometimes known as "The Juice," because of his initials, set an NFL rushing record by gaining 250 yards in today's game between his Buffalo Bills and the New England Patriots. Simpson's total was the most yards rushing by one player in one game, surpassing the mark of 247 yards set by Willie Ellison of the Los Angeles Rams in 1971. By the end of the season, O.J. would have an even more impressive record. He would become the first player to rush for 2,000 yards in a season.

1975 Rennie Stennett of the Pittsburgh Pirates was one of those dependable baseball players who was never a brilliant hitter. Except on this day. Stennett became only the third player in the history of the major leagues to get seven hits in seven at bats in one game. He had four singles, two doubles and a triple. The other players who went seven for seven were Wilbert Robinson of the Baltimore Orioles and Detroit's Cesar Gutierrez. (See June 10, 1892, and June 21, 1970.)

1986 Bobby Witt couldn't keep his wits about him. The Texas Rangers pitcher threw two wild pitches in the first inning of a, 10–6, victory over the Oakland A's. With that, Witt set an AL record for the most wild pitches (22) in a season.

1920 The American Professional Football Association (APFA) was founded today in Canton, Ohio. Ten teams joined now, four teams joined in November. The APFA later became the NFL.

1930 Earl Averill of the Cleveland Indians hit three home runs in a row in the Indians', 13–7, scalping of the Washington Senators. He had one grand slam and two, two-run shots. Then, in the second game of the doubleheader, Averill hit another shot over the wall. His 11 runs batted in set a major league record for a doubleheader.

1944 The Green Bay Packers defeated the Brooklyn Tigers, 14–7, on an unusually hot Sunday in Milwaukee, Wisconsin. Maybe the heat made the players cranky. The two teams set an NFL record for most penalties in a game. The officials called 33 infractions, for a total of 249 yards in penalties.

1957 Ted Williams had just returned to the Boston Red Sox after being out sick for two weeks. Although he was still weak, Williams pinch-hit a home run in his first at-bat. His next at-bat the following day he walked and hit a home run. In fact, over the next five games, Williams reached base every single time he was up. His 16 times on base in 16 trips to the plate set a major league record that still stands.

1984 Reggie Jackson of the California Angels hit the 500th home run of his career in a game against the Kansas City Royals to become the 13th player in major league history to hit 500 homers. Jackson had gotten his first big-league home run exactly 17 years earlier on this very day.

1968 One good no-hitter deserves another. Today, one day after Gaylord Perry of the San Francisco Giants threw a no-hitter against St. Louis, Cardinals pitcher Ray Washburn returned the favor. Washburn no-hit the Giants, 2–0.

1984 Joe W. Kittinger of Orlando, Florida became the first man to cross the Atlantic Ocean alone in a hot-air balloon. Kittinger flew 3,535 miles from Caribou, Maine, to Savona, Italy, in a 10-story-tall balloon, named *Rosie O'Grady's Balloon of Peace.*

1984 This season the Detroit Tigers became only the fourth team in major league history to hold onto first place from opening day through the end of the season. Today, they clinched the AL East Division with a 3–0 blanking of the Milwaukee Brewers. The Tigers went on to win the World Series, beating the San Diego Padres. By the way, the other teams to lead their division from start to finish were all from New York City. They were the 1923 New York Giants, the 1927 New York Yankees and the 1955 Brooklyn Dodgers.

1988 Seventeen-year-old swimmer Janet Evans gave the United States its first gold medal of the Olympics in Seoul, South Korea. The high school senior from Placentia, California, won the women's 400-meter individual medley, when she beat Noemi Lung of Rumania by a full seven feet. Evans was one of the few bright spots for the Americans in women's swimming at these Games. Most events were won by the East Germans.

1925 At the U.S. Open Tennis Championships, Bill Tilden became the first man in the 20th century to win 6 U.S. Open titles in a row. "Big Bill" defeated William M. Johnston in a thrilling five-set battle. Even six wins wasn't enough for Tilden. He won his seventh in 1929. Only two men and two women have won that many. They are Richard D. Sears, William A. Larned, Molla Mallory and Helen Wills Moody.

1943 Finally! The Detroit Lions opened the 1943 season in style, defeating the Chicago Cardinals, 35–17. The victory was their first since November 30, 1941. In fact, their 35 points in today's game almost equaled their point total (38) for the entire 1942 season, when they were one of the worst football teams ever.

1968 The Detroit Tigers defeated the New York Yankees, 6–2. Except for giving up a homer to Mickey Mantle, Tigers pitcher Denny McLain was brilliant. It was his 31st win of the season, tying an AL record set 37 years earlier by Lefty Grove of the Philadelphia Athletics.

1973 Frank Robinson hit his first home run as a California Angel in a game against the Texas Rangers at Arlington Stadium. It was the 32nd major league ballpark in which he had homered. Robinson won Most Valuable Player Awards in both the American and National leagues, was elected to the Hall of Fame, and became the first black manager in baseball.

1931 Evar Swanson, a former pro football and baseball star, set a speed record for running around the bases. In a special exhibition, he started at home and circled the infield in 13.3 seconds. Many players have tried to top that, but none has succeeded.

1970 Farr out, Mann! Mel Farr scored two touchdowns and Errol Mann kicked four field goals as the Detroit Lions bombed the Green Bay Packers, 40–0. It was the first time the Packers had been shut out in 12 years.

1973 When a sexist male tennis player named Bobby Riggs said he could beat any woman, Billie Jean King decided to prove him wrong. King embarrassed Riggs in three straight sets.

1986 SPORTS QUIZ Tony Gwynn of the San Diego Padres stole five bases in a game against the Houston Astros. Gwynn is terrific as a base stealer, but do you know who holds the record for the most stolen bases in a career? Hint: You've already read about him in this book.

A: Lou Brock, who stole 938 bases playing for the Chicago Cubs and the St. Louis Cardinals from 1961–1979.

1964 It was one of the worst collapses in the history of baseball. With 12 games left to play in the season, the Philadelphia Phillies held a comfortable 6½-game lead in the NL. Then disaster struck. The Phillies lost their next 10 games in a row, allowing the St. Louis Cardinals to steal the pennant.

1970 Anyone who cared to tune in tonight saw the first *Monday Night Football* game. Homer Jones of the Cleveland Browns thrilled a crowd of 85,703 fans watching in person and millions more watching on TV when he returned a kickoff for a 94-yard touchdown. The Browns beat the New York Jets, 31–21.

1980 New York Jets quarterback Richard Todd put on a record-setting passing display and still lost the game. In New York's 37–27 defeat by the San Francisco 49ers, Todd set an NFL record by completing 42 passes, including three touchdowns, in 60 attempts. The old record of 37 completed passes (out of 68 attempts) was held by George Blanda of the Houston Oilers.

1982 NFL players walked off the job for the first time in the league's history. Their strike went on until November 17 and became the costliest ever in sports. The NFL's regular season was cut back from 16 games to 9.

1912 When Eddie Collins of the Philadelphia A's set a record, he wanted to make sure people knew about it. In case anyone had missed seeing him set a major league mark by stealing six bases in a game just 11 days earlier, Eddie stole six again today.

1927 This was a heavyweight championship fight Jack Dempsey should have won. In the seventh round, he knocked down Gene Tunney, but failed to go to a neutral corner, as the rules require. So the referee did not start counting Tunney out for several seconds, and Tunney had time to get to his feet. After the 10th round, Tunney won on a decision. He probably would have lost if Dempsey had just gone to that corner.

1968 Hail Cesar! Cesar Tovar of the Minnesota Twins became only the second player in baseball to play every position in a nine-inning game. In so doing, he tied a record set by Bert Campaneris in 1965 (see September 8). As a pitcher in the first inning, Tovar retired the very first batter he faced... none other than Bert Campaneris.

1969 SPORTS QUIZ San Francisco Giants outfielder Willie Mays hit the 600th home run of his career in a game against the San Diego Padres. By the time he retired from baseball, Mays had hit 660 homers. He was only the second player in history to hit 600 home runs. Do you know the first?

A. Babe Ruth.

1897 The city of Cheyenne, Wyoming, went wild with excitement as the first Frontier Days rodeo was held. The highlight of the rodeo was a horse-roping contest, complete with wild horses that had never been roped before. Today, Frontier Days is a nine-day event in Cheyenne. It is the largest outdoor rodeo in the world.

1908 It would be years before New York Giants baseball fans would forget the day Fred Merkle cost his team the pennant. In a crucial game against the second-place Chicago Cubs, Merkle was on first base when a single scored a runner ahead of him with what everyone thought was the winning run. Merkle, seeing the runner safe at home, stopped running and did not touch second base. The alert Cubs second baseman tagged second, Merkle was called out, and the run was erased. The game was declared a tie, and later replayed. The Cubs won the do-over—and the pennant.

1946 Hey, that's not nice! Boxer Al Couture recorded the quickest knockout in boxing history when he punched Ralph Walton with exactly a half second gone in the fight. Walton was still in his corner putting in his mouthpiece when the bell rang and Couture knocked him out.

1988 Jose Canseco of the Oakland A's stole two bases in a game against the Milwaukee Brewers to become the only baseball player to hit more than 40 home runs (he had 42) and steal 40 bases in the same season.

1950 Chicago Cardinals Quarterback Jim Hardy set a record he might like to forget. In a game against the Philadelphia Eagles, eight of Hardy's 39 pass attempts were intercepted by the opposing team! Hardy's eight interceptions remain the most ever thrown by a quarterback in a single game.

1967 Placekicker Jim Bakken of the St. Louis Cardinals must have had a sore foot by the end of his team's 28–14 victory over the Pittsburgh Steelers. In one game, Bakken made seven field goals—an NFL record. I guess you could say he got a kick out of this game.

1972 Jack Tatum, a safety for the Oakland Raiders, set a rather unusual record. In a game against the Green Bay Packers, he ran a fumble recovery back 104 yards. He scooped up a Green Bay fumble in Oakland's end zone and ran it back the length of the field for what turned out to be the winning touchdown. No one has made a longer touchdown run.

1988 Canadian runner Ben Johnson won the 100-meter sprint at the Olympics in Seoul, South Korea. Johnson shattered the world record with an incredible 9.79-second run. But two days later, Johnson was stripped of his medal when it was learned he had used steroids, an illegal drug. Carl Lewis of the United States, who had come in second, was declared the winner.

1989 In the 1970s, Vida Blue had been the star pitcher for the Oakland A's. Today, he was back on the mound again but it wasn't to pitch. It was to get married! Blue and his bride were married in front of thousands of fans at Candlestick Park in San Francisco, California, before today's game. No, the honeymoon wasn't spent in leftfield. That would have made Vida blue.

1955 His nickname was "The Horse." And Alan Ameche of the Baltimore Colts had quite a gallop the first time he touched the ball as a pro football player. Ameche ran 79 yards for his first touchdown in leading the Colts to a 23–17 upset of the Chicago Bears.

1965 Here's a "Paige" for the history books. At age 59, Satchel Paige pitched three shut-out innings for the Kansas City A's against the Boston Red Sox and became the oldest person to play in a major league game. Paige didn't break into the majors until he was 42, because, until then, black players were not allowed in the majors.

1973 Willie Mays, one of the most beloved players in major league baseball, was honored in an emotional ceremony at Shea Stadium today. He had spent most of his career with the Giants in New York and San Francisco, but played with the New York Mets during this last season.

1988 Swimmer Matt Biondi of the United States won his fifth gold medal and seventh medal of any kind at the Olympics in Seoul, South Korea, by helping the U.S. squad win the 400-meter medley relay. The Americans broke the world record for the event set by another U.S. swim team in 1985.

1908 Edward "Big Ed" Reulbach of the Chicago Cubs became the first pitcher to pitch shutouts in both games of a doubleheader. He gave up only eight hits in the two games, and beat the Brooklyn Superbas, 5–0 and 3–0.

1962 Where there's a Wills, there's a way—to steal bases, that is. On this day, Maury Wills of the Los Angeles Dodgers accomplished a feat (in this case, you might as well spell it "feet"). Wills set a major league record of 100 stolen bases in a single season. He would finish this season with a total of 104.

1981 Today, Nolan Ryan became the first major league pitcher to record five no-hitters in his career. The Houston Astros ace struck out 11 and blanked the Los Angeles Dodgers, 5–0. On September 23, 1973, Ryan had entered the record books by striking out 16 Minnesota Twins batters while playing for the California Angels. That day he also got his 383rd K of the season, which set a modern major league record.

1983 The United States had never lost the America's Cup in the yacht race's 132-year history. Until today. The Australian challenger *Australia II* defeated the U.S. yacht *Liberty*, four races to three, to take the Cup away from the Americans for the first time.

1898 It wasn't a pretty win. Boston pitcher Charles A. Nichols gave up 13 hits, but still beat the Baltimore Orioles, 19–10, for his 30th win of the season. It was the seventh season he had won 30 games, and that is still a major league record.

1930 Bobby Jones had already won three major golf events of the year—the British Amateur tournament, the British Open and the U.S. Open. The only one left for a sweep of the top tournaments was the U.S. Amateur tournament in Ardmore, Pennsylvania. Sure enough, Jones won, becoming the first man to win golf's "Grand Slam." (Nowadays two pro tournaments, the Masters and the PGA Championship, have replaced British and U.S. Amateurs in golf's Grand Slam.)

1942 The New York Giants football team didn't get a single first down in their game against the Washington Redskins today, but they still won, 14–7. One of their touchdowns came on a 70-yard interception return and the other scored on a 50-yard touchdown pass. The Redskins got 14 first downs and still lost.

1953 The first field goal of Bert Rechichar's professional football career was a doozy. He set an NFL record by kicking a 56-yarder to help the Baltimore Colts defeat the Chicago Bears, 13–9. The current field goal record is 63 yards, set by Saints Tom Dempsey on November 8, 1970.

1988 Greg Louganis became the first man to win two diving gold medals in two Olympics in a row. In one of the most dramatic moments in Seoul, South Korea, Louganis today barely overtook Chinese diver Xiong Ni on his 10th, and final, dive to win the 10-meter platform event. Only a week earlier, the 28-year-old Louganis had banged his head on the springboard and had needed five stitches. Few people will forget the scene of Louganis, dripping wet, hugging his coach with tears in his eyes after winning the medal.

1941 On the last day of the 1941 baseball season, Red Sox great Ted Williams got six hits in eight times at bat. With that performance, Williams finished the season batting .406. He became only the 6th American League player since 1900 to bat over .400. No one in either league has done it since.

1951 New York Yankees pitcher Allie "The Chief" Reynolds tied an AL record by pitching his second no-hitter of the season. His superb performance against the Boston Red Sox today helped the Yanks clinch their third straight pennant.

1951 Los Angeles Rams quarterback Norm Van Brocklin completed 27 of 41 passes for 554 yards in the Rams' 54–14 win over the New York football Yankees. Van Brocklin, known as "The Flying Dutchman," set an NFL record for most yards in a game.

1968 The Atlanta Chiefs beat the San Diego Toros, 3–0, to win the first North American Soccer League (NASL) championship. Their first game ended in a 0–0 tie. The winner of the championship is the team with the highest combined score from the two games.

1969 Quarterback Joe Kapp of the Minnesota Vikings tied an NFL record by throwing seven touchdown passes in the Vikings' 52–14 victory over the Baltimore Colts. One of the referees at the game was none other than Adrian Burk, who had also tied the NFL record with seven touchdown passes in 1954 when he was a quarterback for the Philadelphia Eagles.

1894 In the last game of the baseball season, Boston center-fielder Hugh Duffy got two hits to help his team beat Pittsburgh, 6–5. Duffy finished the season with an astonishing .438 batting average. The only player in modern times who has even come close to matching Duffy's record is Rogers Hornsby, who hit .424 for the St. Louis Cardinals in 1924.

1984 Imagine how you'd feel if you set a major baseball record—and no one cared. That's what happened to Mark Langston of the Seattle Mariners. He became the first AL rookie pitcher in 29 years to strike out more than 200 batters. He finished the season with 204 K's. Normally, that would be big news. But not this year. Another rookie, hurler, Dwight Gooden of the Mets, was grabbing all the headlines by striking out 276 hitters that year.

1987 First baseman Don Mattingly of the New York Yankees hit his sixth grand slam of the season, to set a major league record. The big hit came on a one-ball, two-strike pitch from Red Sox lefty Bruce Hurst. Bam!

1988 Sometimes it pays to be a Joyner. At the Olympics in Seoul, South Korea, sisters-in-law Jackie Joyner-Kersee and Florence Griffith Joyner set records and won medals as if they were going out of style. Florence (known as "Flo-Jo") today set a world record in the 200-meter dash. Earlier in the Games, Flo-Jo set an Olympic record in the 100-meter dash. She was also a member of the American squad that won the gold medal in the 4 x 100-meter relay. Not to be outdone, Jackie set an Olympic mark in the long jump and a world record in the heptathalon. They left Seoul with five gold medals between them.

1927 New York Yankees great Babe Ruth bettered his own record of 59 home runs in one season. He slammed number 60 off pitcher Tom Zachary of the Washington Senators. Ruth's record was later broken by Roger Maris, who hit 61 homers in 1961. Both men remain in the record books, however, because Ruth set his mark in a 154-game schedule, and Maris's came in a 162-game schedule.

1972 Outfielder Roberto Clemente of the Pittsburgh Pirates smacked a pitch from Mets hurler Jon Matlack off the left-field wall for a double, and became the 11th man in history to have 3,000 hits in his career. Only three months later, on New Year's Eve, Clemente's plane crashed at sea while he was taking food and supplies to earthquake victims in Nicaragua. His body was never recovered. Clemente's historic 3,000th hit, sadly, turned out to be his last.

1973 This is the story of the famous home run that wasn't. Dave Augustine of the Pittsburgh Pirates hit what appeared to be a game-winning homer against the New York Mets in the 13th inning. The ball looked like it cleared the fence, but it really hit the top, fell back in and was declared playable. Mets outfielder Cleon Jones scooped up the ball, threw out the runner at home, and the Mets went on to win the game and the NL East Division title. Augustine never hit another home run in the majors.

1978 A new league, the Major Indoor Soccer League (MISL), was formed with franchises in six cities. The league, which played soccer in basketball and hockey arenas, would have teams in Cincinnati, Ohio; Cleveland, Ohio; Houston, Texas; New York City, New York; Philadelphia, Pennsylvania; and Pittsburgh, Pennsylvania.

1903 The first World Series game ever was held today between the Boston Red Stockings and the Pittsburgh Pirates. The Pirates started the series well, scoring a commanding 7–3 victory, but Boston ended up winning the best-of-nine game series, five games to three.

1932 Babe Ruth hit his last home run in World Series play today, and it's one of the most famous moments in the history of baseball. During Game 3 of the World Series between the New York Yankees and Chicago Cubs, the great Babe stepped to the plate. Suddenly, he pointed to centerfield, as if to say: "That's where I'm going to hit this home run." And then, with the crowd on the edges of their seats, he did.

1961 In the final game of the 1961 season, New York Yankees rightfielder Roger Maris set a record for the most home runs in a season. His 61st of the season sailed over the rightfield wall of Yankee Stadium. The stadium, often called "The House that Ruth Built," was a particularly fitting place for Maris to do this, since it was former Yankee Babe Ruth who had set the previous home run record in 1927. But Ruth did it during a shorter season, so both records are still in the record books. (See September 30, 1927.)

1977 Pelé was the greatest soccer player ever. Today, he appeared in the last game of his brilliant career. More than 75,000 fans packed Giants Stadium in New Jersey to say good-bye, and to watch Pelé play a special exhibition game. He played the first half with his former American team, the New York Cosmos, and the second half with his previous team, the Santos of Brazil.

1988 Donat Gadoury of Quebec, Canada, successfully lifted an 841-pound barbell on a Canadian television show. What made his lift astonishing is the fact that Gadoury was 81 years old.

Bob Beamon, the Olympic long jumper who broke the previous record by almost two feet. (See October 18, 1968)

←————————

1950 Can Bob Shaw of the old Chicago Cardinals football team catch touchdown passes? Shaw he can. In a game against the Baltimore Colts, he grabbed five touchdown passes to set an NFL record. Thirty-one years later, on November 22, 1981, his record was tied by Kellen Winslow of the San Diego Chargers. But no man has ever broken his mark.

1963 Los Angeles Dodgers pitcher Sandy Koufax struck out 15 of the New York Yankees in the opening game of the 60th World Series. Koufax not only won the game, he set a Series record for the most strikeouts in one game. The Dodgers swept the Yankees in four games, but Koufax's record only lasted five years. (Read on.)

1968 Ace pitcher Bob Gibson of the St. Louis Cardinals fanned 17 Detroit Tigers in the opening game of the World Series to set a World Series record for most strikeouts in one game. Behind Gibson, the Cards beat the Tigers, 4–0. The Tigers came back, though, to win the series.

1978 Bucky Dent was an unlikely hero. The New York Yankees shortstop had only hit five home runs all season. But in a special one-game playoff for the AL East Division title, Dent hit a seventh-inning homer over the high leftfield wall (called the Green Monster), in Boston's Fenway Park. Dent's homer shocked the Red Sox, and the Yankees went on to win the game, 5–4. Dent was named manager of the Yankees in 1989. (See August 18, 1989.)

1934 The characters involved sounded more like they should have been in a cartoon instead of a baseball game. The St. Louis Cardinals and the Detroit Tigers met for Game 1 of the 31st annual World Series. The Cardinals eventually won, four games to three. Stars of the series for the Cards were the pitching brothers Dizzy and Daffy Dean, and outfielder Ducky Medwick.

1951 Talk about tension. The New York Giants and Brooklyn Dodgers were playing the final game of a special best-of-three playoff to name the NL pennant winner. It was the bottom of the ninth. The Dodgers led, 4–2, but the Giants had two men on base. Up stepped Giants third baseman Bobby Thomson. Thomson hit a 315-foot shot over the left-field wall. The Giants had pulled out the game and went on to face the Yankees in the World Series. Thomson's homer is still remembered as "The shot heard around the world."

1973 Plans for a new professional football league to compete with the NFL were announced today. The World Football League (WFL) would start in 1974. Franchises were planned for Tokyo, Japan; Toronto, Canada; London, England; and Osaka, Japan; but only Toronto ever fielded a squad. The WFL folded in 1975.

1974 Frank Robinson became the first black manager in major league baseball history. Robinson signed a $175,000-a-year contract not only as manager, but also as a player for the Cleveland Indians. Also on October 3—but in 1989—former All-Pro lineman Art Shell became the first black *football* coach in modern NFL history. He took over the helm of the Los Angeles Raiders.

1955 Johnny Podres [pronounced POD-rays] of the Brooklyn Dodgers pitched an eight-hit shutout in the seventh game of the World Series to beat the New York Yankees, 2–0. It was the first time a team had won a seven-game series after losing the first two games. It's a pity there was no baseball team in San Diego at the time. Then Podres could have played for the Padres.

1980 It had to happen Sooner or later. The University of Oklahoma Sooners defeated the University of Colorado, 82–42. The 124 combined points set a NCAA Division I-A record for the highest scoring college football game. Oklahoma also set records for rushing, with 758 yards, and total offense, by gaining 875 yards.

1920   The scene was the 100-meter dash at the Olympic Games in Antwerp, Belgium. Runners Charles Paddock and Morris Kirksey of the United States were neck-and-neck with only a few feet to go. Paddock and Kirksey. Kirksey and Paddock. Suddenly, Paddock leaped forward toward the finish line, jumping several feet off the ground. His "flying finish," as it came to be known, worked. Paddock won the race by a foot.

1953   The number five was obviously lucky for the New York Yankees. Here they were on the fifth of October, in the 50th World Series, winning their fifth championship in a row. It was the first time a team had won five straight world titles. The Yankees beat the Brooklyn Dodgers, four games to two.

1963   Yogi Berra was smarter than your average batter. But in today's World Series game against the Los Angeles Dodgers, the Yankees pinch hitter failed to get a hit. Bad day or not, Yogi set several World Series records with his appearance, including most Series appearances (14), and most Series games played (75). Berra also holds four other Series marks, including most hits (71).

1974   Wouldn't it have been easier to take a cab? David Kunst arrived back at his home in Waseca, Minnesota, after walking—yes, walking—around the world. He had started out on June 20, 1970. He walked around the world with only a wagon full of his belongings pulled by a mule named Willie-Make-It.

1985   Eddie Robinson became the winningest coach in college football history. Robinson, of Grambling State University, won the 324th game of his career as his Tigers defeated Prairie View A&M in Dallas, 27–7. In his 47 years at the all-black college in Louisiana dating to 1989, Robinson lost only 125 games and tied 15.

1857 The first major national chess tournament was held in New York City. Twenty-year-old Paul Morphy of New Orleans, Louisiana, took first prize. On July 19, 1858, Morphy went to Europe and won the Grand Tournament of the First National Chess Association in England and France.

1947 The New York Yankees today defeated the Brooklyn Dodgers, 5–2, in the seventh game of what many experts call the most exciting World Series ever played. In addition to being the first Series ever televised, the Series included a one-hitter by Floyd Bevens in Game 4 and one of the greatest catches ever. Dodgers outfielder Al Gionfriddo made a one-handed grab of Joe DiMaggio's can't-miss tying home run in the sixth game. By the way, the Yanks have won three different World Series on October 6.

1985 Yankees pitcher Phil Niekro won the 300th game of his career by beating the Toronto Blue Jays, 8–0, on the last day of the season. Only two months earlier, on August 4, Tom Seaver of the Chicago White Sox had notched his 300th win, against the Yankees. It was the first time since 1890 that two pitchers had joined the 300 club in the same year. At 46, Niekro also became the oldest pitcher to throw a shutout.

Wayne Gretzky, holder of 51 NHL records, including all-time leading scorer. (See October 15, 1989)

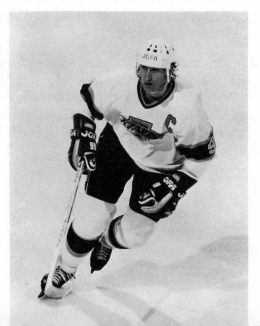

1945 The Green Bay Packers set an NFL record by scoring 41 points in the second quarter. They devastated the Detroit Lions, 51–21. The Packers scored six touchdowns in the second quarter, including four by receiver Don Hutson. Hutson further added to Detroit's embarrassment by kicking seven extra points.

1984 Walter Payton of the Chicago Bears rushed for 154 yards as the Bears beat the New Orleans Saints, 20–7. The performance brought Payton up to an even 12,400 yards gained in his career. That broke the previous mark of 12,312 set by Jim Brown in 1965. By the time Payton retired at the end of the 1987 season, he had rushed for 16,726 yards.

1916
SAD SACKS
OF SPORTS
How's this for a runaway college football game? Final score: Georgia Tech, 222, Cumberland College, 0—the most lopsided score in sports history. Tech, which rushed for 528 yards, was so successful running, they never bothered to throw a pass. Can you imagine what the score might have been if Tech had thrown a few bombs? By the way, the most lopsided *professional* football score was in a 1940 championship game between the Washington Redskins and the Chicago Bears, December 8, 1940. Chicago won, 73–0.

1904 Can you name the first American automobile race to be held on a yearly basis? No, it's not the Indianapolis 500. Beating the Indy 500 by seven years was the Vanderbilt Cup, a 284-mile race held on Long Island, New York. The first winner was George Heath, who drove a Panhard at an average speed of 52.2 mph.

1913 Christy Mathewson didn't look like much of a baseball player. Big, flabby and with a huge neck, he looked more like a wrestler than a major league pitcher. But today, the New York Giants ace went into the record books when he shut out Philadelphia, 3–0, in World Series action. Because he had pitched three shutouts in the 1905 Series, Mathewson became the first pitcher ever to have four World Series shutouts. (See October 14, 1905.)

1929 The World Series contest between the Philadelphia Athletics and the Chicago Cubs started out with a surprise. Connie Mack, manager of the A's, decided to start Howard Ehmke in the important first game. Ehmke had only pitched in 11 games all season. No matter. Ehmke struck out 13 Cubs—a World Series record at the time. He won the game, 3–1.

1956 Nearly 65,000 fans went wild at Yankee Stadium when New York Yankees pitcher Don Larsen hurled the only perfect game in World Series history. Larsen retired all 27 Brooklyn Dodgers he faced in his 2–0 victory in Game 5. Oh yes, the Yanks won this Series, too.

1957 The citizens of Brooklyn, New York, went into mourning today. Their beloved Brooklyn Dodgers announced that they were moving to Los Angeles, California. Several months earlier, on August 19, 1957, the New York Giants had announced they were on their way to San Francisco, California.

1919 The 16th World Series, lost on this day by the Chicago White Sox, remains one of baseball's darkest hours. Eight White Sox players were later accused of accepting bribes to purposely lose to the Cincinnati Reds. All eight men were barred from baseball for life. One of them, "Shoeless" Joe Jackson, may or may not have accepted bribes, but he didn't play like he was trying to lose. He tied a World Series record by collecting 12 hits. Jackson's story was recently featured in the movies *Eight Men Out* and *Field of Dreams*.

1958 The New York Yankees became the first team in 33 years to come back from being behind three games to one to win a World Series. Playing in his record-tying 10th series, Yogi Berra led the Yanks over the Milwaukee Braves.

1960 Dallas Cowboys quarterback Eddie LeBaron set an unofficial NFL record for the shortest touchdown pass in history—two inches. With only inches to go for a touchdown, LeBaron fooled the Washington Redskins defense by tossing the ball to tight end Dick Bielski in the end zone.

1971 The 68th World Series, begun today, was the first World Series to include night games. It pitted the Pittsburgh Pirates against the Baltimore Orioles. The underdog Pirates shocked the baseball world eight days later, winning four games to three. Roberto Clemente of Pittsburgh hit .414 with two home runs.

1988 Blink your eyes five times fast. You just missed Eddie Hill setting a record for the fastest time in an automobile drag race. At a competition in Baytown, Texas, Hill completed the quarter-mile race in 4.936 seconds—less time than it just took you to blink.

1920 His name is hard to spell, but what he did is even harder. Bill Wambsganss, a second baseman for the Cleveland Indians, became the only player in World Series history to turn an unassisted triple play. The Indians were battling the Brooklyn Dodgers, who had men on first and second. Wambsganss made a leaping catch for one out, then touched second for two outs and finally tagged the runner who was on his way from first base to second.

1968 Only eight days after striking out 17 batters to set a record for most strikeouts in a World Series game, Bob Gibson of the St. Louis Cardinals did it again. Even though he fanned "just" eight of the Detroit Tigers batters today, that was good enough for Gibson to set a mark for the most strikeouts in a Series—35. Unfortunately, Gibson lost the game, 4–1, and Detroit won the championship.

1982 The Milwaukee Brewers were counted out. Down two games to none in the best-of-five AL Championship Series, no one expected them to come back against the California Angels. But that's just what they did, capturing the next three games in a row to take the pennant. The Brewers became the first team in history to win a playoff series after losing the first two games. Alas, the Brewers lost to the Cardinals in the World Series, four games to three.

1987 Columbia University set a college football record today, but it wasn't one they were very proud of. The Lions lost to the Princeton University Tigers (it's a jungle out there), 38–8. It was their 35th loss in a row, more than any other Division I football team. Columbia hadn't won a game since October 15, 1983.

1890 John Owen of the United States won the 100-yard dash at the AAU Track and Field Championships in Washington, D.C. His winning time of 9.8 seconds set a U.S. record and he became the first American to run 100 yards in less than 10 seconds.

1972 What a way to lose! In the fifth game of the NL playoffs, Pittsburgh Pirates pitcher Bob Moose threw a wild pitch in the bottom of the ninth that allowed the winning run to score. When Cincinnati Reds runner George Foster ran home from third, the Reds won the game, 4–3, and took the pennant, too.

1978 It was the kind of dramatic ending to a game that baseball fans live for. Game 2 of the World Series between the Dodgers and the Yankees. Top of the ninth, Los Angeles leading, 4–3. Reggie Jackson, one of the greatest home run hitters of all time, was up for the Yanks. Two outs, two strikes. You could feel the tension filling Dodger Stadium. Pitcher Bob Welch wound up and threw the pitch. Jackson took a big swing and . . . missed. The game was over, Los Angeles won. Not to worry, the Yankees went on to win the Series anyway.

1967 The dream came crashing to an end today. It looked like the Boston Red Sox were finally going to win a World Series. After all, this was the year their star slugger, Carl Yastrzemski, had won the batting crown and led the AL in hits, runs scored, runs batted in, home runs and total bases. Yet even the great Yaz couldn't pull this one out. The Sox lost to the St. Louis Cardinals in seven exhausting games.

1986 One little pitch, and it was all over for the California Angels star reliever, Donnie Moore. It was Game 5 of the Angels AL playoff series against Boston, and Moore was one pitch away from sewing up California's first pennant ever. And then it happened. Moore gave up a home run to Dave Henderson. The Red Sox went on to win the game, 7–6, in 11 innings, and won the next two games to win the series. The Angels fans were furious with Moore. Whenever he pitched the next season, they booed. He became terribly depressed and committed suicide two years later. Few people in Southern California remember all his brilliant relief appearances. They just remember that one pitch.

1853

THE GOOD, THE BAD AND THE WEIRD

Maybe nobody ever taught heavyweight boxer Yankee Sullivan his manners. And it cost him. Sullivan was slugging it out for the heavyweight championship with John Morrissey. Between the 36th and 37th rounds, Sullivan suddenly went into the stands to punch some Morrissey supporters. When the bell rang for the next round, Sullivan didn't make it back in time and Morrissey was declared the winner. It doesn't pay to be rude.

1947 The first NHL All-Star Game was held today in Toronto, Canada. The game pitted the previous year's Stanley Cup winner, the Toronto Maple Leafs, against the stars from the league's five other teams. The All-Stars outskated the Leafs, 4–3, before a crowd of 14,169.

1960 In one of the most exciting games in World Series history, the Pittsburgh Pirates defeated the New York Yankees in the seventh game, 10–9. The two teams scored a total of 10 runs between them in the last two wild innings. Pirates second baseman Bill Mazeroski hit a game-winning 400-foot homer in the bottom of the ninth inning.

1982 On this day Jim Thorpe was awarded two Olympic gold medals, but he'd already been dead for 29 years. Actually, Thorpe, part Native American, had won medals in the decathlon and pentathlon at the 1912 Olympics in Stockholm, Sweden. The medals were taken away when it was learned that he had once received $25 for playing minor league baseball. Olympic officials said that made him a professional, not an amateur athlete. On this day, however, the International Olympic Committee finally changed its mind. The medals were presented to Thorpe's children on January 18, 1983.

1905 In a battle of teams that would one day move to California, the New York Giants (now in San Francisco) won the second World Series by beating the Philadelphia (now Oakland) Athletics, four games to one. Giants pitcher Christy Mathewson won all but one of his team's victories, pitching three stunning shutouts.

1945 That loud noise you hear is a sigh of relief. It's coming from the Chicago Cardinals of the NFL. After losing 29 games in a row, an NFL record, they finally beat the Chicago Bears, 16–7. The Cardinals didn't have much time to celebrate. They turned around and lost their last six games of the season. Oh, well.

1964 Billy Mills, part Native American, was given no chance of winning the 10,000-meter run at the Olympics in Tokyo, Japan. No one had ever heard of him. Besides, with only a short distance to go, he was in third place and there seemed to be no way he could catch the leaders. Suddenly, out of nowhere, Mills turned on the speed as he had never done before. He caught the two leaders and crossed the finish line less than a second ahead of them, to set an Olympic record. It was one of the greatest upsets in the history of the Games.

1973 It took 4 hours and 13 minutes, but the New York Mets finally beat the Oakland A's, 10–7, in a World Series game today. The 12-inning game was the longest in World Series history. The two teams also set Series marks for most pitchers used (11) and most players in one game (38). The A's went on to win the Series, though.

1925 Roger Peckinpaugh, shortstop for the Washington Senators, set a World Series record by committing eight errors
in a series. It's no wonder the Senators lost to the Pirates,
four games to three.

1968 Al Oerter of the United States became the first Olympic
athlete to win four consecutive gold medals in the same
track-and-field event. At the 19th Olympic Games, held in
Mexico City, Mexico, he won the discus throw competition.
He had also won in the discus in 1956, 1960 and 1964.

1986 It was the longest playoff game in baseball history—and
one of the most exciting. The New York Mets defeated the
Houston Astros, 7–6, in 16 innings. The Mets batters had
been powerless through the bottom of the ninth inning,
and New York was trailing, 3–0. But the Mets suddenly
tied the game. In extra innings, the Mets took the lead,
only to see the Astros tie it again, with a home run. Finally,
New York scored three times in the top of the 16th, and
held on as Houston scored twice. The Mets took the pennant and went on to win the World Series against the Boston Red Sox in similarly dramatic fashion.

1989 Wayne Gretzky broke his 51st NHL record today—and it
was his biggest. "The Great Gretzky" scored a goal in the
third period of the Los Angeles Kings' 5–4 victory over his
old teammates, the Edmonton Oilers, to become the NHL's
all-time leading scorer. That goal broke Gordie Howe's old
mark of 1,850 points. It took Howe 26 seasons to set the
record. It took Gretzky only 11 to break it.

1989 A six-man bowling team from Mobile, Alabama set a
record by knocking down 186,078 pins on 6 lanes in 24
hours. The previous record for 24 hours was set by a team
from Jennings, Missouri on November 2, 1988. The Missouri team knocked down 126,276 pins.

1912 Poor Fred Snodgrass. How do you live down blowing the World Series? Snodgrass, the New York Giants center-fielder, dropped an easy fly ball in the 10th inning of Game 8. The Red Sox scored two runs and won the Series.

1969 Do you believe in miracles? The New York Mets just per-formed a doozy. They upset the Baltimore Orioles in the World Series when they won the fifth game today, 5–3. During their first seven years in the NL, the Mets had been the laughingstock of baseball. Even this year, the Mets had been 9½ games out of first place in the NL East as late as August 14. Then, the not-so-laughable Mets won 38 of their last 49 games.

1973 At age 67, Victor Morely Lawson of Great Britain decided to try a new career: horse racing. He won his very first race today, and became the oldest rookie jockey ever to win a horse race.

**1985
SPORTS
QUIZ** The NL Championship was on the line. Two out, top of the ninth inning, men on second and third, and the St. Louis Cardinals were trailing the Los Angeles Dodg-ers, 5–4. Up to the plate walked St. Louis slugger Jack Clark, who belted a three-run homer. The Cards not only won the game, 7–5, but they went on to the World Series, which they lost to Kansas City in seven games. Kansas City and St. Louis are on opposite ends of the same state. Can you name it?

A: Missouri. There is also a Kansas City, Kansas, but it is a much smaller city without any pro-sports teams.

1948 The Chicago (now Phoenix) Cardinals flattened the New York Giants, 63–35, in an NFL game that set two major records. The combined 98 points scored was the most ever in an NFL game, although the mark has since been broken. And Chicago kicker Pat Harder established a mark for the most extra points in a game. He kicked nine, a mark that has been matched twice, but never broken.

1954 Adrian Burk became the second man in NFL history to throw seven touchdown passes in one game. He completed 23 of 33 passes for 257 yards in leading the Philadelphia Eagles over the Washington Redskins, 49–21.

1989 Japan beat the United States volleyball team in the final game of a three-game series in Japan. It was the first time that Japan had beaten the Americans in 43 games, dating back to 1984.

1989 The pregame activities at Game 3 of the Oakland-San Francisco World Series caused more excitement than any game ever could. Minutes before the game was supposed to start, a major earthquake hit Northern California, crumbling buildings, killing people and forcing the game to be postponed 10 days. When play finally resumed, the A's swept the Series.

1924 Harold "Red" Grange of the University of Illinois had what many consider the greatest game by one man in the history of college football today. Against the University of Michigan, he ran for a touchdown four times in the game's first 12 minutes, touching the ball just six times. Later in the game he ran for another touchdown and passed for one and rushed for a total of 402 yards. Not surprisingly, Illinois won the game, 39–14.

1956 The NFL voted to outlaw the use of walkie-talkies in huddles. A number of coaches had been using them to relay plays to their quarterbacks. The problem was, opposing teams were buying their own walkie-talkies and listening in.

1968 When long jumper Bob Beamon of the United States set a world record, he wasn't kidding around. At the Olympic Games held in Mexico City, Mexico, Beamon jumped 29 feet, 2 1/2 inches. That was almost two full feet further than the previous mark. When Beamon's record was announced, he collapsed on the ground and began to cry. Beamon's jump is still considered one of the greatest accomplishments in the history of sports. In more than 20 years since that jump, no one has even come close to matching that mark.

1977 Reg-GIE! Reg-GIE! With the New York Yankees leading the World Series three games to two, and thousands of fans chanting his name, New York outfielder Reggie Jackson stepped up to the plate against Los Angeles Dodgers reliever Charlie Hough. BOOM! Jackson got his third home run of the game and, counting one from the game before, his fourth homer in a row on only four swings. Thanks to Reggie, the Yankees took the Series.

1960 Reggie Fleming, a rookie forward for the Chicago Black-hawks, became good friends with the penalty box in a game against the New York Rangers. Fleming received 37 minutes in penalties to set an NHL record (which has since been broken). The old record of 30 minutes had been set by Ted Lindsay of the Detroit Red Wings on October 12, 1952.

1968 Bill Toomey, a 29-year-old English teacher from California, was in the lead going into the 8th event of the Olympic decathlon competition. (There are 10 different track-and-field events in the decathlon.) Then came the most important moment of Toomey's career. In the pole vault, he had missed the opening height of 11 feet, $9^{1}/_{4}$ inches twice. If he missed once more he would be eliminated and would lose the gold medal. Toomey didn't miss. He cleared the bar and went on to make his best vault ever, 13 feet, $9^{1}/_{2}$ inches. Toomey got his gold medal, and set an Olympic record in the process.

1976 Designated hitter Dan Driessen of the Cincinnati Reds had a single, a double, a home run and a walk, and the Reds moved one step closer to sweeping the World Series from the New York Yankees. Their 6–2 win over the Yanks today gave them a 3–0 lead in the Series. Jim Mason's homer for New York in the seventh would be the only home run for the Yanks in the entire Series, which the Reds did indeed sweep.

1987 Haven't we seen this before? After being fired by New York Yankees owner George Steinbrenner for the fourth time in 1985, shazam! Billy returned again. Martin was hired to be manager of the New York Yankees for the *fifth* time. Just like the other times, however, Martin was soon fired. This time he lasted only until June 23, 1988.

1894 Football's first attempt at an organized professional league ended today as a terrible flop. The American Association of Professional Football Clubs cut its first and only season short by several months. The League had already lost $2,000, which in 1894 was a lot of money. The owners decided to end the season before they had no money left at all.

1988 Pitcher Orel Hershiser of the Los Angeles Dodgers became the hero of the World Series. Tonight he went nine innings and allowed only four hits and two runs to win the fifth, and final, game of the Series, 5–2, over the Oakland A's. Hershiser, who had nine strikeouts, had also won the second game, 6–0.

1931
SPORTS
PROFILE
Mickey Mantle is born in Spavinaw, Oklahoma. They say the great ones played their best games when it counted. Well, that was certainly true of this New York Yankees slugger. Whenever the Yankees were in the World Series—and in the 1950s, that was most of the time—Mantle came through with the key hits. He set a number of World Series records that still stand. Take a deep breath and read the list: most runs scored, most extra-base hits, most total bases, most home runs, most RBIs, most walks, most strikeouts. Whew! In 1974, Mantle entered the Baseball Hall of Fame.

1956 George Blanda of the Chicago Bears missed his first extra point attempt in five years when the kick sailed off to the left. Blanda had made 156 points-after-touchdown before the miss, to set an NFL record. Blanda's miss really didn't matter, though, as the Bears ripped the Baltimore Colts, 58–27.

1964 Soviet gymnastic sensation Larissa Latynina took the silver medal in the women's all-around competition at the Olympics in Tokyo, Japan. In three Olympic Games from 1956 to 1964, Larissa collected 18 medals. No other athlete has ever won that many medals in the Olympics.

1964 While Larissa Latynina was setting Olympic marks in gymnastics, runner Abebe Bikila of Ethiopia was doing the same in the marathon. Bikila today became the first athlete to win the marathon twice. After becoming the first gold medalist in the event from a black African nation, and smashing the world record in 1960, he chopped 13.05 minutes off his own mark this year in Tokyo.

1973 The Oakland A's defeated the New York Mets, 5–2, to take the World Series four games to three. Bert Campaneris and Reggie Jackson each hit a two-run homer in the third inning to give the A's the win. Jackson was beginning to be known as Mr. October because of his post-season play.

1979 Roy Green of the St. Louis Cardinals football team was deep in his own territory to take the Dallas Cowboys kickoff. Green caught the ball six yards into the end zone, but instead of taking a touchback, he decided to see how far he could run it out. How about 106 yards—all the way for a touchdown? He did it, and tied a record for the longest kickoff return.

1950 The Los Angeles Rams trounced the Baltimore Colts, 70–27, setting two NFL records and tying two more in the process. The Rams 70-point score was the highest ever recorded by an NFL team in the regular season, as was their 10 extra points. The records tied were most touchdowns (10) and most points after touchdown by one kicker (9). It was the Colts' 11th straight loss, and it was just one of many times the Rams would score a bundle. The next week, they beat the Detroit Lions, 65–24, and on December 3, they walloped the Green Bay Packers, 51–14.

1988 Olympic gold medal winners Janet Evans and Matt Biondi were named coswimmers of the year by United States Swimming, the governing body for the sport. In the 1988 Olympics, in Seoul, South Korea, Evans had won three golds and set a world record in the 400-meter freestyle. Biondi won seven medals, more than any other American at the Games.

1989 Man against machine. World chess champion Gary Kasparov won a special two-match exhibition in New York City today against a very tough competitor—a computer. The computer, named Deep Thought, had beaten a number of chess champions previously, but Kasparov was the highest-rated player in the history of chess.

1884 Long before there were the New York Mets there were...
the New York Mets. The old Mets belonged to the American Association. Today, they were defeated by Providence
of the National League, 6–0, in an early version of the
World Series. The old Mets soon folded. The new Mets
joined the NL in 1962.

1981 Los Angeles pitching ace Fernando Valenzuela had an
unusually bad day in the third game of the World Series
against the Yankees. He gave up four runs, nine hits and
seven walks. But the Dodgers somehow held on to beat
New York, 5–4, and went on to win the Series, four games
to two.

**1940
SPORTS
PROFILE** What? An athlete with only one name? The great Pelé,
whose real name is Edson Arantes do Nascimento, was
born in the South American nation of Brazil today.
Since his youth, he took the nickname "Perola Negra"
(Black Pearl), which became shortened to Pelé. In 18
years as a pro soccer player in Brazil, he scored more
than 1,216 goals—the most in soccer history. When he
signed with the New York Cosmos of the NASL in
1975, most Americans hadn't heard of him. But they
soon would. Pelé's contract paid him a record $7 million over three years, and made him the highest-paid
athlete in any sport. The Cosmos won the NASL title
after Pelé joined them. Pelé is credited with almost
single-handedly popularizing the sport of soccer in the
United States. He was so famous throughout the
world, that a war in the African nation of Biafra was
stopped for two days while he visited.

1857 The first soccer club in the world, the Sheffield Football Club, was founded in England. Six years later, the first soccer league, the Football Association of England, was formed. In Britain, and most other countries of the world, soccer is known as football.

1891 Forty contestants started in the first international six-day bicycle race in New York City's Madison Square Garden. Only six men finished. The grueling race was too much for the rest of the contestants. Today's winner was William ("Plugger Bill") Martin of Detroit, Michigan, who rode one of those old-fashioned bikes with the huge front wheel. Martin covered almost 1,500 miles in the 6 days.

1908 George Robertson became the first American to win the Vanderbilt Cup auto race on Long Island, New York. He covered the 258-mile course in just over four hours, at an average speed of 64.3 mph.

1936 The New York Giants took advantage of an interference call against the Philadelphia Eagles to score a last-minute touchdown and win the game, 21–17. As soon as the game was over, two Eagle players, angry over the interference call, surrounded the referee who had made it, and charged him. Fortunately, the ref wasn't hurt, although his shirt was torn to pieces. Talk about unsportsmanlike conduct!

1981 In the 12th New York City Marathon, Alberto Salazar, originally from Cuba, set a record for the fastest time— 2 hours, 8 minutes, 13 seconds. Meanwhile, Allison Roe of New Zealand went into the record books with the best time for a woman, 2 hours, 25 minutes, 28 seconds.

1986 Impossible. It couldn't happen. There was no way the New York Mets could come back from a 5–3 deficit with two out in the bottom of the 10th inning. It looked like the Boston Red Sox were going to win the sixth game of the World Series, and their first championship since 1918. And then the unthinkable happened. The Mets scored three runs on three hits, a wild pitch and a Boston error. And oh, what an error! Red Sox first baseman Bill Buckner let an easy Mookie Wilson ground ball trickle through his legs, which let Ray Knight score the winning run for New York. The Mets won today's game, and took the Series.

1964
SAD SACKS
OF SPORTS
Jim Marshall must have been pretty excited. The Minnesota Vikings defensive end had just scooped up a San Francisco fumble and run it back 61 yards into the end zone. Only, Jim, that's the *wrong* end zone! Instead of a Viking touchdown, it's a safety for the 49ers. You're lucky, Jim, the Vikes held on to win, anyway.

1912 In a college football game today, the University of Georgia Bulldogs beat the University of Alabama Crimson Tide on a sneaky play. The Bulldogs dressed one of their receivers in street clothes and then had him run onto the field when no one was looking. The Tide didn't even realize he was there, and didn't defend him. Bet you can guess what happened—they threw the ball to the receiver and no one could stop him.

1980 Baltimore Colts quarterback Bert Jones became very friendly with the field today. The St. Louis Cardinals sacked him 12 times, for a new NFL record, and won the game, 17–10. In the Colts' previous seven games, Jones had been sacked only nine times altogether.

1985 Rookie center Patrick Ewing of the New York Knicks made his NBA debut against the Philadelphia 76ers at New York City's Madison Square Garden. Ewing scored 18 points and grabbed 6 rebounds, but the Knicks still lost, 99–89. As a player at Georgetown University, Ewing had been one of the greatest college stars in the game. With the Knicks, he went on to be named Rookie of the Year at the end of the season.

1974 It could have been a scene from a Hollywood movie. On the last play of the game, the New England Patriots trailed the Minnesota Vikings, 14–10, but the Patriots had the ball on the Minnesota 10. Quarterback Jim Plunkett hit Bob Windsor on the two-yard line. Windsor had to make it into the end zone or the Pats would lose. With a desperate leap toward the goal line, he escaped Vikings free safety Paul Krause, who lunged at his legs. Windsor did score the winning touchdown, but at a high price. He tore the ligaments in his knee. He would miss the rest of the season and would never play the same again.

1984 Running back Rueben Mayes rushed for 357 yards to lead Washington State University over the University of Oregon, 50–41. Mayes's total established a college record, beating the mark of 356 set by Eddie Lee Ivery. (See November 11, 1978.)

1928   The first organized men's field hockey game in the United States was played on this day. The Westchester Field Hockey Club of Rye, New York, defeated the Germantown (Pennsylvania) Cricket Club, 2–1. Field hockey is similar to ice hockey, except that it is played outdoors on grass with 11 players on a team.

1962   He was known as "The Bald Eagle." Eagle, because of his great eye as a passer. Bald, because . . . well, you can figure that out yourself. Veteran New York Giants quarterback Y.A. Tittle today became only the fourth man in NFL history to throw seven touchdown passes in the same game. The Giants beat the Washington Redskins, 49–34. Less than two months later, Tittle threw six touchdown passes in a game against the Dallas Cowboys.

1981   Sweet revenge. After losing the World Series to the New York Yankees in both 1977 and 1978, the Los Angeles Dodgers finally got even. They won the 1981 Series, four games to two. For a while, it had looked like the Yankees would win again, however. They won the first two games of the Series before losing all the rest.

1984   The New York City Marathon looked a little like a meeting of the United Nations. Grete Waitz of Norway was the women's winner, and Orlando Pizzolato of Italy took the men's crown. Both runners won the Marathon again the next year, and in 1986 Waitz would again be the first woman, with another Italian man, Gianni Poli, winning the race for the men.

1950 The Los Angeles Rams scored 41 points in one quarter to wallop the Detroit Lions, 65–24. The only good news for Detroit was the fact that kickoff returner Wally Triplett set an NFL record for kickoff return yards with 294.

1973 The Juice was on the loose. Star Buffalo running back O.J. "Juice" Simpson set two new NFL records as he rushed for 157 yards in a game against the Kansas City Chiefs. Simpson's 39 carries broke an NFL mark set in 1966. Simpson also became the first man to rush for more than 1,000 yards halfway through the season (after seven games). He went on to set an NFL record for most yards in a season— 2,003 yards.

1908
SPORTS
QUIZ

At the Olympic Games in London, England, Ulrich Salchow of Sweden won the gold medal, and two other Swedes took the silver and the bronze in the first Olympic figure skating competition. Salchow invented a jump that is now named after him. To do it, you take off from one skate, do a complete turn in the air and land on the opposite skate. Oddly, though, the figure skating event was held in the *Summer* Olympics, and not the Winter. Can you guess why?

A: There *were* no Winter Olympics yet. The first Winter Games were held in Chamonix, France, in 1924.

1954 BUZZZZZZZZ! That's the sound of the 24-second clock going off for the first time in a basketball game. Until 1954, professional basketball teams could hold onto the ball as long as they wanted before shooting. That made for some very low scoring—and boring—games. In this historic game, Rochester beat the Boston Celtics, 98–95.

1988 Quarterback Doug Flutie of the New England Patriots got his revenge. Playing against the mighty Chicago Bears, the team that had traded Flutie the season before, he passed for four touchdowns. The Patriots walloped the Bears, 30–7. At the start of the season, Flutie had been only New England's third-string quarterback.

Pelé, the most popular soccer player ever. (See October 23, Sports Profile)

1948 In a football game against the Boston Yanks, "Slingin'" Sammy Baugh, the quarterback for the Washington Redskins, set a record that stands to this day. He completed 24 passes and gained 446 yards. That's an average gain of 18.58 yards. No one has beaten that average in more than 40 years.

1959 A record college football winning streak came to an end today when the University of Nebraska Cornhuskers defeated the University of Oklahoma Sooners, 25–21. It was the Sooners first loss in their conference in 75 games.

1971 The Houston Oilers played a Halloween trick on the Cincinnati Bengals. They held the Bengals to a total of *minus* 52 yards in their 10–6 victory. No, the Bengals weren't facing the wrong direction. It's just that every time they tried a run or short pass, the Oilers tackled them behind the line of scrimmage.

1986 Dr. J announced he would hang up his stethoscope—er, his basketball sneakers—at the end of the season. That's right, basketball great Julius Erving was about to retire after 16 seasons. Whether playing for the New York Nets of the old ABA or the Philadelphia 76ers of the NBA, Erving was one of the greatest players in the history of both leagues.

1989 Nine years after his last gymnastics competition, gymnast Kurt Thomas announced he was ready for a surprise comeback. Thomas, who in 1978 had become the first American male to win a world gymnastics championship, announced he would try to make the U.S. team for the 1992 Olympics in Barcelona, Spain.

NOVEMBER

1959 It's hard to imagine, but before this day, hockey goalies never wore masks. Their faces were totally unprotected against the speeding pucks that shot at them like bullets. But Montreal Canadiens goalie Jacques Plante changed all that. After getting badly cut early in a game against the New York Rangers, he returned wearing a mask he had been using in practice. With it on, Plante stopped 28 of 29 Ranger shots. The mask stayed.

1913
SPORTS
QUIZ

It was a shocker. Army had one of the best college football teams in the country. Few people had ever heard of a university named Notre Dame. But on this day, the Fighting Irish outbattled Army, 35–13, and popularized the forward pass. Before this, teams usually ran with the ball, or made short, quick laterals. Notre Dame became the first team to rely heavily on long passes. A new hero was born—Notre Dame end Knute Rockne (pronounced "Newt ROCK-nee"). Under his guidance as coach from 1918-1930, Notre Dame became a national powerhouse. His life story was later turned into a movie, *Knute Rockne: All American.* Can you name the famous actor who played George Gipp, a player on Rockne's team, in the film?

A: Former President Ronald Reagan played "The Gipper."

Gordie Howe, the superstar who held hockey's four most important records. (See November 10 1963)

1895 The first official auto race in the United States was held in Chicago, Illinois. Six cars entered the 52-mile race along the city streets from Chicago to the suburb of Evanston. Because of a heavy snowstorm, none of the cars finished. The race was rescheduled for Thanksgiving Day. (See November 28, 1895.)

1969 In an air battle, the New Orleans Saints defeated the St. Louis Cardinals, 51–42. Quarterbacks Bill Kilmer of the Saints and Charlie Johnson of the Cards tossed six touchdown passes each. The 12 touchdown passes in one game set a new NFL record.

1986 Grete Waitz of Norway won the women's division in the 17th annual New York City Marathon. Her time was 2 hours, 28 minutes, 6 seconds. It was her eighth victory in the event. But the biggest star of the marathon was a man who took more than 98 hours to complete the race. That was Bob Wieland, a legless veteran of the Vietnam War, who used his arms to pull himself along the route. It took him four days to complete the 26-mile, 385-yard route.

1961 The Boston Patriots beat the Dallas Texans, 28–21, thanks to the defense of an anonymous Boston football fan. On the last play of the game, Dallas quarterback Cotton Davidson threw the ball into the end zone toward one of his receivers. A defender batted it away, and the game was over. Unfortunately, the defender turned out to be a Boston fan who had snuck onto the field, and immediately ran away before the refs saw him.

1968 Charlie West of the Minnesota Vikings knew which direction to run when he got the ball—toward the goal line. In a game against the Washington Redskins, West took a punt on his own two-yard line and ran it back past a bunch of Washington defenders for a touchdown. The 98–yard punt return tied an NFL record that had been set 35 years earlier by Cincinnati's Gil LeFebvre.

1973 Jay Miller of Brigham Young University set a college football record by catching 22 passes for 263 yards in a game, a 56–21 win over the University of New Mexico. No player had ever pulled in that many balls in one contest, and no one has done so since.

Grete Waitz, the only woman to win the New York City Marathon eight times. (See November 2, 1986)

1947 Ding! The boxing match has begun. Ding! The boxing match is over. One of the shortest fights in history took place today. Mike Collins knocked down Pat Brownson after only four seconds of their Minnesota Golden Gloves bout. The Golden Gloves is a competition for amateurs. A pro would have lasted at least *five* seconds.

1960 Wilt Chamberlain may have been one of the greatest shooters in the history of basketball. But not from the free throw line. On this day, playing for the Philadelphia Warriors, Wilt missed all 10 of his free throws to set an NBA record. In 1967, he almost tied his own sad mark by missing nine attempts from the line.

1965 Don't ever get into a car with Lee Ann Roberts Breedlove and her husband, Craig. That couple likes to drive fast. Really fast. On this day, Lee Ann set a land speed record for women when she drove her rocket-powered car 308.5 mph. Eleven days later, Craig drove the same car more than 600 miles per hour to set a new record.

1973 The Chicago Bears sent Green Bay packing, 31–17, in one of the most embarrassing games in the Packers glorious history. Chicago limited Green Bay to *minus* 12 yards in passing. It was the Bears' best defensive show in 28 years.

1989 Once Martina Navratilova and Pam Shriver were doubles partners in tennis. Today they were rivals. Navratilova beat Shriver for her 24th straight win to advance to the semifinals of the Virginia Slims tournament in Worcester, Massachusetts.

1904 It was one of the weirdest—and wettest—touchdowns in college football history. Giant winds blew an Oklahoma A & M (now known as Oklahoma State University) punt backward, out of OSU's own end zone and into a creek behind the stadium. Halfback Ed Cook of the University of Oklahoma jumped into the water, picked up the ball, and swam back to the stadium. He ran into the OSU end zone for a touchdown. Believe it or not, the touchdown counted. The Sooners beat Oklahoma State, 75–0.

1911 Calbraith P. Rodgers became the first man to fly a plane across the United States. It took him 49 days to make the flight from New York City to Pasadena, California, in a plane designed by the Wright brothers. Rodgers made some crash landings along the way. Today, the same trip would take less than six hours and involve, one hopes, no crash landings.

1966 He could run. He could pass. He could set records. Brigham Young University quarterback Virgil Carter passed for five touchdowns today, as the Cougars trounced Texas Western University, 53–33. Carter passed for 513 yards and ran for another 86 yards. His total 599 yards of offense set a college football record.

1989 Few people expected Juma Ikangaa of the African nation of Tanzania to be the first man across the finish line of the New York City Marathon. Fewer still expected him to set a course record. But that's what he did, shaving a full 12 seconds off the mark set by Alberto Salazar in 1981.

1960 The Cleveland Browns were lucky to get 13 points in their 17–13 loss to the New York Giants. Even with Jim Brown, one of the greatest runners ever, Cleveland was held to a total of six yards rushing. Add that to only 89 yards passing, and the Browns became one of the few football teams in history to gain less than 100 yards in a game.

1971 Paul Kaliades of Columbia University kicked a 34-yard field goal with 54 seconds left to beat Dartmouth College, 31–29, to end Dartmouth's 15-game winning streak. It was the seventh time in as many games that Columbia had won or lost a game by a margin of no more than three points.

1972 Ultimate Frisbee™ is a team sport that's similar to soccer or football only it's played with a Frisbee™ instead of a ball. The first official Ultimate Frisbee™ game was played at New Brunswick, New Jersey today. A squad from Rutgers University beat Princeton University, 29–27. Exactly 103 years earlier, the two schools had played the first intercollegiate football game in the United States. Rutgers won that game too, six touchdowns to four.

1987 The Indiana Pacers lost to the Philadelphia 76ers, 108–95, but Pacers coach Jack Ramsay must have felt proud, anyway. He set a record for the most games coached in the NBA, 1,559. The old record had been held by Dick Motta.

1968 The Philadelphia Flyers were grounded by the St. Louis Blues, 8–0, in a lopsided NHL game. All but two of the goals were scored by the Blues' Red Berenson. But his six goals weren't quite good enough to set an NHL mark. That record is held by Joe Malone, who scored seven goals for the old Quebec Bulldogs in 1920. Berenson, by the way, later coached the Blues. (See January 31, 1920.)

1984 Running a 24-hour race would be too exhausting for most people—especially for those who have heart conditions. But Joe Michaels of Queens, New York, wasn't most people. There he was running in a 24-hour race in Queens— just four years after having double-bypass surgery on his heart. (Bypass surgery is a major operation for people who are in danger of having a heart attack.) What's most amazing is that Michaels had rarely run before his heart problems began. Michaels finished in the middle of the pack. He dedicated the race to his 11-year-old son, Jason, who was born with a birth defect called spina bifida.

1913 It was a play Clair Scott would like to forget. The punter for the Indiana University Hoosiers was trying to kick the ball out of the Hoosiers' end zone in a college football game against the University of Iowa Hawkeyes. Unfortunately, a strong 50-mph wind got hold of the ball and blew it back *into* the Hoosiers' end zone. Leo Dick of Iowa ran under the ball and caught it for a touchdown. It was just one more embarrassment for Indiana, which lost the game, 60–0.

1959 Elgin Baylor of the Minneapolis Lakers set a new NBA record by scoring 64 points in his team's victory over the Boston Celtics. Baylor shattered the old mark of 63 set by Joe Fulks of the Philadelphia Warriors in 1949. That's nothing compared to the record set less than three years later by Wilt Chamberlain. He scored 100 points in a single game. (See March 2, 1962.)

1970 It's up. It's up. It's *still* up. And it's good! Tom Dempsey of the New Orleans Saints kicked the longest field goal in pro football history. His 63-yarder with no time left on the clock lifted the Saints past the Detroit Lions, 19–17. Dempsey was born with only half a right foot.

1978 Imagine playing for both sides in the same basketball game. That happened to three players for the Philadelphia 76ers and the New Jersey Nets. Today, the Sixers beat the Nets, 137–133, but the Nets protested some calls by the referees after the game was over. NBA officials ruled the last 18 minutes had to be repeated. By the time those minutes were replayed, three players had been traded to the other team, so they played the last 18 minutes for the other side.

1895 You've come a long way, baby. The first U.S. Women's Amateur Golf Championship was held at the Meadowbrook Club in Hempstead, New York. Unfortunately, history does not record the winner's first name. She is listed only as Mrs. Charles B. Brown.

1912 The college football career of a young man named Dwight D. Eisenhower came to a close today. Playing for the U.S. Military Academy, Eisenhower broke his kneecap in a game against Tufts University and decided to give up the sport. Ike, as he was known, had better luck in the Army. He commanded the American troops during World War II, and later became President of the United States.

1985 Division I schools like Notre Dame, Oklahoma and Southern Cal grab most of the headlines, but there are hundreds of tiny schools that play in different divisions of the NCAA. Some of their athletes have racked up impressive records, too. Take Joe Dudek. Playing for Plymouth State, a Division III college in New Hampshire, he set three NCAA scoring records in one game. Dudek rushed for the 76th touchdown of his career, scored his 79th touchdown all told and picked up his 474th career point in Plymouth's 43–7 win over Curry College of Milton, Massachusetts.

1989 The Milwaukee Bucks defeated the Seattle SuperSonics, 155–154, after five overtime periods. The game took 4 hours and 17 minutes to complete, making it the third longest contest in NBA history. The longest: Indiana's six-overtime 75–73 win over Rochester on January 6, 1951.

1928 It was halftime at the college football game of the year, and Notre Dame University trailed the U.S. Military Academy, 6–0. In the Notre Dame lockerroom, coach Knute Rockne delivered one of football's most famous and inspirational speeches to fire up his team. "Win one for the Gipper!" Rockne told his players. He was referring to the team's beloved star quarterback, George Gipp, who had died of pneumonia eight years earlier at the age of 25. Notre Dame came out of the locker room determined, and won, 12–6.

1963 A grand slam...in hockey? Well, sort of. Gordie Howe of the Detroit Red Wings captured hockey's "grand slam" by breaking yet another of the NHL's four most important records. Howe's goal today against the Montreal Canadiens was the 545th of his career, breaking the mark set by Maurice Richard of the Canadiens. Earlier, Howe had set records for the most points, the most assists and the most games played in a career.

1985 Few things are more exciting than the sight of a wide receiver catching a short pass and going all the way for a touchdown. The Philadelphia Eagles had their backs against the wall in an overtime game against the Atlanta Falcons. With the ball on their one-yard line, the Eagles were in danger of becoming the first team to lose an overtime game by a safety. Then, quarterback Ron Jaworski threw a pass to wide receiver Mike Quick, who lived up to his last name. Quick ran all the way downfield to become the sixth player in the history of the NFL to take a pass in for a 99-yard touchdown.

1988 Pitcher Orel Hershiser, the Los Angeles Dodgers World Series star, won the NL Cy Young Award today. He received all 24 first place votes from the sportswriters. Hershiser became the ninth man in NL history to win the pitching award unanimously.

1868 The first indoor amateur track-and-field meet was held, at a skating rink in New York City. Spiked shoes were worn by the contestants for the first time. Oh yes, the ice had been removed and was replaced with a regular track.

1911 Harvard University was a football powerhouse in 1911. Which is why many people regard its loss today to the tiny Carlisle Indian School as one of the greatest upsets in college football history. As the name suggests, the Carlisle school was attended by Native Americans. Its star was Jim Thorpe, one of the greatest athletes of all time. Carlisle beat Harvard, 18–15.

1978 How could you not like Georgia Tech tailback Eddie Lee Ivery? He was an awesome runner. In a game against the Air Force Academy, Ivery rushed for 356 yards, including touchdowns of 80, 73 and 57 yards. That broke the NCAA single-game rushing record set by Eric Allen of Michigan State University in 1971.

1988 The University of Dallas beat John Brown University, 76–68, to finally end college basketball's longest losing streak. Before beating John Brown, Dallas hadn't won in 86 games, dating back to November 11, 1985.

1892 William "Pudge" Heffelfinger became the first professional football player today. He was paid $500 for his first game with the Allegheny Athletic Association. Football had previously been played only by college players and amateurs. Today Heffelfinger recovered a fumble by his opponents, the Pittsburgh Athletic Club, and returned it for the game's only touchdown. At the time, touchdowns were worth four points. Allegheny won, 4–0.

1920 Judge Kenesaw Mountain Landis was elected major league baseball's first commissioner. Landis ruled for 23 years, enacting a number of rules changes to speed up the game. His most famous act, though, was to ban eight Chicago White Sox players for throwing the 1919 World Series. (See October 9, 1919.)

1955 There wasn't exactly a huge crowd for today's college football game between Washington State University and San Jose State University. In fact, only one fan bothered to show up. The temperature was around zero degrees and the winds were fierce. It was the smallest "crowd" ever to watch an NCAA football game.

1964 It's a jet. It's a car. It's a jet-car! Whatever you called it, it was fast. Paula Murphy of California set a women's land speed record when she drove her 10,000-horsepower jet car 226.37 mph on Utah's Bonneville Salt Flats.

1875 You call this football? Harvard University defeated Yale University today in the first "football" game. The game was played by some rather strange rules, known as the "Boston" Rules. The field was 140 yards, including end zones, not 120. There were 15 men on a side instead of 11, and the ball was flat, rather than . . . well, football-shaped. These rules didn't last long.

1964 Forward Bob Pettit of the St. Louis Hawks became the first NBA player to score 20,000 points in a career. By the time he retired after 11 seasons, Petit had scored 20,880 points. It may not seem like much compared to the 37,639 Kareem Abdul-Jabbar had when he retired in 1989, but it was impressive in its time.

1966 Quarterback Don Meredith of the Dallas Cowboys completed 21 of 29 passes for 406 yards to lead the Cowboys to a thrilling 31–30 victory over the Washington Redskins. Meredith completed four of five crucial passes in a desperate last-minute drive to set up the game-winning field goal. "Dandy Don," as he was known, later became a commentator on ABC's *Monday Night Football.*

1985 Lynette Woodard, the first woman to play for the Harlem Globetrotters, the zany pro basketball team, made her U.S. debut tonight. She scored seven points in a game in Spokane, Washington, as the Globetrotters trotted all over the Washington Generals, 81–65.

1987 The Washington Bullets hardly needed to hit any field goals in their 108–101 win over the New York Knicks. The Bullets made 60 free throws in 69 attempts. That broke a 38-year-old NBA record for most free throws attempted in one game.

1889 America's first golf course was opened in Yonkers, New York. The six-hole course was built on a cow pasture. Fortunately, all the cows had been removed long before the first golfer teed off.

1893 The University of the South had only 97 students, and just 12 players on its entire football squad. But today, that team won its fifth game in six days, blanking Mississippi State University, 12–0. The five earlier games had been shutouts, as well. This is one case where quality really was more important than quantity.

1943 Here's a football record that will probably *never* be broken. That's because it was set in the days when players often played both offense and defense. In a 42–20 victory over the Detroit Lions, Washington Redskins quarterback *and* defensive end Sammy Baugh became the only man in NFL history to pass for four touchdowns and also intercept four passes. Unless quarterbacks start playing defense again, no one will ever beat that record.

1943 Quarterback Sid Luckman of the Chicago Bears passed for a record 453 yards and set another mark for touchdown passes by tossing seven. He led the Bears over the New York Giants, 56–7. Four other quarterbacks have thrown seven touchdown passes in a game since, but no one has ever thrown more.

1971 It was a battle of field goals. The Washington Redskins kicked five field goals and the Chicago Bears had three to tie an NFL record of eight in one game. The Bears may have lost the field goal contest, but they won the game, 16–15. They scored the only touchdown, on a 40-yard run by Cyril Pinder.

1949 The football team from Dewey High School in Wisconsin did something today that they hadn't done in years—they won a game. Dewey's 31–20 victory over Avoca High School snapped a 92-game losing streak.

1950 If you remember the entry from January 18, 1958, you'll recall that Willie O'Ree was the first black player in the NHL. But the first black man to play for any professional hockey team was Arthur Dorrington. He signed with the Atlantic City (New Jersey) Seagulls of the Eastern Amateur League today. He played for them in 1950 and 1951.

1964 Willie Brown may have been the greatest cornerback ever to play football. In 16 seasons in the NFL, most of them with the Oakland Raiders, Brown intercepted at least one pass each year. That's a record. Today, he tied another league record by intercepting four passes in one game for the Denver Broncos. In Super Bowl XI, played in 1977, he became the second player in a Super Bowl to return an interception for a touchdown.

1940 In one of college football's greatest blunders, Cornell University scored a game-winning touchdown against Dartmouth College...on a *fifth* down. Referee Red Friesell miscounted and didn't realize Cornell had already used its four downs. Cornell scored a touchdown on the extra play. Cornell later agreed to forfeit the game, since the play should not have been allowed.

1957 The University of Oklahoma's football team had put together an amazing 47-game winning streak. It ended, though, on this cold day in Norman, Oklahoma. Notre Dame quarterback Bobby Williams faked a handoff to Nick Pietrosante and tossed a pitchout to Dick Lynch for the day's only score, with four minutes left in the game. The final score: Notre Dame 7, Oklahoma 0. The Sooners' 47-game streak has never been matched.

1960 Los Angeles Lakers forward Elgin Baylor broke his own NBA record for most points in a basketball game. He scored 71 points against the New York Knicks at New York City's Madison Square Garden. Baylor's record was later shattered by Wilt Chamberlain well before Chamberlin's famous 100-point performance.

Paula Murphy, the driver who set the women's land speed record. (See November 12, 1964)

1954 Boxer Jimmy Carter became the first man to win the world lightweight title three times when he knocked out Paddy DeMarco. Carter is not to be mistaken for former President Jimmy Carter who lost his title of President on election night, 1980, when he was knocked out by Ronald Reagan.

1956 The Syracuse University Orangemen beat arch-rival Colgate University, 61–7, and never once had to punt. Why should they? They had brilliant All-America running back Jim Brown. Brown ran for six touchdowns and kicked seven extra points. His 43 points in one game set an NCAA record that still stands.

1968 It is still known as the "Heidi" game. When an important game between the New York Jets and the Oakland Raiders ran late, NBC stopped televising the game in order to show the movie *Heidi*. In a thrilling finish that no one in TV land saw, Oakland scored twice in nine seconds and beat the Jets, 43–32. Football fans were furious because they had missed the best part of the game. The TV networks promised never to let that happen again. Now, when football games run long, they continue covering the game.

1982 A two-month strike by the NFL players finally came to an end today. The strike forced the 16-game schedule to be cut to nine games. In addition, the usual playoffs were canceled and a special "Super Bowl Tournament" featured the 16 teams with the best records.

1945 Don Hutson of Green Bay caught a 10-yard touchdown pass in a pro football game against the Boston Yankees. It was Hutson's 99th touchdown.

1954 It was the biggest trade in the history of baseball. In all, 18 players switched between the New York Yankees and Baltimore Orioles. One of the minor players was a pitcher named Don Larsen, a 3-21 pitcher for the Orioles who went on to pitch the only perfect game in World Series history for the Yanks.

1972 Johnny Rodgers of the University of Nebraska tied an NCAA record for running back the most kick returns for touchdowns. Starting in 1970, Rodgers ran back seven punts and a kickoff for a total of eight touchdown returns.

1978 Placekicker Uwe von Schamann of the University of Oklahoma set an NCAA mark today. In his last game, against Oklahoma State, he hit all eight extra points in the Sooners' 62–7 rout. That gave him a total of 125 points-after-touchdown in a row.

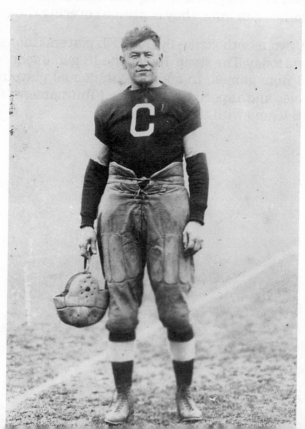

Jim Thorpe, one of the greatest all-around athletes of all time, and the captain who led his team to victory in the world football championship. (See November 25, 1916)

1929 Defensemen generally aren't expected to score many goals in hockey. Surprise! Today, defensemen Johnny McKinnon of the Pittsburgh Pirates and Clarence "Hap" Day of the Toronto Maple Leafs each scored four times. Pittsburgh won, 10–5.

1950 It looked like the Baltimore Colts were on their way to an easy win. They led the New York Giants at halftime, 20–7. The Giants coach must have said something good in the locker room, because the Giants scored 48 points in the second half. Final score: New York, 55; Baltimore, 20.

1978 New York Giants fans call it simply "The Fumble." The Giants were leading the Philadelphia Eagles, 17–12, with only 30 seconds left. They had the ball on their own 26-yard line. All they had to do was fall on the ball and the clock would run out. Instead, quarterback Joe Pisarcik attempted a handoff and fumbled the ball. Herman Edwards of the Eagles picked up the ball and ran it back for the winning touchdown.

1983 Forever Young. Brigham Young University quarterback Steve Young threw six touchdown passes to lead his team to a 55–7 thrashing of the University of Utah. It was the 22nd game in a row over two complete seasons in which Young had thrown at least one touchdown pass.

1961 SPORTS QUIZ Quarterback George Blanda of the Houston Oilers set an AFL record by throwing seven touchdown passes in one game. The Oilers trounced the New York Titans, 49–13. Today, both teams are part of the NFL, but the Titans have another name. Do you know what it is?

A: The New York Jets.

1969 The New York Rangers certainly kept Los Angeles Kings goalie Gerry DesJardins busy. They peppered him with 51 shots, including 23 in the final period. No wonder the Rangers won, 4–2.

1975 Bob McAdoo scored 50 points as the Buffalo Braves erased a 23-point deficit to defeat the Cleveland Cavaliers, 118–115. It was a season high for McAdoo, who set a basketball record for most points scored at the Cleveland Coliseum in Ohio. McAdoo had set the previous Coliseum record of 49 points the year before.

1977 Chicago Bears running back Walter Payton set an NFL record for rushing when he ran for 275 yards in a single game against Minnesota. The Bears held on to beat the Vikings, 10–7. By the time he retired in 1987 after 12 seasons, Payton had set a mark for most yards gained in a career: 16,726.

1982 It was the final play of the game and it's remembered as "The Play." The University of California Bears were trailing Stanford University, 20–19, and California had the ball on a kickoff return. That's when they got smart...and crafty. The California players knew that the minute any of them was tackled with the ball, the game was over. So they tossed each other laterals (quick, short tosses sideways or backward). After five laterals, the Bears finally scored the winning touchdown. The last California runners had to dodge the Stanford band, which had come onto the field thinking the game was over.

1925 The annual Yale-Harvard college football game ended in a 0–0 tie. Time ran out with the Bulldogs on Harvard's five-yard line. It didn't have to but the Yale players were fighting in the huddle, and no one thought to call time out.

1971 What a period! The New York Rangers set an NHL record by scoring eight goals in the third period on their way to a 12–1 blowout of the California Golden Seals. Ten years later—on March 19, 1981—the Buffalo Sabres broke the Rangers' mark by scoring nine goals in the second period of their 14–4 thrashing of Toronto.

1975 Bob Atheney, Jr., of St. Petersburg, Florida, set an exhausting record that didn't even count. Atheney had begun bowling on November 9 and didn't stop for 265 hours. At the time, it was a record, but the ABC later ruled that it was not an official event. Would you want to be the one to tell the poor guy he just bowled 265 hours for nothing?

1981 You have probably heard of Jim McMahon. The flashy quarterback made headlines, and enemies, when he was with the Chicago Bears. But did you know that as college quarterback for Brigham Young University, McMahon set or tied 70 NCAA records? In his last game, against the University of Utah, he threw for four touchdowns, and set marks for most yards gained in a three-year career (9,640) and most points (568).

1917 The National Hockey League was formed at a meeting in Montreal, Canada. The new league was really a larger version of an all-Canadian hockey organization called the National Hockey Association of Canada, Limited, and the four original teams in the NHL were Canadian, too.

1950 BOOOOORING! In the lowest-scoring game in the history of professional basketball, the Fort Wayne Pistons beat the Minneapolis Lakers, 19–18. This was four years before the 24-second rule went into effect. Each team was allowed to hold the ball as long as it wanted before shooting.

1962 Rarely before had the nation seen the mighty Green Bay Packers so humiliated. All the Pack could do was manage two meaningless last-minute touchdowns in losing to the Detroit Lions, 26–14. The Lions defense was awesome, sacking the great Green Bay quarterback Bart Starr 11 times and holding him to 58 yards passing.

1956
SPORTS
QUIZ

This year's Summer Olympics, held in Melbourne, Australia, actually took place in November and December. Do you know why?
A: Australia is located south of the equator. That means its seasons are reversed from those of places north of the equator. Australia has summer when we have winter.

1947 The first interracial football game in the history of the South was held in Durham, North Carolina. The all-black Willow Tree Athletic Club of Washington played the all-white Vulpine Athletic Club of Philadelphia to a 6–6 tie. It was a small step toward racial equality.

1975 Quarterback Fran Tarkenton of the Minnesota Vikings set an NFL record for pass completions as he led the Vikings to a 28–13 win over the San Diego Chargers. In the second quarter, Tarkenton completed the 2,831st pass of his career—more than any other quarterback. But Tarkenton was not through. By the time he retired in 1978, he had completed 3,686 passes, a record that still stands.

1984 Don't touch that dial! The televised showdown between Boston College and the University of Miami turned out to be one of the most exciting college football games in history—and one for the record books. Between them, Boston quarterback Doug Flutie and Bernie Kosar of Miami passed for 919 yards. In the final quarter, the lead swung back and forth, until it looked like Miami had finally locked up the game. But then, with six seconds left, Flutie threw up a 64-yard bomb to Gerard Phelan in the end zone. Despite being covered by three defenders, Phelan somehow caught the pass. Boston won, 47–45.

1987 It was the end of a streak—sort of. For 33 straight games, the Boston Celtics had won at home. Tonight they lost, 107–102, to the Chicago Bulls. The game was not *really* played at home, though, since it was held at the Hartford Civic Center in Connecticut, and not the Boston Garden. The Celtics play a number of home games in Hartford each year.

1949 The Syracuse Nationals and the Anderson (Indiana) Packers played the longest NBA basketball game ever. Syracuse won after five overtime periods, 125–123. Two years later, Indianapolis defeated Rochester, 75–73, in *six* overtime periods. That is still the longest game in NBA history. (See January 6, 1951.)

1954 Less than a week earlier, Italian race-car driver Umberto Maglioli had won the Pan-American road race by driving 1,908 miles at 107.9 mph. Six people were killed in the dangerous race, which goes through several countries in North and South America. Maglioli didn't get a scratch. Today, however, as he was about to meet some of his fans, he injured his hand on a taxi door. Maglioli would have been better off staying in his race car.

1960 Wilt Chamberlain of the Philadelphia Warriors set a pro-basketball record by grabbing 55 rebounds in one game. Despite Chamberlain's efforts, the Warriors (now the Golden State Warriors) lost to the Boston Celtics, 132–129. "Wilt the Stilt" broke the record of 51 rebounds set by Bill Russell of the Boston Celtics the previous season. Guess who guarded Chamberlain this game? That's right. Bill Russell.

1905
THE GOOD,
THE BAD
AND THE
WEIRD
The University of Iowa and Iowa State University have always had a great football rivalry. Today, some University of Iowa students came up with a way to make sure their team won. They invented a giant noisemaking machine. Every time their opponents had the ball, the students turned the machine on, which let out a deafening sound. It was so loud, the State players couldn't hear the quarterback's calls. They didn't score a touchdown all day.

1908 Back on July 25, 1908, John Hayes of the United States was declared the controversial winner of the Olympic marathon after Dorando Pietri of Italy was helped across the finish line. Today, Pietri got his chance for a rematch, and he made it count. He beat Hayes by 60 yards at a marathon in New York City's Madison Square Garden.

1916 Captain Jim Thorpe led his Canton, Ohio, football team to victory in the world football championship against another Ohio team, Massillon. And he won a $2,500 bet in the process. The day before, Thorpe had heard a Massillon fan bragging that his team would win. Thorpe challenged him to a rather expensive $2,500 bet. The next day, Jim was richer and the other man had learned a lesson about bragging.

1951 Dub Jones, the right halfback for the Cleveland Browns, tied an NFL record by scoring six touchdowns in the Browns' 42–21 victory over the Chicago Bears. Jones was one of the thinnest men ever to play football. He was 6'4" tall but he weighed only 205 pounds.

1965 University of Tulsa quarterback Bill Anderson turned the last game of the season into a record-breaker. Anderson led Tulsa past Colorado State, 48–20, with four touchdown passes. He set records for the most passes attempted in a season, the most passes attempted per game, the most passes completed per game, and the most plays per game. All this from a player who had been a bench warmer and almost never played before this year.

1944 Football coaches will tell you that when a team commits too many penalties, it will lose the game. Well, not always. The Chicago Bears set an NFL record by being penalized for 170 yards, but they still beat the Philadelphia Eagles, 28–7.

1956 Bob Richards couldn't move. He had just pole-vaulted 14 feet, 11½ inches, at the Olympics in Melbourne, Australia, and now he lay on his back in the pit below watching the bar shake above him. If it stayed up, Richards would not only win another gold medal for the United States, but he would also set a Olympic record. If it fell.... Finally, the shaking stopped. The bar stayed up. Richards had his gold medal.

1964 University of Tulsa quarterback Jerry Rhome attempted 198 passes over a seven-game period without once being intercepted. Rhome completed that record streak today when he threw two touchdown passes to lead Tulsa past Wichita State University, 21–7.

1976 It was raining at Three Rivers Stadium in Pittsburgh, Pennsylvania, and the artificial turf was slippery and wet. But that didn't stop the University of Pittsburgh's star running back, Tony Dorsett, from carrying the ball for 224 yards in Pittsburgh's 24–7 victory over Pennsylvania State University. All told, Dorsett set 28 Pitt records and 11 NCAA records, including most yards gained rushing— 6,082. A few weeks after the game, he received the Heisman Trophy as the best college football player in the country.

1960 Gordie Howe made an assist for the Detroit Red Wings in a 2-0 win over the Toronto Maple Leafs to bring his career points total to 1000. In hockey, points are awarded for both goals and assists.

1966 The referees in this game must have gotten tired of raising both arms in the air. Between them, the New York Giants and the Washington Redskins set an NFL record for scoring the most touchdowns in one game. The Redskins crossed the goal line 10 times and the Giants did it 6 times. Washington won the amazing 72–41 rout. The Redskins' 72 points was the highest ever for one team. The previous high was 70 points, racked up by the Los Angeles Rams when they blew away the Colts 70–27 in 1950.

1897
THE GOOD,
THE BAD
AND THE
WEIRD
In its earliest days, professional football seemed anything but professional. Take today's game between teams from Latrobe and Greensburg, two Pennsylvania towns. It was delayed for 1 hour and 20 minutes while the two teams argued on the field about whether one of the players should be allowed in the game. Finally, both squads left the field, got in their buses and began to drive away. Then, they got out of the buses and began to argue again. Finally, as the sun was about to set, the game began, but had to be shortened because of darkness.

343

1895 The first *completed* auto race in the United States was held in Chicago, Illinois. The weather at an earlier race had been so terrible, no one finished. This time, the results were better... a little. Two cars actually completed the 55-mile race. The winners were J. Frank Duryea and his brother Charles, who drove a car the two of them had built. Their average speed was a whopping 7.5 mph.

1929 Never say Nevers. As the running back, kicker and coach, Ernie Nevers *was* the Chicago Cardinals. In this game against the crosstown rival Chicago Bears, he not only coached his team to victory, but he scored all their points. He ran for a record six touchdowns and kicked four extra points as the Cards won, 40–6.

1959 The name St. Louis University is not usually included in a list of the powerhouses of college sports. But it should be. The Billikens of St. Louis University won the first NCAA soccer championship by beating the University of Bridgeport (Connecticut), 5–2. The Billikens have won 10 NCAA soccer titles since.

1979 Billy Smith of the New York Islanders became the only goaltender in the history of the NHL to score a goal while playing goalie. It happened in the third period of a game against the Colorado Rockies. With an Islander in the penalty box, the Rockies pulled their goalie to add another forward. Smith stopped a shot and the puck ricocheted off his stick. It kept going, and going, until it went into the empty Rockies goal.

1941 Bobby Yandell of the University of Mississippi made a brilliant tackle in a game against Mississippi State University. Unfortunately, he tackled his own teammate! The score was tied, 0–0, when Yandell's teammate, end Ray Poole, pulled in a pass and started running toward the end zone. Yandell thought the ball had been intercepted and stopped his own player from scoring the game-winning touchdown. Mississippi lost, 6–0.

1980 The three-point line was used in college basketball for the first time. Ronnie Carr of Western Carolina University sunk the first three-pointer in a game against Middle Tennessee University. Both teams belonged to the Southern Conference, which was experimenting with the new shot. The three-pointer is now used in all college and professional basketball games.

1987 Defensive back Vencie Glenn of the San Diego Chargers intercepted Denver quarterback John Elway's pass in the Chargers' end zone. Most players would have taken a touchback so their team could get the ball on the 20. But Glenn decided to run it out. And run he did...for a 103–yard touchdown. Glenn's run set an NFL record for the longest interception return. Four players had on earlier occasions returned interceptions for 102 yards.

1987 Fourteen-year-old Chrissy Wolking set a women's bowling record by playing 173 games in 18 hours without a break. The resident of Riva, Maryland, averaged almost 10 games per hour.

1989 The University of Oklahoma basketball team scored 97 points tonight...in the first half. The Sooners set an NCAA record for the most points in a half, and most shots in a game (147). They smothered U.S. International University, 173–101.

1905 The University of Chicago football team defeated the University of Michigan on a safety on the very last play of the game. With the score tied 0–0, the Michigan punt returner decided to run the punt out of his end zone and try for a touchdown. He was met immediately by two Chicago players and thrown back over his goal line for the safety.

1941 With the Washington Redskins leading the Green Bay Packers, 17–0, at halftime, the Redskins were confident. But Packers end Don Hutson caught nine passes in a row, scored three touchdowns, and kicked two extra points. Hutson accounted for 20 of the Packers' 22 points as Green Bay won the game, 22–17.

1946 Running back Glenn Davis of the U.S. Military Academy took a pitchout from quarterback Arnie Tucker, and zigged and zagged through the Naval Academy's defense for a 13-yard touchdown. It was Davis's final game, and it placed him in the record books. He had carried the ball 358 times for 2,957 yards in his college career. That's an average of 8.26 yards per carry. No one has matched that average yet.

1956 Don't mess with Tamara Tyshkevich of the Soviet Union. At 244 pounds, she was *huge!* Her nickname wasn't "Fatty" for nothing. On this day, Fatty set an Olympic record for the shot-put competition, and won the gold medal with a toss of 54 feet, 5 inches.

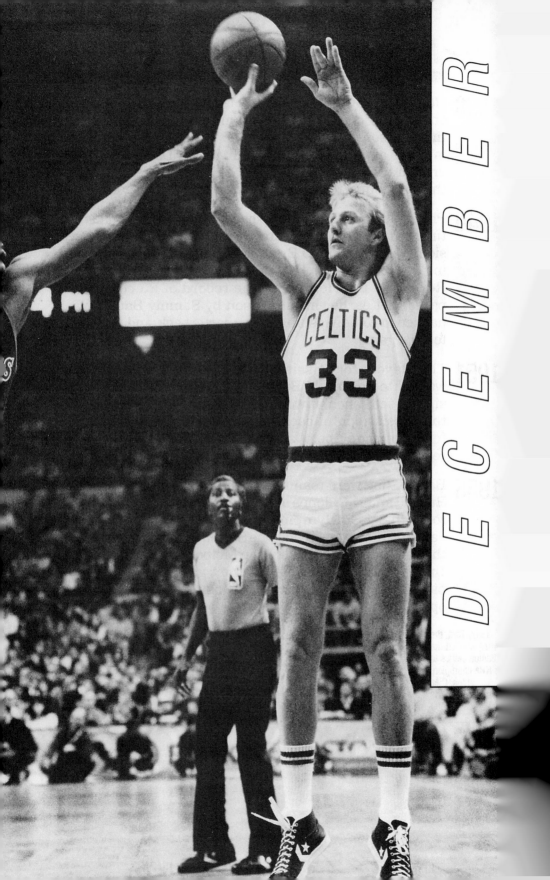

1898 Here's the key to a happy marriage, at least according to one strange couple: Bicycle around the world together. On this day, some 3 years, 7 months, 21 days, 2 hours and 55 minutes after they left, Mr. and Mrs. H. Darwin McIlrath arrived back home in Chicago, Illinois. That made them the first couple to ride around the world together on bikes.

1940 Philadelphia Eagles quarterback Davey O'Brien made the final game of his NFL career count. In the Eastern Division championship, O'Brien set an NFL record by completing 33 passes in the Eagles' 13–6 loss to the Washington Redskins. O'Brien broke the record of 23 completed passes set earlier in the season by Sammy Baugh, who happened to be Washington's quarterback and kicker in today's game.

1951 The players for Mississippi State University probably wanted to tie Arnold Boykin of the University of Mississippi to the bench. It would have been the only way to stop the Mississippi fullback in today's game. Boykin rushed for all of the Rebels' seven touchdowns, a new college record, in their 49–7 romp.

1956 Before they were teammates on the Boston Celtics, Bill Russell and K.C. Jones led another basketball team to victory: the U.S. Olympic Squad. Today, the Americans defeated their arch-rivals, the Soviet Union, 89–55, to take the gold medal at the Games in Melbourne, Australia. The United States won all eight of their games in these Olympics, averaging more than twice as many points as their opponents.

Larry Bird, the forward who led the Boston Celtics to three NBA championships. (See December 7, Sports Profile)

←

1950 More than 101,000 spectators, including President Harry Truman, watched in amazement as the U.S. Naval Academy beat the U.S. Military Academy, 14–2. It was Navy's first win in seven years in the bitter football rivalry. Army was the second-ranked team in the nation, and hadn't lost a game since 1947!

1950 There's an expression in boxing called "throwing in the towel." When the fighter's manager throws his towel into the ring, he wants the referee to know his boxer is giving up. Well, today, in a contest for the world bantamweight championship, challenger Danny O'Sullivan refused to throw in the towel against champion Vic Toweel. O'Sullivan was knocked down 14 times, but kept coming back. Finally, in the 10th round, Toweel knocked him out for good. Nowadays, the ref would stop the fight much earlier.

1972 The University of Southern California's Anthony Davis had one of those days every college football player dreams about. First, he tied an NCAA record by returning two Notre Dame kickoffs for touchdowns. He ran one back for 97 yards and the other for 96 yards. He also rushed for four more touchdowns in Southern Cal's 45–23 victory. Davis had scored all of Southern Cal's touchdowns.

1933 The Brooklyn Dodgers took on the Cincinnati Reds today. Baseball in December? Well, no, these Dodgers and Reds were football teams, although neither is around any longer. Anyway, in today's *football* game, the Reds punt returner, Gil LeFebvre, set an NFL record by returning a punt 98 yards for a touchdown. Since then, two other players have done the same thing (Charlie West of Minnesota in 1968, and Dennis Morgan of Dallas in 1974), but nobody has ever returned a punt farther.

1950 His name was Tom Fears, but it was his opponents who had reason to be afraid. The great Los Angeles Rams receiver was unstoppable in today's game against the Green Bay Packers. Fears set an NFL record by catching 18 passes in one game—four more than the previous record. The Rams whipped the Packers, 51–14. Fears's mark still stands. You could say the Rams' opponents had nothing to fear but Fears himself.

1936 Norman Skelly and John Shefuga arrived in Los Angeles California, today after traveling across the country—on rollerskates. Skelly and Shefuga made the trip from Boston, Massachusetts, in just over two months. Skelly, by the way, owned a roller rink. Maybe that explains why he did it.

1960 Quarterback Johnny Unitas of the Baltimore Colts threw touchdown passes of 80 and 38 yards in a win over the Detroit Lions. It was the 47th game in a row in which he had thrown a touchdown pass. The streak, which had started four years earlier, came to an end in the Colts' 10–3 loss to the Los Angeles Rams the next week.

1971 Running back Greg Pruitt of the University of Oklahoma gained 189 yards in his team's 58–14 victory over Oklahoma State University. Pruitt finished the season with 1,665 yards on 178 rushes. That's an average of 9.35 yards per carry, and an NCAA record.

1987 The Milwaukee Bucks held Kareem Abdul-Jabbar to only seven points in their 85–83 squeaker over the Los Angeles Lakers. It was the first time in 787 straight games the great center had been held to fewer than 10 points. The last time Jabbar had scored fewer than 10 points was on October 18, 1977, also against the Milwaukee Bucks.

1987 Larry Bird of the Boston Celtics missed his first free throw in 60 attempts in a game against the Detroit Pistons today. The string of 59 straight free throws was the fourth-longest consecutive free throw streak in NBA history. Oh yes, the Celtics lost the game, 128–105.

1868 Can you imagine going to school to learn how to ride a bicycle? On this day, the country's first bicycle school was opened in New York City. Students learned how to ride, race and take care of their bicycles. In those days bicycles were a lot more difficult to handle because they had huge front wheels.

1971 Running back Willie Ellison of the Los Angeles Rams burst free for an 80-yard touchdown run early in Los Angeles' 45–28 drubbing of New Orleans. And that was only the start. By the time the game was over, Ellison had set an NFL record by rushing for 247 yards on 26 carries. The mark is now held by Walter Payton of the Chicago Bears, who ran for 275 yards in a game against the Minnesota Vikings on November 20, 1977.

1975 Yogi Berra returned as coach of the New York Yankees after an 11-year break. Berra, a former star catcher for the Yankees, had been fired as the Yankees manager in 1964, even though his team had won the pennant. Just four months before being rehired by the Yankees today, he had been fired as manager of the New York Mets. He had led the Mets to the World Series in 1973.

1976 The University of San Francisco captured the NCAA soccer title for the second year in a row by defeating Indiana University, 1–0. It was the Hoosiers' first soccer loss of the season. Until the championship game, they had won 20 in a row.

1984 A record winning streak in tennis came crashing to an end today when Martina Navratilova lost to Helena Sukova in the semifinals of the Australian Open. Before losing this match, 1–6, 7–3, 7–5, Navratilova had won 74 matches in a row.

1925 A record pro-football crowd of 70,000 fans crammed into the old Polo Grounds in New York and saw the Giants lose to Chicago, 19–7. The fans had turned out to see the Bears' star running back, Red Grange. He didn't disappoint them. After a weak start, Grange scored a touchdown late in the last quarter. In addition to the 70,000 fans in the stadium, 20,000 lined the rooftops of buildings outside the Polo Grounds.

1960 Rafer Johnson and C.K. Yang were friends. Both were students at UCLA, where they trained together for the Olympic decathlon competition. But in this year's competition at the Olympics in Rome, Italy, they found themselves competing against each other, and representing different countries. Johnson represented the United States, but Yang had been born on the island of Taiwan. Johnson beat Yang in what turned out to be the closest decathlon competition in Olympic history. Yang's silver medal was the first medal ever won by Taiwan.

1987 In leading his team to victory over the Green Bay Packers, San Francisco's quarterback Joe Montana completed 22 passes *in a row,* without a single miss. That easily broke the record of 20 consecutive passes set by Kenny Anderson of the Cincinnati Bengals in 1983.

1969 The Kansas City Chiefs scored only one touchdown, and they still beat the Buffalo Bills, 22–19. Most of the Chiefs' points came from their kicker, Jan Stenerud, who kicked five field goals. That gave Stenerud 16 straight field goals without a miss—and set an NFL record. The old mark had been held by Lou Groza, who hit 12 consecutive field goals with the Cleveland Browns in 1953.

1985 The Heisman Trophy has been given to the top college football player in the country by the Downtown Athletic Club of New York every year since 1935. This year's voting by the nation's football writers, though, was the closest in the history of the trophy. Auburn halfback Bo Jackson edged Iowa quarterback Chuck Long by only 45 votes.

1956 SPORTS PROFILE Larry Joe Bird was born in the small Indiana town of French Lick. The man who would become best passing forward in basketball almost didn't make it through college, much less into the NBA. He dropped out of school twice before settling down at Indiana State University, and leading them to the finals of the NCAA Tournament in 1979. In the championship game Indiana State lost to Michigan State and Bird's rival Magic Johnson. Bird then became the highest-paid rookie in the history of professional sports, when the Boston Celtics signed him to a five-year, $3.25 million contract. He has since led the Celtics to three NBA championships.

1940 Would you believe this was a championship game? The Chicago Bears defeated the Washington Redskins by an incredible 73–0 score to take the 1940 NFL football title. The Bears scored 11 touchdowns. The key was the Bears' new "T" formation. In the "T" formation, the Bears offense lined up with the quarterback and the running backs standing in a straight column behind the front line to form the shape of a T. Previously, teams had lined up in other formations, including a box-shaped formation, which did not work as well as the T.

1961 For one game anyway, Larry Costello of the Syracuse Nationals was perfect. In a loss to the Boston Celtics, he hit all 13 field goals and all 6 foul shots he attempted. By the end of the game, Larry scored 32 points without a single miss!

1968 Ooops, what down was that again? The Los Angeles Rams lost a crucial NFL game to the Chicago Bears, 17–16, when the referees forgot what down it was. With time running out and the Rams trying for a winning score, they had to give up the ball after a third-down pass was incomplete. The refs incorrectly thought the missed pass had been the fourth down. For their mistake, all six officials were not allowed to work any games for the remainder of the season.

1987 Detroit Pistons forward Adrian Dantley scored his 20,000th point in the NBA in the Pistons' 127–117 win over the Portland Trail Blazers. The historic bucket, a layup, came with only 13 seconds left in the game.

1934 Things looked dismal for the New York Giants. They trailed the Chicago Bears, 10–3, at halftime on a bitterly cold day at New York's Polo Grounds. The players were slipping all over the place, because their cleats couldn't dig into the frozen ground. Then, at halftime, the coach had a brilliant idea. He told his backfield to take off their football shoes and put on basketball sneakers with rubber soles. It worked! New York got a grip on things and went on to win, 30–13.

1951 Bob Waterfield of the Los Angeles Rams was known as one of the greatest quarterbacks in football. Today, though, he went down in the record books not for his arm, but for his foot. In a game against the Detroit Lions, Waterfield became the second player to kick five field goals in a game. The current record for field goals is held by Jim Bakken, who hit seven for the St. Louis Cardinals on September 24, 1967.

1978 The first professional basketball league for women was called, fittingly enough, the Women's Professional Basketball League. In its first game, played today, the Chicago Hustle beat the Milwaukee Does, 92–87. Like a number of other attempts to bring women's basketball to the public, the League didn't last very long. It ended in 1981.

1984 In only his second season as a pro, running back Eric Dickerson of the Los Angeles Rams set a single-season rushing record. He gained 215 yards in the Rams' 27–16 victory over the Houston Oilers to break O.J. Simpson's mark of 2,003 yards rushing in one season. Dickerson ended the season with a total of 2,105 yards.

1938 Many people think it's only recently that American football teams began playing exhibition games in other countries. Not true. Today, two U.S. all-star football teams played in Paris, France. The game wasn't exactly a hit. Only 2,000 fans showed up.

1971 Dumb, dumb, dumb. In a trade they would live to regret, the New York Mets traded pitcher Nolan Ryan to the California Angels for infielder Jim Fregosi. Ryan went on to become one of the greatest pitchers in the history of the game.

Dan Marino, the quarterback who made the most touchdown passes in one season. (See December 17, 1984)

1877 You've heard of professional wrestling. You've heard of mud wrestling. But have you ever heard of bear wrestling? For the first time, wrestling matches between men and bears were held at New York City's Madison Square Garden. In the first of two contests, a wrestler named William Heyster took on a brown bear who was wearing a muzzle and had had his claws filed. The bear was too heavy to throw to the ground and it refused to do anything but just sit in the ring. The match was declared a draw. For the hundreds of fans in attendance, the contest was no doubt un-bear-able.

1949 Johnny, be good. Quarterback Johnny Lujack really put the ball in the air today, as he led the Chicago Bears to a decisive 52–21 victory over their crosstown rivals, the Chicago Cardinals. Lujack tossed six touchdowns and set an NFL record by throwing for 468 yards.

1960 The Los Angeles Rams defeated the Baltimore Colts, 10–3, in a game that was memorable for what *didn't* happen. Colts quarterback Johnny Unitas did not throw any touchdowns. It was the first time in 47 games that had happened, dating back to 1956. No one has yet matched Unitas's record.

1977
SAD SACKS
OF SPORTS

The Tampa Bay Buccaneers were a bad team. Since joining the NFL the previous season, they had lost their first 26 games. Today, all of a sudden, the Bucs bucked the odds. They played like champions, beating the New Orleans Saints at the Louisiana Superdome, 33–14. Then they won their final game of the season, beating the St. Louis Cardinals, 17–7. Two years later, they advanced to the NFC title game, where they lost to the Rams, 9–0.

1925 The Chicago Bears lost to the Detroit Panthers, 21–0, because their star linebacker, Red Grange, was sidelined with an injury. The Bears' management thought it would only be fair to refund everyone's money. The club ended up refunding $18,000 to the pleased fans.

1965 One NFL record was set and another tied in the Chicago Bears' 61–20 drubbing of the San Francisco 49ers. The Bears' running back sensation, Gale Sayers, tied a mark by scoring six touchdowns, including one on an 80-yard reception. Not to be outdone, Chicago placekicker Tommy Davis set a record by kicking his 234th extra point in a row without a miss.

1982 It was the Great Snowplow Play. The Miami Dolphins and New England Patriots were playing in the middle of a bad snowstorm. Neither team had been able to score in the terrible conditions. Patriots kicker John Smith was sent out to try to kick the game-winning field goal from 16 yards. All of a sudden, a snow plow, ordered by New England coach Ron Meyer, came onto the field. It cleared all the snow away from where Smith had to stand to kick the ball. Smith scored the field goal and the Patriots won, 3–0.

1987 You've probably heard of the Twin Towers. They are those two giant skyscrapers in New York City. Houston's Ralph Sampson and Akeem "the Dream" Olajuwon were called the Twin Towers of basketball. Both were more than seven feet tall and both were human dunking machines. Together they helped Houston make it to the 1986 NBA finals. But today, the Twin Towers were torn down. Sampson was sent to Golden State for Eric "Sleepy" Floyd and Joe Barry Carroll. The Twin Towers in New York, however, still stand.

1936 No, this isn't a mistake. The old Brooklyn Dodgers of the NFL really did beat the St. Louis Terriers, 100–0, in an exhibition game. The Dodgers gained 300 yards passing, and 274 rushing. They scored at the rate of almost two points a minute.

1983 You could have hurt your neck watching the ball go up and down the court. The Detroit Pistons outshot the Denver Nuggets, 186–184, in a wild NBA game. The combined point total of 370 set a record for the most points in one game that still stands. It's doubtful, though, that any NBA team will ever be able to match the highest team score in an international basketball game. At the Asian Games in 1982, in New Delhi, India, Iraq "squeaked" by Yemen, 251–33.

1887
THE GOOD,
THE BAD
AND THE
WEIRD
You may have heard of a three-ring circus, but a two-ring boxing match? It happened when Irish boxer Jack Dempsey defended his world middleweight title against an American fighter named Johnny Reagan. The match began outdoors in Huntington, Long Island, New York. But halfway through the fight, a nearby river overflowed, and the ring flooded. Everyone had to get on a ship and float to another ring downstream to continue the fight. When it was over, Dempsey was still the champ... and everyone was very wet.

1952 In the Los Angeles Rams' 28–14 victory today over the Pittsburgh Steelers, the Rams' Dick "Night Train" Lane set a NFL record when he intercepted three Pittsburgh passes. It was Lane's 14th interception of the season, a mark that still stands.

1969 Receiver Lance Alworth caught a nine-yard pass from San Diego quarterback John Hadl, and the Chargers blitzed the Bills, 45–6. It was the 96th game in a row in which Alworth had caught a pass. That broke the mark set by Green Bay's Don Hutson in 1945.

1985 It was the longest soccer game in college history. In the NCAA soccer championship match, UCLA scored the game's only goal in the eighth overtime period to beat American University, 1–0.

1988 It was a long time coming, but the Miami Heat finally won its first NBA game, beating the Los Angeles Clippers at the Los Angeles Sports Arena. In losing their first 17 games, the not-so-hot Heat set an NBA record for most defeats in a row at the start of a season. It was the Heat's first year in the NBA.

1925 The Montreal Canadiens beat the Americans from New York, 3–1, in a hockey game that marked the formal opening of the third Madison Square Garden in New York City. More than 17,000 fans, including New York's Mayor John F. Hylan, were on hand to see the first game in what was then the world's largest and most impressive ice hockey arena.

1946 It was a scandal that rocked the NFL. A gambler from New York City was arrested for trying to fix the league championship game between the Chicago Bears and the New York Giants. He offered $2,500 to two Giants players *not* to play their best in the game. The players refused the bribes. As it turned out, *none* of the Giants played their best; they lost, 24–14.

1963 The great Jim Brown of the Cleveland Browns ran for 125 yards on 28 carries today to become the first man in NFL history to rush for more than a mile in one season. His performance against the Washington Redskins brought his season total to 1,863 yards—103 yards over the mile mark.

1968 Placekicker Jim Turner of the New York Jets booted a 49-yard field goal in New York's 31–7 victory over the Miami Dolphins. It was his 34th field goal of the season, which was good enough for a new record. Turner's mark has since been passed by the New York Giants' Ali Haji-Sheikh, who made 35 field goals in 1983.

1987 Adrian Dantley of the Detroit Pistons hit 19 free throws without a miss today to tie an NBA record. In 1961, Bob Pettit of the St. Louis Hawks sank 19 foul shots in a row. New York's Bill Cartwright did the same in 1981, but no one has broken the record yet.

1878 Today thousands of people jammed Mozart's Hall in Brooklyn, New York, to watch an English woman known as Madame Anderson begin her attempt to walk 750 miles in 750 hours. When January 13 came around, she had completed her task, and was carried out of the building by the swarming crowd.

1973 In a game against the New York Jets, Buffalo Bills running back O.J. Simpson became the first man ever to rush for 2,000 yards in a season. He broke the record of 1,863 yards set by Cleveland's Jim Brown exactly 10 years and one day earlier. Simpson ended up the season with 2,003 yards. His mark has since been passed by Eric Dickerson, who ran for 2,105 yards for the Los Angeles Rams in 1984.

1979 Defensive end Jim Marshall of the Minnesota Vikings retired today. In his final game, Marshall set a number of NFL records, including more seasons with one club (Minnesota) than any other man in the history of the game. In 19 years, he played a total of 282 games for the Vikings, for another NFL record. He also recovered more opponents' fumbles—29—than anyone else.

1984 Washington Redskins receiver Art Monk caught 11 passes, two of them for touchdowns, in Washington's 29–27 victory over St. Louis. The final catch was his 106th reception of the season. That's an NFL record that has yet to be matched.

1960 He was called "The Golden Boy," partly because of his blond, curly hair, and partly because he came up with the big plays when the Green Bay Packers needed them. Today, in a game against the Los Angeles Rams, Paul Hornung went into the record books. The running back and kicker ran for one touchdown and kicked five extra points in the Packers' 35–21 victory to bring his point total for the season to 176. That's more points than any other player has scored in a season.

1979 Hold on tight! The highest speed for a land vehicle with wheels was set today at Edwards Air Force Base in California. The rocket-engined contraption, driven by Stan Barrett, went an incredible 739.666 mph. That's more than 13 times faster than the speed limit on most highways! It was the first time any land vehicle had broken the sound barrier.

1983 It was a crucial game for the Washington Redskins and the New York Giants. The final game of the season, it would decide the division champs. Several NFL records were set as the Redskins beat the Giants, 31–22. Washington running back John Riggins went down in the history books for scoring his 24th touchdown rushing for the season. The Redskins set another record for scoring the most points in a season (541).

1984 It was a familiar story during the 1984 season. In the final minute of play, quarterback Dan Marino of the Miami Dolphins connected with his favorite receiver, Mark Clayton, for the winning touchdown. This time the Dolphins beat the Cowboys, 28–21, and Marino set an NFL record with his 48th touchdown toss of the season.

1932 The NFL held its first playoff in history, with the Chicago Bears taking on the Portsmouth (Ohio) Spartans. Unfortunately Wrigley Field was frozen so the game was moved indoors to Chicago Stadium, a basketball arena. There was only enough room for an 80-yard field and that went right up to the walls. To protect the players, the goalposts were moved from the back of the end zone to the goal line. They remained there for all teams for the next 40 years, before the NFL again moved them back.

1949 The Philadelphia Eagles defeated the Los Angeles Rams, 14–0, to take the NFL championship for the second year in a row. Only 22,245 fans showed up at the giant Los Angeles Memorial Coliseum, due to a pouring rain. But those who did show up saw Philadelphia's Steve Van Buren set an NFL record by running for 196 yards on the muddy field. That was the most ever in a championship game.

1886
SPORTS
PROFILE
Ty Cobb, considered by many the greatest baseball player of all time, was born Tyrus Raymond Cobb in Narrows, Georgia. He joined the major leagues as an outfielder in 1905, and played 22 years for the Detroit Tigers and 2 for the Philadelphia Athletics. By the time Cobb retired in 1928, he had set more records than any other player. Although many of his records have since been broken, no one has beaten his mark for the highest lifetime batting average, .367. In 1911, he batted an amazing .420. Anything over .300 is considered good these days. Cobb was among the original five players inducted into the Baseball Hall of Fame in 1936.

1965   Gale Sayers, Chicago's brilliant rookie running back, won the season's scoring title today in the Bears' 24–17 loss to the Minnesota Vikings. Sayers plunged in from the two-yard line for his 22nd touchdown of the season.

1965   Jim Brown of the Cleveland Browns set a record today by scoring the 126th touchdown of his career in Cleveland's 27–24 victory over the St. Louis Cardinals. One of the best players Cleveland ever had, Brown had already set records for the highest rushing average and the most seasons leading the league in both rushing and touchdowns.

1970   Ken Houston of the Houston Oilers tied an NFL record when he returned two interceptions for touchdowns in a game against the San Diego Chargers. They were his third and fourth touchdown interception returns of the season. Houston also holds the mark for the most touchdown returns in a career. He had 9 in 14 years.

1984   No one ever seems to care much when a coach sets a record, but here's one worth mentioning. Today, Scotty Bowman of the Buffalo Sabres became the winningest coach in NHL history. The Sabres beat the Chicago Black-hawks, 6–3. It was Bowman's 691st career win, against only 285 losses and 202 ties. He had begun his career with the Montreal Canadiens.

1964 The Buffalo Bills won the Eastern Division title of the AFL with a 24–14 victory over the Boston Patriots today. Buffalo quarterback Jack Kemp scored two touchdowns and passed for a third to win the game. If the name Jack Kemp sounds familiar, that's because he went on to become a U.S. congressman, a presidential candidate, and the Secretary of Housing and Urban Development.

1975 The Minnesota Vikings had two opponents in today's game: the Buffalo Bills and snowballs. With Buffalo trailing, 35–13, Bills fans became restless and began throwing snowballs at the Viking players. It didn't stop two Minnesota stars from playing well, though. Quarterback Fran Tarkenton threw two touchdowns to set an NFL record of 291 career scoring passes. And Chuck Foreman ran for his 13th touchdown of the year, becoming league leader for that season.

1980 "Welcome to today's football clash between the New York Jets and the Miami Dolphins. Your play-by-play announcer will be: no one. Providing expert commentary will be: no one. Along the sidelines to interview players is: no one." NBC's experiment at airing a football game without any commentary seemed like a good idea at the time. Who ended up liking it? You guessed it: no one.

1981 Left wing Doug Smail of the Winnipeg Jets didn't waste any time today. Smail scored a goal after only five seconds against the St. Louis Blues. That is the fastest goal ever scored after the opening whistle of an NHL game. Three years later, Bryan Trottier of the New York Islanders did the same thing in a game against the Boston Bruins. (See March 22, 1984.)

1974 With 26 seconds remaining in an AFC playoff game, the Oakland Raiders trailed the Miami Dolphins, 26–21. But the Raiders were threatening. Oakland quarterback Ken "The Snake" Stabler threw a pass into the crowded end zone and hoped for the best. The best happened. Clarence Davis came down with the ball and Oakland won, 28–26.

1981 This one sure was long. Real long. The University of Cincinnati beat Bradley, 75–73, after seven overtime periods. It was the longest game in college basketball history. The game almost went into an eighth overtime period, but Doug Schloemer hit an 18-foot shot with one second remaining, to give Cincinnati the victory.

1957 An important lesson came out of today's NFL Western Conference playoff game: Never give up. The Detroit Lions might have given up when they were trailing the San Francisco 49ers at halftime, 27–7. Instead, they came out and scored 24 points while shutting down the 49ers completely. The Lions won the game, 31–27. The key play was also a "don't give up" daring fake-punt when the Lions had the ball fourth down on their own 20.

1973 Franz Klammer of Austria recorded the fastest time ever for a downhill ski race today. In a competition in Schladming, Austria, he skied the 3,145-meter (10,000-foot) course in 1 minute, 41.77 seconds. That's an average speed of more than 69 mph! Klammer would go on to win the gold medal for the downhill at the 1976 Winter Olympics.

1985 Wide receiver Stephone Paige of the Kansas City Chiefs was not the man you would expect to set a record for most yards gained on pass receptions in a game. He was playing in pain, with bruised ribs. But Paige caught eight passes for a total of 309 yards, including two for touchdowns. That broke a 40-year-old record. The Chiefs beat the Chargers, 38–34. Not bad for a guy in pain.

1985 Roger Craig of the San Francisco 49ers today became the first man in NFL history to collect 1,000 yards rushing *and* receiving in the same year.

1921 A new sport is introduced to the United States: judo. The inventor of this form of martial arts, Jigoro Kano, gave the first demonstration in the United States at the New York Athletic Club. The crowd watched the beautiful, slow-moving exhibition politely, but a little confused.

1951 The Cleveland Browns had won five straight NFL championships. The fifth one, in 1950, had come against the Los Angeles Rams. But this year, Los Angeles got its revenge. An exciting 73-yard pass from quarterback Norm Van Brocklin to left end Tom Fears iced a 24–17 victory, and broke the Browns' hold on the championship.

1972 It would become one of the most famous receptions in NFL history. In an AFC playoff game between Pittsburgh and Oakland, the Raiders were leading, 7–6, with only 22 seconds left to play. The Steelers had the ball at their own 40 and it was fourth down. The game was all but over. Then Pittsburgh quarterback Terry Bradshaw faded back and threw up a desperate pass to running back John Fuqua. The ball bounced off an Oakland defender, and into the hands of the Steelers' Franco Harris. Harris caught the ball, and ran 34 yards for an unbelievable touchdown.

1967 New York Jets quarterback Joe Namath passed for 343 yards and four touchdowns to lead the Jets to a 42–31 victory over the San Diego Chargers. The man known as "Broadway Joe" finished the season with 4,007 yards to set a pro football season passing record. Namath broke the NFL mark of 3,746 yards set by Washington's Sonny Jurgensen just the week before.

1968 Center Garry Unger played his first game on the way to an NHL record. Unger would play in each of his team's next 914 games without missing a single game. Unger's record stood until 1987, when Doug Jarvis of the Hartford Whalers set his own mark of 962 consecutive games.

1977 In one of the longest, and most exciting, games in NFL playoff history, the Oakland Raiders defeated the Baltimore Colts, 37–31, in double overtime. The game-winner finally came when Oakland's Dave Casper jumped high in the air to make an amazing catch of a Kenny Stabler pass that had been thrown well over Casper's head.

Joe Namath, the quarterback who set the pro-football season passing record. (See December 24, 1967)

1862 On Christmas Day in the middle of the Civil War, two Union Army teams played a strange new sport. It was called baseball. Some 40,000 people watched the two squads play in Hilton Head, South Carolina. This game was more important than you might think. When the war ended, the soldiers brought it to their homes all over the country and helped spread its popularity.

1894 It was a long trip, but it was worth it. The University of Chicago became the first college football team from the East or Midwest to travel to the West Coast. Chicago beat Stanford University, 24–4, in San Francisco, California.

1971 The Miami Dolphins defeated the Kansas City Chiefs, 27–24, in the longest game in NFL history. Garo Yepremian kicked a 37-yard field goal for the Dolphins more than 22 minutes into sudden-death overtime to win the AFC playoff game.

1908 Jack Johnson became the first black heavyweight world boxing champion today. He knocked out Tommy Burns in the 14th round in a fight held in Sydney, Australia.

1930 It was the worst hockey fight of its day. Twelve police officers had to rush onto the ice to break up a brawl between the Boston Bruins and Philadelphia Quakers. The Quakers were probably in a bad mood because they were trailing, 8–0, at the time. Seven players were penalized and fined $15 each.

1936 Less than eight months after winning four medals at the Olympics track star Jesse Owens decided to take on a four-legged opponent. A crowd of 3,000 in Havana, Cuba's Tropical Stadium watched in amazement as Owens defeated a racehorse named Julio McGraw in a 100-yard dash.

1943 Of all the nerve! Imagine the surprise of the Chicago Bears coaches when they looked down their bench and saw the owner of the Washington Redskins. Convinced that he was trying to steal plays, the Bears trainer called the police to have him escorted back to his box seat. Chicago won the game, 41–21.

1960 Chuck Bednarik of the Philadelphia Eagles was the last of a dying breed. He was a football star who played both offense and defense in the same game. Bednarik played all 60 minutes against the Green Bay Packers in the 1960 NFL championship game. With time running out, Bednarik tackled Jim Taylor on the 10-yard line to stop a possible game-winning touchdown. Thanks to Bednarik, the Eagles held on for a 17–13 win.

1953 Rookie defensive back Carl Karilivacz of the Detroit Lions intercepted a last-minute Cleveland Browns pass to give the Lions their second straight NFL title. Only minutes earlier, Lions receiver Jim Doran had caught the game-winning 33-yard touchdown pass.

1959 The Baltimore Colts scored three touchdowns and a field goal in a 10-minute span for a come-from-behind victory in the NFL championship game. For the second year in a row, the Colts beat the New York Giants, this time by the score of 31–16. The Giants dug their own graves by throwing three interceptions that led to Colt scores in the final quarter.

1987 Steve Largent of the Seattle Seahawks caught six passes to become the NFL's all-time leading receiver. The 752nd catch of his career broke the mark set by Charlie Joiner.

**1975
SPORTS
QUIZ** An American record crowd of more than 15,000 people attended a Jai Alai match in Miami, Florida. Jai Alai— originally an Italian game—is played by two people who catch a ball in a wicker basket and slam it against the wall. The ball can travel at tremendous speeds. The record is 188 miles per hour, or almost twice the speed of the fastest recorded fastball ever thrown in baseball. That fastball was clocked at 100.9 mph. Can you name the pitcher who threw that ball?

A: Nolan Ryan, who threw the pitch while playing for the California Angels on August 20, 1974.

1958 It's been more than 30 years since the New York Giants football team took on the Baltimore Colts in the NFL championship game, but many fans still remember it as one of football's greatest contests. It was also the first one to ever go into overtime. Colts fullback Alan "The Horse" Ameche plunged into the end zone from the one-yard line eight minutes into the sudden-death overtime to give the Colts a thrilling 23–17 victory.

1969 In an NFL game against the Cleveland Browns, the Dallas Cowboys had finally scored their first touchdown late in the game. Still trailing, 38–7, they decided to try an onside kick. Dallas kicker Mike Clark tried to squib the ball the necessary 10 yards required for a kickoff. But he missed, and the ball remained in the kicking tee. On his second attempt, Clark did not kick the ball far enough. Finally, Clark gave up and kicked the ball deep. Those 10-yard kicks can be killers.

1975 The capacity crowd of Minnesota Vikings fans sat in stunned silence. Quarterback Roger Staubach of the Dallas Cowboys had just thrown a 50-yard desperation pass with only 24 seconds left to play in an NFL playoff game. Somehow, despite double coverage, Drew Pearson caught the pass for a touchdown, and the Cowboys beat the Vikings, 17–14.

1960 Here's a college basketball tournament for all you scientists. In the Rochester Institute of Technology's third "Tech Tournament," West Virginia Tech toppled Indiana Tech, and Illinois Tech trounced the Newark College of Engineering. I won't tell you who won the championship, but Tech did beat Tech.

1963 American tennis stars Chuck McKinley and Dennis Ralston brought the Davis Cup back to the United States for the first time in five years. They beat the Australian team, three matches to two. Unfortunately, the next U.S. Davis Cup victory wasn't until 1968.

1974 The Los Angeles Rams had no one but themselves to blame for their 14–10 loss to the Minnesota Vikings in the NFC championship game. The Rams had seven penalties, three fumbles and two interceptions. And all those mistakes stopped Los Angeles scoring drives.

1978 Woody Hayes was one of the greatest college football coaches ever. The tough, outspoken leader of the Ohio State University Buckeyes was also one of the most controversial coaches around. Hayes's career came to an end today when he punched a Clemson University player on the sidelines during the Buckeyes' 19–15 loss in the Gator Bowl. Ohio State decided to fire Hayes for the incident. Still, he remains the fourth winningest coach in NCAA football, with 238 victories. The winningest major college coach was Alabama's Paul "Bear" Bryant, whose teams won 323 games. Hayes died in 1987.

1936 Hank Luisetti again made history. The talented Stanford University basketball player had already become the first man to score 50 points in a college game. Today, he cracked the record books by becoming the first in the pro or college ranks to sink a shot using one hand. Before, players shot using both hands. Luisetti scored 15 points as Stanford beat Long Island University, 45–31. LIU had been undefeated in 43 games. His one-handed style quickly caught on.

1962 Brrrrrrrrr! The Green Bay Packers and New York Giants faced off today for the NFL championship in 13-degree weather and 40-mile-per-hour winds. The Packers won this icicle bowl, 16–7, on three field goals by Jerry Kramer.

1935
SPORTS
PROFILE
Baseball great Sandy Koufax is born in Brooklyn, New York. Koufax grew up listening to the Dodgers on the radio and had his dream come true when he joined the Brooklyn club in 1955 as a pitcher. In 12 seasons, the lefthanded pitcher became known for his fiery fastball and wicked curveball. Koufax became only the eighth pitcher in NL history to throw a perfect game when he blanked the Chicago Cubs, 1–0, on September 9, 1965. He also struck out 23 New York Yankees in the 1963 World Series to set a four-game Series record. He probably would have set many more records had he not been forced to retire in 1966 at the age of 30 because of an arm injury. He was elected to the Hall of Fame in 1972.

1961 Four weeks before this day, the Green Bay Packers squeaked by the New York Giants 20–17 in a regular season meeting of the NFL's two top teams. In the championship game today, the Packers left little doubt as to who was football's toughest squad as they mowed down the Giants 37–0. What a difference a month makes!

1978 The Los Angeles Rams defeated the Minnesota Vikings in an NFC divisional playoff game, 34–10, in the last game of Minnesota quarterback Fran Tarkenton's brilliant career. In 18 years in the league, playing for the Vikings and the New York Giants, Tarkenton completed more passes (3,686) than any other player in the history of football.

1985 Ooops. Jockey Jorge Velasquez made a terrible error that cost his horse, Southern Sultan, the Display Handicap at New York's Aqueduct Racetrack. With Southern Sultan in the lead, Velasquez began digging in his heels to make Sultan go as fast as possible toward the finish line. Unfortunately, Velasquez had made a mistake, and the finish line was still a mile away. By the time he really did finish, Southern Sultan was so exhausted that he was nowhere near the lead. The lesson: When you really want to win, don't horse around.